CW00521933

A PERFECT GENTLEMAN

A PERFECT GENTLEMAN
The Sir Wilson Whineray Story

BOB HOWITT

Harper*Sports*
An imprint of HarperCollins*Publishers*

HarperCollins_Publishers_

First published 2010
HarperCollins_Publishers (New Zealand) Limited_
P.O. Box 1, Auckland, 1140

HarperCollins_Publishers_
31 View Road, Glenfield, Auckland 0627, New Zealand
25 Ryde Road, Pymble, Sydney, NSW 2073, Australia
A 53, Sector 57, Noida, UP, India
77–85 Fulham Palace Road, London W6 8JB, United Kingdom
2 Bloor Street East, 20th floor, Toronto, Ontario M4W 1A8, Canada
10 East 53rd Street, New York, NY 10022, USA

National Library of New Zealand Cataloguing-in-Publication Data

Howitt, Bob, 1941-
A perfect gentleman : the Sir Wilson Whineray story / Bob Howitt.
ISBN 978-1-86950-817-3
1. Whineray, Wilson James. 2. All Blacks (Rugby team)
3. Rugby Union football captains—New Zealand—Biography.
I. Title.
796.333092—dc 22

ISBN: 978 1 86950 817 3

Cover design by David Faulls, ExPress Communications Limited
Cover image: Fairfax Media
Typesetting by ExPress Communications Limited

Printed by Bookbuilders in China

CONTENTS

FOREWORD

Whenever I think of Wilson Whineray, I think of Mount Rushmore in the USA, that monumental granite sculpture of four former presidents of the United States — George Washington, Thomas Jefferson, Theodore Roosevelt and Abraham Lincoln — carved out of the mountainside in the state of South Dakota.

Wilson Whineray is the face of New Zealand: granitic in quality, unchanging over the years, a trifle amused, mildly sceptical, self-reliant, not a loner but not necessarily a joiner. He is what New Zealand is all about; he is what its people are all about.

It's people like him who make New Zealand such an enchanting place to visit, and if one is lucky, to tour as a rugby footballer. I first went there in 1959. I knew little of New Zealand, other than the heroism of its men at Gallipoli and the incredible exploits of the Second Division of the New Zealand Army under General Bernard Freyberg in the Second World War.

There is a story, which may be slightly apocryphal, of General Hans Von Arnim, the German Commander-in-Chief, advising General Erwin Rommel about troop deployments in the desert in 1942. He pointed to where various regiments were, and finally he said, 'And that's where the New Zealanders are.' Rommel's alleged reply was, 'I think we'll give that place a miss.'

Add to this a quotation from Alan Moorehead's book *African*

Trilogy. Moorehead was a brilliant Australian writer and, like many of his fellow countrymen, he was not given to either the Poms or New Zealanders. The passage in question is set after El Alamein and towards the end of the North African Campaign in Tunisia.

> At last we cut through a field of cactus and beyond the main road north of Sousse. With the main road we saw the New Zealand Division coming head on towards us in the way the enemy would have seen it coming. They rolled by with their tanks and their guns and their armoured cars. The finest troops of their kind in the world, the outflanking experts, the men who had fought the Germans in the desert for two years, the victims and the victors of a half dozen pitched battles.
>
> They were too gaunt and lame to be handsome; too hard and sinewy to be graceful; too youthful and physical to be perfect, but if you wished to see the most resilient and practised fighter of all the Anglo-Saxon armies, this was he.

Wilson Whineray is like these men. He is in their tradition, but in a less martial atmosphere.

Prior to my initial visit I had also read *A History of New Zealand* by Keith Sinclair, which depicted the brief, but eventful, history of New Zealand and its ceaseless quest for democracy and *égalité*. In this, they have been hugely successful under all administrations. Again, when you seek a figure who symbolises those aspirations, you think of Wilson.

He has served with me on the boards of various companies, and I have had an opportunity to listen to the cadence of his voice; the measured, deliberate way he addresses a topic; the calm, conclusive way that he reaches his judgments; and the overall feeling is one of fairness and reasonableness.

That is what Wilson Whineray is all about, and that is what New Zealand is all about.

I joke with him about the '59 Lions and the fact that under the modern scoring system we would have split the series, 2–2, by winning that first test. We scored four fine tries against the mighty Don Clarke's six penalty goals. He always demurs.

The other memorable thing about Wilson is that he doesn't change, apart from suffering from the eternal front row forwards' affliction, which is back and hip problems.

Like all recollections of friends, one's thoughts inevitably focus on a single incident, and mine of Wilson will delight him in that, for all his sterling play in a fine New Zealand pack in the '59 series and again in Great Britain and Ireland in 1963–64, I recall his spectacular and indeed impertinent dummy to score under the posts at Cardiff Arms Park in the final match of the tour against the Barbarians. To this day, he still secretly believes that he was a fleeting, elusive centre three-quarter who just happened to end up in the pack.

New Zealand and world rugby are lucky to have him as a symbol of all that is good and upright in the land of the long, white cloud. This book will confirm it.

Sir Anthony O'Reilly
June 2010

AUTHOR'S NOTE

It can be revealed that Wilson was a most reluctant book subject. For four decades following his retirement as probably the All Blacks' most distinguished and successful captain, he steadfastly resisted approaches from publishers, authors and writers — and there was a heap of them — to present his story in book form. And he does have a most remarkable story to tell.

Why would he not allow his achievements as an iconic New Zealander to be chronicled? It seems another celebrated rugby player who also made it big in business and was also knighted, Sir Anthony O'Reilly, may have influenced his thinking. O'Reilly, who would get Wilson involved in a couple of directorships as well as a remarkable international advisory committee, made it be known he regretted having ever written a book. O'Reilly had written critically of others, and the comments had come back to haunt him.

Wilson, for whom the word 'diplomatic' might well have been invented, had throughout his business career, if not so much his rugby career, been suspicious of the media, believing that on too many occasions it didn't understand the issues involved. So this was possibly also a factor in his decision. Add to that the fact that Wilson is a modest, humble fellow, a man who is most comfortable when talking about other people's achievements. A classic example is given by Jonathan Mason, an American finance expert who joined the Carter Holt Harvey group when Wilson was the chairman of the board. He confesses that for a long time he had no idea that Wilson was an iconic New Zealand rugby player, because whenever they were together — including on trips to Australia — Wilson talked animatedly, and authoritatively, about everything except himself.

So how did *A Perfect Gentleman* come about? Because, given his exceptional achievements, in sport and business, there *had* to be a Whineray book — which I wanted to write. And, while I told Wilson I would prefer to write this with his co-operation, whether he said yes or no I was going to write it anyway.

At which he said, 'Well, go for it.'

Wilson was insistent that it must be my book about him, which it is, thanks to the fantastic assistance and co-operation from every family member, relative, business colleague, rugby teammate and neighbour I approached.

What emerged from the dozens of interviews I conducted was that no one has an unkind, let alone critical, word to say about Wilson. In the boardroom, he impressed them with his business acumen and fairness; on the rugby field, he was a leader *par excellence*; as a neighbour, he mucked in and got things done.

This book has been an absolute delight to write, and, although Wilson was a reluctant subject to begin with, he came to accept the inevitable, and kindly made available his scrapbooks — the one his mother kept, starting in the 1950s, is a national treasure — and photo albums.

It was his great friend Colin 'Pinetree' Meads who unwittingly came up with the title. Over lunch in the Meads household in Te Kuiti, after relating one of his countless on-tour tales about Wilson, he paused and said: 'You know, he was always a perfect gentleman.'

Well said, Pinetree.

Bob Howitt
June 2010

ACKNOWLEDGEMENTS

This book would not have been possible without the enthusiastic input of all members of the Whineray family: Beth — who qualifies for the title of Lady Whineray, but who prefers to remain simply Beth — for providing so many personal insights into her illustrious husband's life; son, Jim, who brought enlightenment when the chapter on Wilson's business career was starting to read like a boring financial report, directing me towards Wilson's venerable associates who would reveal all; daughter Susan (who has marvellously remembered every story her father has ever told her) for providing the 'missing chapter' on Wilson the father and home handyman; Scott, for delivering me four pages of fascinating anecdotes about his older brother; plus eldest brother Grant and daughter Kristen, who both chipped in with valuable material.

The number of fresh rugby anecdotes involving Wilson was amazing … thanks to the recall of such rugby luminaries as Sir Colin Meads, John Graham, Adrian Clarke, Ralph Caulton, and Sir Brian Lochore.

Likewise, the business chapter would have been thoroughly forgettable had it not been for the input of Americans Jonathan Mason and David Oskin, for the man from Matamata who now runs General Motors, Chris Liddell, and for high-achieving Auckland businessmen John Maasland and Peter Springford. They gave me their valuable time because they all simply love Wilson.

Others who were so helpful in the compilation of this book include Brian Gaynor (*New Zealand Herald* business writer), Dr Mark Orams (author of an insightful book on Sir Peter Blake), Gordon McLauchlan (who features Wilson in his book *Loving All of It*), rugby statistician Geoff Miller, and Wilson's former neighbour and great old mate, Tom Marshall.

The illustrations that decorate the book have been supplied by the New Zealand Rugby Museum, Fairfax Ltd, and by the Whineray family from the superb scrapbook compiled by Wilson's mother.

INTRODUCTION

A lot of people wonder 'what happened' to Wilson after he completed his illustrious term as the All Black captain in the 1960s. Reason being that Wilson didn't follow the predictable pattern of eminent sportspeople in New Zealand and progress into coaching and administration, maintaining a high public profile along the way. It wasn't that Wilson wouldn't have enjoyed doing those things — coaching at club, provincial and perhaps even international level, and/ or helping guide the fortunes of New Zealand rugby where he could have made a massive contribution. It was simply that his calling was in a different direction: the world of business.

When the opportunity to study at Harvard University in the United States occurred, courtesy of a Harkness Fellowship, Wilson jumped at it, setting in motion a business career that would match, if not surpass, anything he'd achieved on the rugby field. If you think that's an exaggerated statement, consider this: he has been inducted into the International Rugby Hall of Fame, the New Zealand Sports Hall of Fame, and the New Zealand Business Hall of Fame, making him a truly unique individual.

He became deputy managing director and subsequently chairman of the board of Carter Holt Harvey, one of New Zealand's great companies. If Wilson had permitted his name to go forward, he would undoubtedly have become the Governor-General of New

Zealand. It's no secret that Helen Clark's Labour Government was looking for a male who hadn't been a judge, and Wilson was their preferred choice.

Those who know him well have no doubts he would have been a stunning success as a Governor-General, because he is who he is — a warm, witty, welcoming person with an unbelievable capacity to engage people at all different levels. It matters not whether he's in the company of royalty, politicians, sportspeople, businesspeople, freezing workers or forestry workers, he engages them all in animated conversation and leaves them feeling good about themselves. While the Governor-Generalship eluded him, he did become a knight, the first All Black so honoured. To his delight, he has since been joined by Sir Brian Lochore and Sir Colin Meads.

Wilson enjoyed rich success in rugby, and, in the same way that Sir Edmund Hillary was acknowledged almost exclusively as the man who conquered Mount Everest — his humanitarian achievements in Nepal largely being ignored — Wilson is remembered predominantly for his leadership of the All Blacks in the 1960s, when the All Blacks were the pre-eminent team in the world. Certainly, the All Blacks were a fearsome force in the 1960s; their record in 50 internationals was an amazing 41 wins, 6 losses and 3 draws, a feat unmatched in any decade before or since.

Wilson led his country on major tours of South Africa and Great Britain at a time when tours were monumental undertakings: the South African tour extending for more than three months; the UK venture for more than four months. Wilson not only held his own against some of the most formidable opponents in the world and guided his team to many treasured victories, he also stamped himself as an exceptional speaker. Teammate John Graham goes as far as to brand him a distinguished orator.

Wilson was only 30 when he stepped down from the international rugby scene. Given his strength and resilience — he never missed a test because of injury — he could have played on for at least another couple of seasons; after all, Colin Meads was still wearing the black jersey at 35. But Wilson, intelligent enough to attain a Bachelor of Commerce while still playing rugby, had ambitions beyond the sporting field, and within three years of playing his final international (against the Springboks at Eden Park in 1965) he had achieved a Master of Business Administration (MBA).

The number of New Zealanders who graduate from Harvard with an MBA are few indeed, and Wilson would ensure his qualification would be put to good use. Pretty soon he held a managerial position with Alex Harvey Industries, and, when that company was absorbed by Carter Holt, he stepped up to board level. Eventually, he would become chairman of the board and would guide it through a fascinating stage of its existence after it was taken over by the American giant, International Paper.

The Americans admired Wilson. They held enormous respect for any individual with an MBA from Harvard, but they just loved Wilson the man. Jonathan Mason, from Boston, who would join the company as a financial advisor and who is currently chief financial officer of Fonterra, another of New Zealand's business goliaths, speaks glowingly of Wilson.

'He would have been a successful corporate executive regardless of his rugby achievements,' he says. 'That's how talented he was. He would have become chairman of Carter Holt Harvey regardless; he was of such quality. He was a very good chairman, a no-nonsense person committed to the shareholders, someone who could get to the essence of an issue.'

After Mason completed his term in New Zealand and returned to the United States, every year he received a handwritten Christmas card from Wilson. 'Every year I'd get this card telling me how things were going in New Zealand, inquiring how I was getting on — it was remarkable.'

Chris Liddell — who served on Wilson's board and became chief executive, and has since gone on to achieve international recognition, first as chief financial officer of Microsoft and more recently (and stunningly, for a Kiwi kid from Matamata) as the chief financial officer of General Motors — is another with nothing but praise for Wilson.

'In the boardroom, he applied the same skills that made him such a great captain,' he says. 'He moulded the board of directors into a strong, focused, coherent team. He was masterful in balancing the needs of a large majority shareholder with the minority shareholders. It would have been easy to simply do what International Paper wanted to do, given their size and voting power, but he always had an eye out for the small guy.

'He was a great mentor to me as CEO at the time. He challenged me to be the best I could, gave me advice when I sought it, and most of all made it clear that he was there whenever I needed him. I grew enormously as a person over that period, and give him a lot of credit for his approach and friendship.' Strong words from a man destined to take financial control of the company that at one point in its existence was the most powerful in the world, General Motors.

Despite his success, Wilson has never been a material person. Not for him ostentatious cars. He wouldn't drive a Mercedes-Benz or BMW, because he believed they sent the wrong signals. And when he was dealing with forestry workers or aluminium-window-frame makers, he regarded it as vital to engage those people on an equal footing.

Nothing has ever caused Wilson to lose his cool. Yes, he might have plonked one on his deadly rival Piet du Toit in South Africa in 1960, but Du Toit's devious scrummaging tactics would have tested the patience of Job, and Wilson was told by the All Black management that if he didn't deal with Du Toit, they would consider replacing him with someone who would.

In a life stretching 75 years, Wilson will admit, if pressed, that he has never lost his temper: 'I could never see the point in losing your temper,' he says with startling innocence. We are not dealing here with someone who retreated to a monastery when life's temptations challenged him, but someone who, after growing up in a family of five boys, boxed and went on to play 240 first-class games of rugby, plus probably that many games again at club level, who has been married for half a century and brought up a son and two daughters, who managed several companies while working for Alex Harvey Industries, and chaired the board of Carter Holt Harvey for 10 years, during which time he had to deal with a strike at the Kinleith Paper Mill.

There must have been plenty of challenges that might have stretched the temperament of mere mortals to breaking point, but throughout his life Wilson has remained delightfully even-tempered. His approach has always been to search for the best in every person he has encountered. It's a philosophy that has endeared him to his sporting and business colleagues.

The Wilson Whineray story is a remarkable one, of a likeable lad from a humble family in Auckland, who showed independence and determination by leaving home at 16 to become an agricultural cadet with State Advances. He became a rugby player of exceptional quality, a prop who was plainly ahead of his time in his eagerness to run with the ball. He was arguably the All Blacks' greatest captain and certainly its greatest ambassador, wowing the Brits with his oratory and receiving a standing ovation from the crowd at Cardiff Arms Park as they sang 'For he's a jolly good fellow' at the conclusion of the 1963–64 tour. With glittering credentials as a rugby player behind him, Wilson then committed himself 100 per cent to his business career. The MBA from Harvard had companies eager to acquire his services. He chose Alex Harvey Industries, and went on to become an icon in the New Zealand business world. Already a legend through sport, he handsomely completed the double. Precious few New Zealanders ever achieve that.

1

GIVE-EVERYTHING-A-GO KIND OF KID

Technical College Old Boys was never one of the fashionable rugby clubs of Auckland. Founded in 1922, it barely survived the war years, when many of its most valuable players were overseas on combat duty, but faithful members kept it buoyant. It resuscitated well in the post-war years, and there was enormous satisfaction when the club took out the Senior Second Division title in 1949.

On many a Saturday, starting in 1946, a cherubic-faced young lad, always immaculately attired, would venture along to Puriri Drive in Mount Eden, position himself atop the fence that ran along one side of the field, and watch enthralled as the Technical COB team, resplendent in bottle-green jerseys with gold trim, did battle for the Thistle Cup. This young fellow, Wilson Whineray by name, was especially taken with a Technical COB front-rower named 'Snow' Johnson, who was the club's only regular Auckland representative. The energy and obvious exuberance displayed by Johnson, who would contribute to the club in many capacities for 50 years, made a deep impression on young Wilson.

So, too, did the 'crowd'. Well, it seemed like a crowd to an 11-year-old. If truth be known, probably the average turnout at Puriri Drive was less than 100. But to a bright-eyed schoolboy — who at that particular point in his life wasn't sure which sport he favoured most out of soccer, rugby and swimming — upwards of 80 fans cheering their team on certainly represented a crowd. It so stirred him, especially when they roared their approval of any Technical COB score, that he knew he wanted to one day play in front of such a turnout.

The Technical COB club was in 1950 renamed Cornwall, later joining forces with Grafton to become Carlton, which ultimately amalgamated with Grammar Old Boys to create Grammar Carlton, now one of the most successful and prosperous clubs in Auckland.

Fast-forward 14 years and, as Wilson stood to attention for the playing of the national anthems prior to kick-off in the opening international of the epic 1960 series between the All Blacks and the Springboks at Ellis Park in Johannesburg, he permitted himself a nostalgic reflection. He thought of those 80 fans who had captured his imagination at Puriri Drive. Surrounding him right now were about 80,000 wildly enthusiastic spectators. He'd sure got his wish: 80 × 1,000 = 80,000.

Wilson, born on 10 July 1935 to Bruce and Ida Whineray, was the third of five sons, all of whom, benefitting from loving, devoted and astute parents, would become achievers. Grant would manage the Newmarket Club (a club that catered to sportsmen and businessmen) for almost a decade, Bruce would captain New Zealand at hockey, Wilson would become a famous All Black and be knighted for his services to sport and business, Scott would become a nuclear physicist, and Murray would pilot Vampire jets.

Although their parents never had a surplus of money, all five boys were loved, well clothed and fed, and received what in the 1940s and 1950s could be termed the ultimate education if you lived in the Queen's City: they were enrolled at Auckland Grammar. And they were encouraged to play sport.

Grant was startled one day when his father said to him, 'I'm going to fill you with sport until you can't stand any more.'

'And, by God, he did,' Grant would acknowledge some five decades on.

The boys' father, who worked as a secretary and accountant, having grown up on a farm, had played soccer in his youth, but the sport that captivated him was swimming. He became president of, and the driving force behind, the Newmarket Swimming Club, and ensured all his sons would not only swim adequately but would be competitive also. Wilson relished the challenge, and not only did he win club titles, but in 1950 he progressed to the final trials for that year's Empire Games in Auckland. Finishing eighth of eight in the backstroke, however, brought an abrupt conclusion to his aspirations as a swimmer. Oh well, there were plenty of other activities and sports to pursue.

The Whinerays bought their sons a horse, which they grazed on Mount St John Domain, a small volcanic cone a short walk from their home in Epsom. The son who appreciated the purchase most, because he was a fearless, give-everything-a-go kind of kid, was Wilson. This city boy, whose infectious enthusiasm for anything he undertook rubbed off onto others, would go on to become a most accomplished horse rider. Initially, however, there was fair bit of hit and miss about Wilson's horsemanship. Rona, as the horse was named, was responsible for removing Wilson's toenail when she stood on his foot and twisted around. On another occasion she gave him a 'facial' by galloping, with Wilson in the saddle, under a low-hanging tree.

Rona, who was half draught horse, was 14 and Wilson not much older when he chose to enter her in a gymkhana at Pakuranga. Nothing wrong with that, except that the Whinerays didn't possess a horse float, so Wilson rode her from Mount Eden to Pakuranga, a distance of about 20 kilometres. It goes without saying that poor Rona was jiggered by the time she lined up for her event. Not surprisingly, Rona and Wilson finished last by a country mile. Wilson's father had driven out to make sure they'd arrived safely. Standing among the spectators, he was mortified to hear a chap next to him exclaim, 'Hell, there's a bloody draught horse in the race — poor creature!' He feigned an expression of disbelief.

The parents set strong moral standards, to which the five boys dutifully adhered. 'These are the rules,' their father told them. 'You don't answer back, you don't get drunk, you're always courteous to visitors, you're home by the time we agree upon, you give whatever sport you play everything you can, but you're always fair.'

They were ideals that Wilson would absorb and retain throughout his career. What his father never said in so many words, but which Wilson would abide by, was that in sport, and life generally, regardless of the circumstances or provocation, you would never lose your cool. He never did.

Boxing certainly helped in this respect. When Wilson was about 15, his ever-enthusiastic father bought the boys two sets of boxing gloves. Not red ones like Rocky made famous in his movies — these were basic brown ones. There wasn't much interest from anyone in the family except Wilson, who was enchanted by the gloves. His initial challenge was to find a sparring partner, younger brother Scott being the chosen one. Because of the height discrepancy, Wilson kneeled while Scott stood. It all ended predictably when Scott hit the . . . well, floor, because the Whinerays didn't run to a canvas, and their concerned mother intervened.

'That'll be enough of that,' she warned Wilson, after tending to Scott's bloodied nose. 'If you're going to box, you can do it at the gymnasium.'

'Yes, Mother.'

Boxing wasn't something Ida Whineray approved of, to be honest. The boxing gloves would have gone back if she'd had her way. She couldn't see any merit in the sport whatsoever. And she certainly couldn't see in Wilson the potential that would win him the New Zealand Universities heavyweight crown.

Ida was a strong, determined mother who cared for her sons like a lioness would her cubs. Mightily proud of them all, she made sacrifices to ensure they never missed out. No matter how many times they dirtied their gear playing sport or working, she dutifully laundered their clothes and ironed every item, even their underpants. When one of her sons went off to work one day leaving his lunch behind, she thought nothing of travelling into the city to get it to him, even though it meant going on three different buses to achieve it.

Ida's parents, Harry and Eva, had emigrated out to New Zealand from Hull, Yorkshire, in 1904. Intriguingly, they bore the same surname — Billany — because they were cousins, but sufficiently removed from each other for it not to have caused any complications. Harry died young in 1939; Eva lived for another 24 years. The Whinerays have traced their family tree back several generations and discovered a Swedish connection dating from 1794.

Bruce's parents, James and Lillian, who grew up in Ulverston, Cumbria, emigrated to New Zealand from Liverpool in 1903, just one year before Ida's parents. James was a man of the land who farmed in the Waikato. Lillian, whose maiden name was Ludlow, was an elegant, well-educated woman, who lived until 1963. The Whinerays endeavoured to establish a connection with Ludlow Castle, but never did.

When Wilson was about 10, he gave his grandmother, who was a gracious lady, a Christmas present. With a twinkle in his eye and a cheeky grin, he handed her the present with a card in which he had written: *To Lilly from Willy*. She was absolutely thrilled.

The north of England connection on the grandparents' side plainly influenced the choice of Christian names. It was not uncommon to use forebears' surnames as Christian names. Interestingly, all five Whineray boys were christened with surnames — Grant, Bruce, Scott, Wilson and Murray.

Ida skimped on housekeeping for more than a year to help buy a piano that became a family favourite. Wilson could beat out a few tunes, although it was Scott who displayed the greatest affinity with the keyboard. Sometimes it seemed Sergei Rachmaninov himself was performing in the Whinerays' lounge as Scott delivered flawless renditions of great classical works. His music teacher was so impressed with his talent that he approached the Whinerays suggesting Scott should consider a career as a concert pianist.

Scott was tempted, but the call of science and physics was greater. While Wilson was attracted to outdoor pursuits, Scott was more into indoor experiments. Not exactly mad-professor stuff, but activities that often left the remainder of the Whineray family bemused. As on the occasion when the mixing of volatile ingredients produced an explosion that resulted in the room under the house being strewn with shattered glass. Ida assured Scott that that would be the last experiment he conducted at home.

While Scott would attend the University of Auckland and achieve a Master of Science in physics, and go on to study nuclear physics at McMaster University in Ontario, Canada, a centre that had its own nuclear reactor, Wilson was, academically speaking, a humble achiever. He was middle-of-the-road in most subjects, not flunking any, but not eliciting much excitement from his teachers either. He was a nice boy, that Wilson, a most promising sportsman, mature for his age, with an infectious humour, almost charismatic. His fellow students related well to him. He seemed to be a natural leader.

Three individuals who graced the same Third Form class at Auckland Grammar would, remarkably, all go on to become knights of the realm. Besides Wilson, there was Ron Carter, who would obtain a Master of Engineering from the University of Auckland, become one of Auckland's and New Zealand's most prominent business leaders, contribute massively to engineering and business administration, and receive a Living Legend Award; and there was Kenneth Hayr, who would dedicate his life to a flying career, rising to the rank of Air Marshal, and be responsible for much of the planning of the RAF's part in the recapture of the Falkland Islands, before assuming the post of Commander British Forces Cyprus, and receiving a double knighthood.

The subjects that preoccupied Wilson in his fourth and final year at Auckland Grammar School, at the conclusion of which he was accredited with University Entrance, were English, chemistry, mathematics, history and geography, with history the only one that flicked his switch. He was fascinated with events that shaped the face of history, and particularly with the leaders whose decisions influenced those happenings.

He demonstrated a certain crude business acumen as a youngster, once buying brother Scott's four budgies for half a crown (about 25 cents in today's money), promptly on-selling them to the Farmers Trading Company for two shillings (about 20 cents) each!

It was sport, however, not study, that consumed Wilson as a teenager. His world revolved around sport. He swam, he boxed, he ran; in summer he played cricket, and on Saturdays in winter he played soccer in the morning and rugby in the afternoon. He was a pretty efficient soccer player, winning selection for several Auckland grade teams, but, in his second year at college, soccer and rugby began to clash. One had to be sacrificed and it was soccer, Wilson reasoning his temperament was better suited to rugby.

Right up to and including his first year in the First XV, he was a halfback; indeed, there was a memorable occasion when Auckland Grammar School did battle with New Plymouth Boys High at Grammar's home ground — Wilson featured at halfback for the one side, and John Graham, who would become an All Black forward a year after Wilson, operated at first-five for the other.

Wilson's performance was marginally superior to Graham's, whose display was greeted with stony silence by his coach JJ Stewart. Stewart, who would go on to coach the All Blacks in the early 1970s, subsequently wrote to Graham — probably an unusual thing for a teacher to do in those days — telling him he was too slow for a back but very quick for a forward. 'From next season,' wrote Stewart, 'you will be a flanker.'

Graham, who rather fancied himself as a playmaking inside

back, was miffed. At the commencement of the next term Stewart confronted him.

'Did you get that letter, son?'

'Yeah.'

'Then start practising your skills as a loose forward.'

'Yes, sir.'

Graham would go on to play 53 matches for the All Blacks, including 22 tests, as a loose forward. He would deputize for Wilson as New Zealand captain in 1964 and become an intimate colleague of the 1950 Auckland Grammar halfback, whom he never personally met on the occasion of their first encounter, although he concedes he probably tackled him at some stage. They would have strong influences on each other's careers.

Demonstrating greater diplomacy than JJ Stewart, Jim Bracewell transplanted Wilson from halfback to the forwards after an earnest discussion following training one day.

'Your talents are more attuned to the forwards,' he said. 'I think you could make it as a No. 8 or prop.'

Because there was another strong candidate for No. 8, Wilson moved comfortably into the front row, from where he helped Auckland Grammar take out the championship. The team was masterfully prepared by Bracewell, who in later years would become a close personal friend of Wilson's.

Many, many years later, in celebration of a new pavilion at Auckland Grammar, the school would bring out a publication in which a number of its most illustrious graduates were invited to contribute articles. Wilson would write of Jim Bracewell:

> Jim's approach was to do the basics well — strong forward play aiming at some dominance upfront, play at one end of the field, no dropped passes, no missed one-on-one tackles, kick where you mean the ball to go, run straight after the initial break. Do the simple things well. More than this, Jim stood for fair play — win, try to win at all times

but always within the rules and spirit of the game. And above all, with dignity and grace. I treasure his memory.

One senses that Jim Bracewell had an enormous influence on the man who would go on to become New Zealand's most illustrious All Black captain.

By the end of 1951, with UE in the bag, Wilson decided he'd had enough of college education. His mother encouraged him to commit to another year at Grammar, but Wilson yearned for the outdoors. During his last two years at Grammar, when he wasn't playing sport he'd grabbed every opportunity to go duck-shooting, ride his horse, and get involved in outdoor activities. He was no office boy. And now he was ready to quit the nest.

He applied for a rural cadetship, a five-year course run by the government in association with the State Advances Corporation, a course that led to a Diploma of Valuation and Farm Management. Over five years, candidates worked for five government departments involved in agriculture — Lands and Survey, Valuation, Maori Affairs, Department of Agriculture, and State Advances. The diplomas were awarded by the University of Lincoln College, near Christchurch, which throughout the cadetship was effectively the cadets' headquarters.

Wilson was told that at 16 he was too young to enter the cadet scheme, but as a city boy he could prepare for it by spending a year on a farm.

'Ideal,' said Wilson. 'Will you select a farm for me?' he asked the man at the State Advances office.

'Yes.'

'It would be nice if it wasn't too far from Auckland where my family live.'

'We'll see what we can do.'

When notification arrived of his farm posting, Wilson needed to refer to a map of New Zealand. Where the hell was Waikaia?

Certainly not close to Auckland. It turned out to be a small settlement 80 kilometres north of Invercargill, about as far from Auckland as a domestic posting could possibly be!

His parents drove him to Whenuapai Airport and farewelled him.

'You'll write regularly now, won't you?' said his mother.

'Yes, Mother.'

As Bruce and Ida watched the DC-3 take off across Auckland, carrying Wilson into the unknown, they could little have suspected that their independent, eager-to-get-going, 'outdoors' son would manage much, much more than merely keeping in touch. Through his remarkable achievements as a rugby player, and subsequently as a businessman in the coming years, he would become a household name throughout the land and generate incredible pride for the whole Whineray family.

Wilson had never flown before. He had plenty of time to contemplate his future as the DC-3 lumbered along from Auckland to Wellington to Christchurch and eventually to Dunedin, keeping him airborne for more than six hours. After landing at Dunedin's Momona Airport, he then had to get himself into Dunedin city to catch a train to Gore, where he was met by the son of the farmer who was employing him. Eventually, in the time a modern-day traveller could fly from Auckland to Los Angeles, he arrived in Waikaia.

The Waikaia senior rugby coach's eyes lit up when he realized a promising new footballer had come into the district, a prop no less. Props were in short supply, and this kid looked pretty useful. Apparently he'd toughened himself up with boxing, and his manual work on the farm meant he was qualified for anything Southland rugby might throw at him. Only four clubs comprised the Northern Southland senior competition — Riversdale, Lumsden, Balfour and Waikaia — and they seemed to play each other an inordinate number of times in the senior competition each season.

Wilson held his own in the front row, and it wasn't long before the characteristic bursts, ball in hand, that throughout his career would distinguish him from most other props, would come to the attention of the Northern Southland sub-union selectors, who selected him for the first sub-union contest of the season.

What no one had bothered to mention to the selectors was that young Whineray was only 16. Sixteen? Hell, no one was playing senior rugby in Southland at 16, let alone packing down against the tough critters that existed in the front row. Many of them were twice Whineray's age and at least twice as mean. The experience helped develop the front-rower's philosophy Wilson would retain throughout his rugby career: get the ball quickly into the scrum, get it out, and get away from there. Spend the bare minimum amount of time in one-on-one combat with your opponent.

It was only in post-match discussions, following Northern Southland's opening game, that the selectors became aware of Wilson's extreme youthfulness. They convened a special meeting and resolved that, in his better interests, he should limit his appearances to club rugby. Wilson merely shrugged his shoulders when informed of their ruling. If they wanted him, they wanted him; if they didn't, they didn't. *C'est la vie.*

Having grown up in the subtropical climate of Auckland, Wilson found his first winter in deepest Southland challenging. The fun of 'skating' in hobnail boots on frozen ponds balanced out against having to drive a fearfully slow tractor around the Waikaia farm in often sub-zero temperatures. One country dance he attended afforded a dramatic change of focus for several of the men present, when a sweeping torch revealed a deer eating turnips. Wilson was among those who raced to retrieve a gun, tearing his pants on the fence in the process!

Late in the year, Wilson reapplied to the government for his rural cadetship and was accepted. His posting was to a hill-country sheep farm at Stoney Creek, east of Featherston in the Wairarapa, where he would work as a farmhand.

Waikaia had been remote, but at least it claimed a reasonably sized township, fielded a senior rugby team, and featured on the map. Stoney Creek didn't rate a mention at all on Wilson's map, and he understood why when his farmer-boss, a fellow in his 30s, drove him — and the two well-bred sheep dogs he'd brought with him upon discovering that a shepherd's rate of pay was greater if he had his own dogs — away into the backblocks towards the Pacific Ocean. The farmstead was about 8 kilometres from the nearest neighbour along an unsealed road, as isolated as it could be. They received mail once a week.

Before taking up the posting, Wilson was summoned to Lincoln for a crash course in horse-riding — which he felt he was well qualified for, although not on the alarmingly steep slopes that would confront him at Stoney Creek — and in shearing and killing sheep.

The first time he exited the main gate at Stoney Creek, his destination was the Linton Army Camp in the Manawatu for three months of compulsory military training. That really toughened him up, and when he returned he was immediately drafted into the Martinborough rugby team's front row, word of his rugby prowess having spread north from Waikaia. Luckily, the manager of the farm on which he was working also played for Martinborough, or Wilson might have encountered difficulties making it to matches, so remote was the property.

Wairarapa's sole selector soon became aware of the now 17-year-old's impressive performances, and drafted him into the representative squad for the final three matches of the season. Incredibly, given his age, Wilson made his debut at the Showgrounds Oval in Carterton against Poverty Bay without having attended a solitary practice. That was because access from Stoney Creek was too difficult, and his manager couldn't spare him anyway. Most days at Stoney Creek, Wilson was away in the hills from 7 o'clock in the morning until after 5pm, effectively operating as a shepherd.

Holding his own in the front row against Poverty Bay was

less demanding than the second assignment allocated him by the Wairarapa coach: to stop Poverty Bay's legendary lock 'Tiny' White from winning the ball in the lineout.

What a laugh. Wilson tried everything — well, everything a 17-year-old knew — but it made not a speck of difference to White, who continued to win the ball with consummate ease. Years later, Wilson thanked White for being such a gentleman. A meaner-minded individual might have taught him a salutary lesson. Wilson survived his three outings for Wairarapa, managing to score a try against Wanganui, but completed the season without experiencing the joy of victory.

Perhaps the greater achievement was surviving the year at Stoney Creek. He would describe it to friends as 'steel-making stuff'. As on the occasion a neighbouring farmer told Wilson and his manager that, for any of the wild cattle that were living in a remote gully that they could flush out, he would pay half the value of each beast when they were delivered to his farm. As there were approximately 30 cattle involved, Wilson reasoned it was worth a try. If they retrieved most of them, the reward would represent a new car.

Wilson and his manager saddled up their horses, whistled up their most experienced dogs, and headed for the gully. They knew if they were to salvage any of the wild beasts, they had to herd them through a gate and away from the gully, rendering them more tenable. With Wilson on one side of the valley, his manager on the other, and the dogs on full patrol, the operation began. After two hours of frantic endeavour, during which one of their best dogs was mauled to death, Wilson and his manager admitted defeat. They went back to their property and the cattle went back to the gully. They would remain the other farmer's problem.

The next stop on rural cadet Whineray's roster, after another freshen-up at Lincoln, was a cropping farm at Dorie, close by the Rakaia River north of Ashburton, where he spent a large part of 1954 sitting on a tractor tending crops. Dorie, like Waikaia, did rate a mention in his map book, although the settlement was basic in the extreme. No pubs, no shops, just a spattering of homesteads.

He joined the Rakaia club, was welcomed by the Mid Canterbury selector, and played all nine matches on the representative calendar, making an impact on a good few people along the way. His maiden first-class win came against Golden Bay-Motueka at Ashburton, with Mid Canterbury, more than two decades prior to the advent of a national provincial championship. Chalking up an impressive six wins for the season, the 'Mighty Mids' beat Taranaki and won the Hanan Shield. Wilson's contribution didn't stop with helping to hold the front row together. He was the leading try-scorer with five, and even kicked a conversion in the match against Marlborough; indications that this teenager was something special.

Among those who concurred with this assessment were the national selectors, Tom Morrison, Jack Sullivan and Arthur Marslin. In the season ahead they had an important duty to perform — they had to select a New Zealand under-21 team to undertake a tour of Australia and Ceylon. Teenage props with two years' representative experience were just what they were looking for.

Before the Ceylon adventure became a reality, Wilson was deployed to Massey College, Palmerston North, to familiarize himself with dairy and pig farming. Much of the study was conducted in the classroom and, just when he should have advanced to the practical, on a dairy farm at Edgecumbe in the Bay of Plenty, he was off overseas with the New Zealand Colts. Before then, he got to represent his third union in three seasons, Manawatu, featuring in seven of the team's first eight fixtures of the 1955 season. By the time he was summoned to Wanganui for the New Zealand Colts trial, he was, at the tender age of 19, a well-established representative footballer.

2

ONE SERVANT
OR TWO?

In the 1950s the New Zealand Rugby Union (NZRU) only really dealt with the main rugby nations of the world — the four Home Unions, and France, South Africa, Australia and its near neighbours in the Pacific Islands. It had briefly embraced the United States and Canada, but that was about it.

So when the NZRU received an invitation from the Ceylon Rugby Union to despatch a team there to promote the code, it was more than a little perplexed. Ceylon had specified that the team should not be too strong. What to do? Despatch a Colts team, the national body determined, up-and-comers under 21.

Ceylon, now Sri Lanka, was in many respects still a British outpost in the 1950s, which meant that the grand old game of rugger was administered there by UK expats, who certainly knew how to organize events and host visitors. They couldn't guarantee fearsome opposition for the New Zealand visitors, but, by God, their visitors would not want for hospitality or friendship. Ceylon offered the NZRU five matches, which the NZRU accepted, expanding the programme by three by arranging games *en route* in Australia, at Melbourne, Adelaide and Perth.

When the New Zealand Colts triallists assembled at the Grand Hotel in Wanganui, in July 1955, they were allocated two to a room, the pairings being made on a completely random basis.

'Wilson Whineray, you'll be sharing with Colin Meads,' announced the NZRU official organizing things. Wilson knew nothing about the rangy King Country forward he'd been coupled with, and Meads had never heard of Wilson Whineray. Was it fate or incredible luck that these two emerging heroes — the one who would become arguably the most famous All Black of all, the other who would become his country's most distinguished captain — should be placed together?

Their careers would parallel each other's, freakishly. After the Ceylon experience, they would go on to make their All Black debuts and also their test debuts alongside each other; they would share the same international successes and setbacks for countless years; they would each become national icons; they would each be knighted; and they would remain the closest of buddies for more than half a century.

But in 1955, they weren't Sir Wilson or Sir Colin. They weren't even Pinetree or Noddy, simply Wilson and Colin, two teenage kids readying for a marvellous rugby experience. When they arrived in Wanganui, they were strangers.

'G'day,' said Colin, shaking Wilson's hand. 'Where you from?'

'Well, home is really Auckland, but I'm studying at Massey College in Palmerston North. And you're from where?'

'Te Kuiti — I work on a farm.'

'Good to meet you.'

'Yeah, same.'

'Be good if we could both be selected for the tour.'

'Yeah. Where the hell's Ceylon, anyway?'

Wilson looked at the towering fellow in front of him. His sleeves were several inches too short for his arms. He was definitely a rural kid, almost a caricature of a gangling sheep farmer, uncomfortable in a formal setting. But there was something about him, the way he sort of glowered at you. He had stature, and he obviously had strength.

Wilson decided he would rather have this fellow Meads in his side than among the opposition.

Meads immediately related to his room-mate, whom he found to be forthright, intelligent and wonderfully accommodating and considerate. Meads would admit later that he felt like a country bumpkin in the presence of an experienced professional. It didn't take him long to appreciate that this bloke Whineray was a leader.

One hundred and fifty-five nominations were received for the Colts team, and only 30, plus a handful of reserves, got to participate in the trial at Spriggens Park in Wanganui, in which the South Island XV, captained by AJ Duncan, defeated the North Island XV, captained by WJ Whineray, by 19 points to 11.

The New Zealand Press Association representative who covered the game wasn't blown away by what he observed, but he did identify a couple of stars of the future. 'The trial was not productive of good football,' he wrote. 'The biggest weakness was close to the scrum and there was an absence of thrust, speed and initiative. The backs were too often flat-footed. One thing was obvious — there were no Johnny Smiths or Ron Elvidges, but no doubt a useful team will be assembled to visit Ceylon and Australia. Two of the most conspicuous forwards were W.J. Whineray, who scored a try, and C.E. Meads.'

When the touring party was named, both Meads and Whineray were included. Interestingly, neither of the trial team leaders made it as captain. The selectors, in their wisdom, decided to invest the leadership in Southland's Ack Soper, a loose forward, who at 18 was one of the youngest players in the 22-strong squad; however, he had captained the Waitaki Boys' High School First XV. The Canterbury halfback, Mark Whitta, was appointed vice-captain.

Soon after he returned to Palmerston North, Wilson received a letter from the NZRU:

The NZRU extends its congratulations on your being chosen for the Ceylon Tour. We are sure you will have a happy and enjoyable trip. You will depart by air from Christchurch on 25 August and arrive back in New Zealand on 12 October.

Players must make their own travel arrangements to Christchurch for assembly. Players selected must pay their union £250, required by 28 July.

Ceylon is paying £750 towards the fares and our estimate of total costs including £50 pocket money is £250 per player. If it costs less than that, the difference will be refunded.

The team will be supplied with a black blazer (pocket silver fern with NZ Colts Ceylon 1955), tie, grey slacks, white shorts, black socks with white tops. The cost of this gear is included in your £250.

Mr Alan Lindsay of Southland has been appointed manager, Mr J.J. Stewart of Wanganui assistant manager and Dr A. Russell will travel as an honorary medical officer. The captain is Ack Soper, the vice-captain Mark Whitta.

Yours, George Geddes, secretary.

An addendum to the letter said that probably £50 would adequately cover any expenses, and explained that one Ceylon rupee equalled approximately 1 shilling and 6 pence (about 15 cents) in New Zealand currency. From information supplied by AR Cutler, the Australian High Commissioner in Ceylon, English cigarettes, razor blades and toilet accessories were apparently expensive, with beer costing 5 shillings (50 cents) a bottle, and imported spirits 3 to 4 shillings (30 cents to 40 cents) a glass.

Telling the players what to expect on the field, High Commissioner Cutler said that an average first-grade club team in New Zealand could walk away from the All-Ceylon team. 'People here expect open football,' he said. Of the food, he said that most Europeans in Ceylon did not eat pork or lettuce, and water should be consumed only if it had been boiled or filtered.

Wilson's £250 was generously paid on his behalf by the Manawatu Rugby Union, even though he had been under their jurisdiction for only a matter of months and upon his return would be relocating to Canterbury.

The team flew out of Christchurch with Tasman Empire Airways on 25 August as scheduled, but didn't get far, as this item in the Christchurch *Press* the next day explained:

> The DC-6 carrying the New Zealand Colts rugby team turned back half an hour after leaving Christchurch for Melbourne. A mechanical fault developed in the port engine which has to be changed before the aircraft leaves today. Fuel was jettisoned five miles off the east coast of the South Island. There was difficulty finding accommodation for the 49 passengers and crew of eight because all Christchurch hotels are fully booked for the Ranfurly Shield match [against Auckland] on Saturday.

While the Canterbury officials managed to locate sufficient beds for the entire touring party, the time it took to get a new engine to Christchurch and have it fitted to the DC-6 meant that the players were a wearied, under-prepared lot by the time they finally touched down at Essendon Airport in Melbourne at 5am on the Saturday, allowing them no more than three hours' sleep before they had to prepare for their opening encounter. Besides sleep deprivation, many of the players were also reacting to their vaccinations.

Nonetheless, they managed to defeat Victoria by 17 points to 3 and flew on to Adelaide, where three days later they did battle with South Australia, under lights. Well — they were called lights, but they were so dim that the players had difficulty identifying anyone more than 5 metres away. After a scoreless first half, the New Zealand Colts were in danger of failing to defeat the low-ranking South Australians until a certain prop named Wilson Whineray drop-kicked a goal. He explained to his coach later that, because there was nothing else on, and points were needed, he decided to 'have a whack'. His team won

9–6. It's doubtful if any prop representing New Zealand at any level before or since has drop-kicked a goal.

Two days later, the Colts wrapped up the Australian segment of their tour with a decisive 24–0 defeat of Western Australia in Perth, and then prepared for their journey through to Ceylon. No flight this time; they travelled from Fremantle aboard the SS *Stratheden*, a trip that lasted seven days before they disembarked in Colombo. It was a special time for the young Kiwis, who participated in everything going and, one player would write later, never stopped laughing.

For the wide-eyed Kiwis, most of whom had never been outside their country, Ceylon was an unbelievable experience. The players were billeted in alphabetical order, meaning Wilson was paired off with Eddie Wheeler, a loose forward from Wellington. They were introduced to their host, a Scottish businessman, who ordered his servant to carry their bags across to his car, which just happened to be a Rolls-Royce. After they arrived at his estate and unpacked, he gave Wilson and Eddie a quick introduction to the property.

'Now, you'll have a car each,' he said. 'Just let the servants know when you're ready to go somewhere, and they'll be ready for you. Now, Whineray, how many servants do you want — one or two?'

'Er, we don't have servants back in New Zealand — I'm quite happy to look after myself.'

'Nonsense, my boy — one servant or two?'

'One, thanks.'

'Wheeler, what about you — one servant or two?'

'One, thanks.'

Their host introduced them to their servants.

'Right-ho, guys, you shout if you have any problems. Enjoy your stay.'

Wilson kind of hoped the servants would keep to themselves and allow himself and Eddie to behave like normal New Zealanders, who relished their independence. However, the next morning Wilson woke to a gentle tapping on his shoulder.

'Excuse me, sir, but it is time to wake up. Your bath is running.'

Wilson looked about. The dirty training gear he had dropped on the floor the night before had been laundered. His shirt had been washed and ironed. His shoes had been polished. His bath was running. Hmm, so this is how the Raj operates! Oh well, relax and enjoy it. When in Rome . . .

At the Colombo Rugby Club, the Colts, who were warned by their management not to drink beer before 6pm and to stay away from spirits completely, settled in for a beer-drinking session one evening. Maurice Raureti, Terry O'Sullivan, Brian Frederikson and Wilson shared a table, and to ensure good service they generously tipped their waiter, a Goanese, who they nicknamed Fang. Their actions became embarrassing as the tour progressed, because 'Fang' brought them double helpings of everything. He looked hurt when they declined, but they certainly got the service they wanted.

Team manager Alan Lindsay may not have been aware of these sessions, because in an interview with a Colombo newspaper, in seeking to account for the difference in playing standards between New Zealand and Ceylon, he said, 'You cannot win rugger matches on beer. While Ceylon players were guzzling beer, whisky and gin at a Colombo Club, the New Zealanders were content with soft drinks. The amount of beer drunk by our team during the whole tour will not drown anyone.'

Obviously a wholesome fellow, Mr Lindsay also sounded off to the local reporter about smoking. 'Folks say that smoking is not harmful,' he said, 'but you never hear of smoking having done anyone good!'

Free of the evils of alcohol and smoking, at least in their manager's eyes, the New Zealand Colts waltzed through their five matches in Ceylon, three of which were played in Ceylon, one in Kandy, and one in Radella. Their average winning score was 32 points to 3, the team scoring 39 (three-point) tries to one. The leading try-scorer (with seven) was Alan McEnaney, a winger from West Coast; he was followed (on five) by Maurice Raureti, a highly promising five-eighth from the Bay of Plenty, Stan Goodwin, a winger from Mid Canterbury, and a certain prop from Manawatu, Wilson Whineray.

Unquestionably, JJ Stewart was the perfect coach for this collection of aspiring New Zealand footballers. A teacher at New Plymouth Boys' High School, he was just 32 when he toured Ceylon, very much in his prime, a gifted, innovative rugby coach with an engaging personality and strong wit. He would eventually coach the All Blacks but, sadly, not until he was 50.

In an interview with the New Zealand Press Association following the tour, he lavished praise on Wilson, who had turned 20 a month before the trip. 'He was indeed a tower of strength,' declared Stewart. 'We tried to develop an intensive backing-up game using backs and forwards to attack, and Whineray's speed and experience were exemplary in this respect and the others learned a lot from him. Whineray scored many times and his success in this area merely indicated how close he kept to the ball at all times. Off the field he was wonderful. The team had a grand team spirit and I feel this was in no small way due to his personality and his influence on other players. He was a fine team man and I cannot speak too highly of him. I am sure he will go further in the game and I'll be surprised if he does not go right to the top. I cannot praise the Manawatu union highly enough for assisting Whineray to make the trip.'

Coach Stewart also had kind words for the skipper, Ack Soper. 'At half-time at Melbourne, I came on to the field and Soper was talking to the team. He spoke about three minutes in his slow, deliberate way and he was putting his finger right on the spot. Frankly, I was staggered. He then turned to me and said, "Do you want to add anything?" and all I could say was "No".'

The rugby completed, the players still had to get back to New Zealand. No Jumbo jet service for them. Instead, they boarded the SS *Orontes* at Colombo, and 17 days later docked in Sydney, from where they had to make their way to the airport for a flight through to Auckland.

Wilson was a diligent letter-writer. He'd promised his mother when he left home at 16 that he would communicate regularly, and he did. Bruce and Ida received frequent despatches from him, including several from Ceylon. But theirs wasn't the only New Zealand address he sent letters to while overseas on rugby duty. There was, you see, this charming girl in Palmerston North — Beth, short for Elisabeth, Seymour.

They had met at a party in Palmerston North where Beth worked as a nurse, having grown up in the town. The party, at a private home, pitched a collection of nurses with a group of students from Massey. Wilson was rather taken with this fair-haired lass and asked if he could see her home. She agreed and he delivered her to her front door in what Beth recalls was 'a funny little car'.

They did a couple of movies together before Wilson headed to Christchurch to join the Colts team. Neither Beth nor her family were into rugby, but she thought Wilson was a nice, wholesome fellow with a pleasant personality. She didn't know whether she'd ever hear from him again as he departed for Ceylon, and was surprised when a letter arrived. A couple more bearing Ceylon postmarks were delivered over the next couple of weeks. They weren't exactly *billet-doux* but they did reflect an obvious interest on his part. In conversation with her family and mates, Beth referred to him as 'my friend Wilson'.

The pattern set in 1955 would survive for a couple of years, after Wilson relocated to Lincoln in Canterbury. He would write occasional letters, and, as his rugby commitments allowed, would make brief stopovers in Palmerston North to catch up with 'his' Beth.

As his stature as a rugby player was enhanced, his visits to Palmerston North began to create great excitement among Beth's girlfriends. To Beth, he was simply Wilson, the lovely fellow who wrote sweet letters and obviously fancied her; to her girlfriends, he was that rugby player who was always in the news. The girlfriends always wanted to know when he was next coming to town!

Following the Colts tour, Wilson scarcely had time to unpack before he was off for six months' experience on a dairy farm at Edgecumbe in the Bay of Plenty, the others on his rural cadet scheme having been deployed more than a month earlier. As his involvement in Edgecumbe fell outside the rugby season, he missed the opportunity to play for a seventh provincial union, Bay of Plenty.

Also living on the Edgecumbe property that Wilson had been assigned to was an elderly fellow who was rather demanding of the workers. In rather grizzled fashion, he told them he wanted a small table built outside his house where he could take his morning cup of tea.

'Righto,' said Wilson, 'we'll get on to it.'

It wasn't the only chore demanded of them that day. A cow had died and the boss requested that Wilson and his colleague bury it.

Rather wickedly, they decided they would kill two birds — or one cow, or something — with one stone. While the old codger was away, they dug a large hole in front of his home into which they dumped the cow, upside-down. They then nailed planks to the cow's hooves, creating a novel piece of Kiwiana.

While Wilson and his mate thought it hilarious, the old codger was outraged and the boss failed to see the humour of the situation, and demanded they instantly dig the cow out and give it a respectable funeral, which they did.

From Edgecumbe, Wilson was posted to Lincoln, where he would spend the next two years. A fair percentage of that time was spent in the lecture room, but there were practical components also, as he was introduced to the art of buying sheep and cattle. For one of those sessions he was based at Helensville, northwest of Auckland, giving him the opportunity to reacquaint himself with family members.

While the time spent at Lincoln would be important to his business career, it would have far greater significance for Wilson Whineray the rugby player, because, while he had garnered useful credentials playing for Wairarapa and Manawatu, those unions didn't rate too highly on New Zealand rugby's Richter scale. Canterbury was a completely different scenario. Not only were the red-and-blacks year in and year out among the most potent sides in the land, at the commencement of the 1956 season they were also the proud possessors of the Ranfurly Shield, which they'd won off Wellington back in 1953. In the 1950s, that was almost the ultimate in New Zealand rugby, guaranteeing massive crowds at Lancaster Park and focusing nationwide attention on the Canterbury team, not least from the All Black selectors.

Rugby interest was intense as the 1956 season approached, because the mighty Springboks, the only team the All Blacks had never defeated in a test series, were touring. Not a day went by without some reference in the daily newspapers to the upcoming tour and how the All Blacks might best prepare themselves to finally overcome this fearsome opponent. The tour would extend to 23 matches, and besides the four internationals would feature two games that were of particular interest to Wilson: those against Canterbury and New Zealand Universities. He was eligible for both.

Wilson began his Canterbury sojourn playing senior club rugby for Lincoln College, a team of modest standard that featured one distinguished player, John Buxton, who had become an All Black in 1955. Wilson certainly gave the side a lift, but given Canterbury's resources he doubted whether he could win representative selection, notwithstanding the excellent reviews he'd received for his performances with the New Zealand Colts. What he didn't know was that the 'senior pros' associated with the Canterbury team had been monitoring his progress closely. 'We had you tabbed,' Tiny Hill, an established member of the side, would tell him years later.

Wilson's great good fortune was that Ed Bullmore, who'd been a front-row anchor of the Canterbury scrum throughout 1955, had transferred out of the district. A schoolteacher and artist, he'd headed north, creating a major opening. It was rare for a player to break into top-level rugby at 20, especially for a major union like Canterbury, but Wilson had been making ripples for quite some time. Canterbury was ready to embrace him.

The Canterbury coach, who'd taken over from a notable achiever in Jack Rankin in 1954, was an astute fellow named Neil McPhail, who had played prop for Canterbury before the war and had been regarded by many as a certainty for selection for the abandoned All Black tour of South Africa in 1940. Captured by the Germans in the Western Desert in 1941, he spent years in prisoner-of-war camps in Germany and Italy before becoming a leading figure in the Kiwi Army team that toured the United Kingsom following the cessation of hostilities in 1945. Phil Gifford, author of *The Passion*, a book that chronicles the 125-year history of Canterbury rugby, describes McPhail as being extremely humble and a perfectionist, illustrating the claim with two delightful stories.

Gifford says that McPhail's humility became evident on the 1963–64 tour of the United Kingdom and France — a tour on which he and Wilson would combine marvellously as coach and captain — when he refused to wear the All Black tie because, he argued, he had never played for the All Blacks. The perfectionist side of McPhail was revealed after he and veteran journalist Terry McLean clashed following an inter-island fixture in which McPhail's South team won courtesy of a late try scored by the team's first-five, Neil McAra, who had been loitering out near the wing when a clearing kick lobbed his way. After trapping the ball with his foot, he scampered across for the winning try in the corner.

McPhail later asserted that McAra shouldn't have been there. 'He was out of position, he should have been closer to his forwards,' he told McLean.

'Would you rather he hadn't got the ball and scored for South to win?' asked McLean.

'Certainly,' replied McPhail.

'That's barmy,' said McLean.

McPhail didn't hesitate to pitch Whineray into his pack, a pack featuring such toughened and celebrated performers as Dennis Young, Bob Duff, Tiny Hill, Hugh Burry, and John Buxton.

Wilson celebrated his 21st birthday in the lead-up to Canterbury's game against the Springboks. Because of the importance of the looming contest, Wilson took himself off to bed at 9pm. When some of his rugby colleagues realized this, they came visiting, waking him up and insisting he celebrate the occasion worthily. They offered him a glass of beer. Wilson took it, downed a couple of mouthfuls and said, 'Thanks, fellas — now would you mind turning the light out as you go, because I've got a terribly important game coming up.'

Twenty-one might seem an extremely young age to debut for a major representative team as a prop, but Kevin Skinner first turned out for Otago at 19, 'Snow' White was 20 when he donned the Auckland jersey, and Ken Gray was 20 when he made his Wellington debut. Perhaps more pertinently, one of the Springbok props, Piet du Toit, who would become Wilson's most notorious career opponent, was 20 when the tour kicked off.

Canterbury had just one warm-up fixture, against a Hanan Shield XV in Timaru, before engaging the South Africans. And what an occasion the Springbok encounter was. Thousands slept outside Lancaster Park to guarantee their place on the terraces. Ninety minutes before kick-off the gates were closed, on police orders. By then, 45,000 people were in the ground, but fans were so desperate to get in that they climbed fences and pushed down a gate.

Those were the days when the International Rugby Board (IRB) declined to allow replacements in international fixtures. When Canterbury's fullback, Kevin Stuart, dislocated his right shoulder in the 13th minute, he should have been taken to hospital for treatment. Instead, after the team doctor had pushed the shoulder back into place and fashioned a sling, Stuart courageously returned to the field. Late in the game, he dislocated the shoulder again while making a heroic tackle. It was again pushed back into place, and he was still on the field at the final whistle. Perhaps not surprisingly, he never played for Canterbury again.

But he, and new chum Whineray, would have a glorious victory over South Africa to celebrate. After the scores were locked together at 6-all at half-time, Canterbury edged ahead eight minutes from time through a penalty goal by Buddy Henderson.

Henderson wasn't fazed when the penalty was awarded.

He laconically offered the ball to Wilson. 'Do you want to take the kick?' he asked.

Wilson most certainly did not. 'You'll do the job,' Wilson replied. And Henderson did, landing the goal that brought Canterbury a famous 9–6 victory.

South African manager Dr Danie Craven was not a happy chappie at the outcome, asserting the referee had given his team a raw deal with the awarding of the late penalty that Henderson goaled. 'I do not begrudge Canterbury their victory,' he said, 'but I feel we should not have been defeated by an easy penalty. The refereeing in the North Island was excellent, but down south the standard seems quite different.'

So Wilson's first international experience brought a famous victory and much controversy. There would be plenty more of both in the years ahead.

The player Wilson marked that afternoon at Lancaster Park was Jaap Bekker, a powerful prop and at 31 a veteran of the Springbok scrum. Wilson couldn't get over the size of his neck, which measured 22 inches — 5 inches more than his own. Bekker wasn't into intimidating opponents. He simply challenged them with his considerable strength — unlike Piet du Toit, whom Wilson would soon confront. As a prop, Du Toit was the devil incarnate.

Terry McLean captured the essence of Canterbury's victory vividly in his tour book, *The Battle for the Rugby Crown*:

Eight red devils surged wherever the ball went, friend and enemy who intervened were mowed down like ripe wheat, a relentless, exhilarating attack was made upon the South African goal and all, all was fire and spirited and determination and manliness and unquenchable courage. You may have your 300-yard drive at golf, your sensational backhand winner at lawn tennis, your weathering of the fleet at yachting and your four-minute mile in athletics, but there is nothing in all of sport to compare with the sight of eight rugby forwards who are really moving forward and who are resolved and relentless. One will always remember the tall, gaunt men Duff and Hill, the fresh newcomer Whineray (who had his sleeves rolled up so high he might have been a butcher making a killing), the chunky hooker Young, the loose forwards Buxton, Burry and Roberts and the last and perhaps the finest of them Hern.

A week after the Canterbury game the Springboks plunged the nation into deep despair by winning the second test in Wellington, in the process causing much embarrassment to the All Black front row, which was bullied and battered into submission. The players who had been selected to pack down opposite Bekker in the first two tests — Mark Irwin and Frank McAtamney — both finished with cracked ribs.

A more powerful scrum was essential before the teams clashed again in Christchurch, or yet another series against the Springboks would be squandered. Who could the All Blacks call upon to reinforce the front row? One of the names bandied about was Wilson's. Despite his youth, he'd comfortably handled every assignment allocated him, including holding his own against these very same Springboks in the Canterbury match. But it would be the persuasive chairman of the NZRU, Tom Pearce, who would influence the selection of the team for the critical third test. He summoned an urgent meeting with the national selection panel (comprising Tom Morrison, Jack Sullivan and Arthur Marslin) — something that has never happened before or since — and convinced them of the need to get some 'steel' into the scrum. The Springboks were intimidating the All Black forwards. That couldn't continue. Kevin Skinner is back in training, he reminded them. Who better to sort these bloody South Africans out? And while you're at it, get 'The Boot' involved as well — Don Clarke.

It is not recorded if Tom Pearce had his foot on the chest of the chairman of the panel when they conceded to his requests, but Tom, who'd gone to the brink of All Black selection as a prop himself in 1937, was a mightily persuasive fellow, for sure.

When the line-up for the third test was announced, there were four changes in the pack. Skinner, then aged 29, was in at prop; Ron Hemi was the new hooker; 'Tiny' Hill, one of the hardest men ever to pull on an All Black jersey, was on the side of the scrum; and Peter Jones was in at No. 8. And, oh yes, The Boot was at fullback. The All Blacks would go on, famously, to win the series, finally wresting the mythical world crown from the Springboks.

Four days after the volatile third test, Wilson would confront the Springboks again, this time wearing the New Zealand Universities (NZU) jersey in a midweek fixture at Athletic Park in Wellington, a game that attracted a crowd of 40,000. Coming off the defeat at Lancaster Park, the Springboks were in low spirits, but they were still expected to account for the so-called students, who had never previously been awarded a fixture against an international opponent.

An oddity of selection was that only those who played their club rugby for a University team were eligible for selection. When he later lived in Auckland and played for Grammar, Wilson wasn't eligible, even though he was studying at university. In 1956, he qualified, however, because he was playing his club rugby for Lincoln College.

The NZU game would live long in the memory as a classic encounter, both for the quality of the rugby and for the stunning victory achieved by the Universities team, which scored four tries to two (and had another — the most spectacular of them all — by winger Ron Jarden, disallowed because he'd stepped into touch). It was a rip-snorter of a match, one that suited the mobile Whineray, who spent a fair percentage of the game running about like a loose forward. His opponent, a year his junior, was Piet du Toit. Like Wilson, he was learning his trade. Rushing about like a flanker wasn't his thing. He preferred one-on-one combat in the front row. Over the next four years, he would develop nefarious ways of frustrating opponents and slowing them down.

The Springboks didn't conclude their tour until the beginning of September, finally allowing New Zealand to return to a degree of normality. But there was still plenty of rugby excitement down Canterbury way, with the Ranfurly Shield to defend. Wanganui, West Coast, South Canterbury and Southland were comfortably sent packing, bringing the successive number of defences to 24, one short of the record set by Hawke's Bay in the 1920s.

The opportunity to establish a fresh mark came in the season's finale, against Wellington, but the Wellingtonians never allowed Canterbury into the game, winning 8–0. The Wellington coach, Clarrie Gibbons, was a staunch advocate of running rugby, but these tactics had failed miserably when his team last challenged for the shield. When, in its final training session in Christchurch, Wellington threw the ball around in carefree fashion, it was obvious to every red-and-black enthusiast that the men from the capital city had learnt nothing.

But the Wellingtonians were a cagier lot than Canterbury gave them credit for. In a three-hour training session in Timaru they had concentrated exclusively on a kicking game. And that's exactly what they hit Canterbury with on match day. It was a cunning plan that caught Canterbury by surprise, and, although it made for a boring contest, it resulted in the Ranfurly Shield finally being prised away from Christchurch.

Not everyone was sad to see the shield depart. Tiny Hill would later concede that, after three years, Canterbury was pleased to see it go. 'Playing for the shield creates terrific tension,' he said. 'Our players were singing in the changing room after Wellington's win.'

One of Wellington's points-scorers was midfielder Kara Puketapu from the Petone club; not someone Wilson had any dealings with at the time. But a decade later, they would find themselves sitting beside each other as candidates for Harkness Scholarships to Harvard.

3

AUSTRALIA, HERE WE COME!

Wilson was attracted to boxing from the moment his father arrived home with a set of boxing gloves. None of his brothers shared his enthusiasm for the sport, neither did his mother, but the sport certainly captivated Wilson.

To his delight, he found boxing to be a sporting option at Auckland Grammar, and soon immersed himself in it. Many people find boxing unappealing to the point of being abhorrent, and struggle to understand why it is categorized as a sport and why its supporters refer to it as a science. Wilson soon came to appreciate that it was not only a worthy sport, but very much a thinking man's sport, that it was indeed scientific and a sport that kept his brain switched on and senses well-tuned. And, as he developed his skills, he found, particularly in a rugby context, that opponents treated him warily. No one was going to deliver a cheap shot to an opponent who had proven himself in the boxing ring. It was an attitude that would accompany him through to rugby's highest strata.

The sport so fascinated Wilson that he found he needed to know more of its origins, and began researching it, with greater enthusiasm and intensity, if truth be known, than he put into his school homework!

Boxing, he discovered, was also known as 'pugilism' or 'the

sweet science' and had roots dating back to ancient Greece. Back then, fights took place without gloves, but with leather taped to the combatants' hands, which resulted in some gruesome, often deadly, battles. The first documented boxing match took place in Britain in 1681, when the Duke of Albemarle organized a fight between his butler and his butcher.

The first rules were set in 1743, after Jack Broughton, known as the father of boxing, killed an opponent; but the most revolutionary change came in 1865, when John Sholto Douglass, the Eighth Marquess of Queensbury, drew up the rules of boxing that transformed it into the sport it is today. He became known as the patron saint of the sport. The Queensbury Rules specify that boxing shall be a stand-up contest in a 24-foot ring; that no wrestling or hugging be allowed; that rounds be of three minutes' duration; that if either man falls he must get up unassisted inside 10 seconds; that a man hanging from the ropes in a helpless state with his toes off the ground shall be considered down; that no seconds are allowed in the ring during rounds; that gloves are to be fair-sized, of the best quality, and new; that a man on one knee is considered down, and if an opponent strikes him he forfeits the fight; and that no shoes or boots with sprigs are permitted.

Primed on the Queensbury Rules, Wilson made rapid progress in the sport, and won the School Cup in the heavyweight division at Auckland Grammar as a Fifth Former, weighing 8-stone-something (a bit more than 50 kilograms), his opponents including Sixth and Seventh Formers. He repeated the feat in his final year at the school.

His next opportunity to fight competitively came during his compulsory military training stint at Linton Camp, by which time he was weighing in at around 12½ stone (79 kilograms). He claimed the camp heavyweight title and fought successfully against boxers from Palmerston North.

Over the next few years, interspersed with his rugby commitments and rural cadet work, he competed at the Universities Easter tournament, initially representing Massey (which for tournament purposes combined with Victoria University of Wellington), and subsequently Lincoln (which combined with Canterbury). Wilson took out the Universities heavyweight title in both 1954 and 1955, and was seeking to complete a hat-trick of successes at Easter 1956. All was going well as he progressed to the final at the Wellington Town Hall, where his opponent was a powerfully-built medical student from Dunedin, Jim Samisone. Wilson was working his way into the fight when a momentary lapse in concentration resulted in him taking a heavy blow from Samisone. In an instant he was flat on his back on the canvas, looking at the lights. After about six seconds, he clambered to his feet.

'I'm alright, referee, I'll carry on.'

'No, you're not — fight over.'

Wilson Whineray, boxer, had just recorded the first defeat of his career, which left him grumpy. And it left his mother grumpier, because she heard the outcome on the late evening news: that her son had been 'knocked out' in the final. Ida had never seen any merit in boxing, and for her this was the last straw. When she next spoke with Wilson she wanted him to assure her that he would hang up his boxing gloves. Wilson listened sympathetically to her argument but said he couldn't give her that assurance.

When 1957 rolled around, Wilson knew he was a leading contender for All Black selection, given the number of senior players who had retired after the Springbok series. With a tour of Australia coming up, it promised to be an exciting season, one in which Wilson undoubtedly wanted to be involved. But there was a little unfinished business in the boxing world he first wanted to address. A certain Jim Samisone would be defending his New Zealand Universities heavyweight boxing title in Dunedin at Easter, and Wilson felt he couldn't let this opportunity to regain his crown pass. There was just one complication: the contest in Dunedin clashed with the South

Island rugby trial in Christchurch. They were both scheduled for the same day in April, the rugby kicking off at 3pm, the fight timed for around 8pm, with some 360 kilometres separating the two venues.

What to do? A Lincoln College colleague of Wilson's volunteered to drive him south, if he could get away from the rugby trial by half-time. That presented a ray of hope, because Wilson's trial team was being prepared by Neil McPhail, his Canterbury coach.

'Er, Neil, if I play the first spell well enough, do you think you could possibly release me at half-time?' asked Wilson.

'Why?'

'Because the New Zealand Universities heavyweight boxing title is at stake if I can beat this Fijian fellow who decked me in Wellington last year. But the fight's in Dunedin, starting at eight o'clock.'

'Don't you want to be an All Black?'

'Oh yes, but I also want the chance to win back this boxing title. It will be the last time I fight competitively.'

'Well, if you're silly enough to drive all the way to Dunedin after playing in a rugby trial, go for it.'

'Thank you, Neil.'

And that's what happened, believe it or not; surely the only instance in the history of All Black rugby where a player has been released from a trial game to go and compete in a boxing event.

Wilson relaxed and mentally re-attuned himself as his friend drove him south in his trusty Vauxhall Velox. There were a couple of other Lincoln students occupying the back seat who fortunately had remembered to pack Wilson's shoes and singlet. They made good progress and arrived at the Dunedin Town Hall with plenty of time to spare.

But there was to be a disappointment. Jim Samisone was in the audience watching, having declined to defend his title. Wilson found himself up against a different opponent, whom he duly defeated, giving him back his NZU heavyweight crown. He and his Lincoln cronies celebrated in style that evening, identified a place to sleep, and returned, leisurely, to Lincoln College the following day. Surprisingly — well, maybe it wasn't surprising because who the hell would have considered it remotely possible — neither of the Dunedin daily newspapers twigged to the fact that the fellow who took out the New Zealand Universities boxing title was the same chap who'd been battling for All Black selection in Christchurch a few hours earlier.

Many years later, Wilson attended a Fijian Sportsman of the Year dinner in Suva and was settling in for the formalities when a tall, good-looking fellow approached him.

'How are you, Willie?'

It was Jim Samisone, now Dr Jim, a practising physician. He would later be appointed to a Pacific Island diplomatic post in Brisbane.

There would be no more compromises at rugby-trial time for Wilson, who was now firmly committed to winning All Black selection. To his delight, he was named in the main trial at Athletic Park, the other props being Snow White, Ian Clarke and Frank McAtamney.

If a genie had materialized in Wilson's world in 1957 and granted him one wish, he couldn't have manufactured a more satisfactory outcome to the trial. Wherever he went, the ball went. He scored a try, he ran like a centre three-quarter, his team won, his scrum was strong. He was on fire. Well before the selectors had completed their deliberations and announced the touring party in the after-match 'dungeon' that was Athletic Park, Wilson was assured by countless colleagues that he could safely start packing his bags.

He was, at the tender age of 21, duly named in the 25-strong team to tour Australia. Right there with him was his good mate from the Ceylon Colts tour, Colin Meads, plus the captain from that venture, Ack Soper. The captain this time was the shortest man in the side, at 5 foot 3 inches: halfback 'Ponty' Reid. The coach was Dick Everest from the Waikato; the manager, Bill Craddock from Buller.

Wilson attracted a lot of attention for his barnstorming display in the final trial, and some were beginning to compare him with Kevin Skinner, the player he'd succeeded. PJ Sheehan, however, writing in the *Weekly News*, proffered this opinion:

> The claim that Wilson Whineray is another Skinner is hardly correct. He is reminiscent of the Kevin of 1949 but the aplomb of the mild-mannered Skinner in massed play is not a characteristic acquired in a year or two. Whineray is a ball of fire nevertheless and an impudent young fellow to boot. In the closing stages of the trial in Wellington when his elders were beginning to feel the strain and their feet were dragging wearily beneath them, Whineray was still full of energy. And suddenly he has developed into the lineout expert of his side, becoming a nuisance to the Possibles team as he went plunging and bucking through the line.

At the request of the Australian Rugby Union (ARU), the All Blacks' 13 matches were played under the kick-into-touch dispensation in vogue in Australia, where, unlike New Zealand, there was fierce competition from league. Australia's administrators were always seeking ways to make the game as attractive and appealing as possible. Having to operate under a law dispensation that the IRB would not adopt universally for more than another decade didn't handicap the All Blacks, who swept through the tour undefeated. All Black manager Bill Craddock became an enthusiastic backer of the dispensation, claiming it brightened up the game considerably without detracting from true forward play.

Wilson made his All Black debut against New South Wales at the Sydney Sports Ground wearing jersey No. 23, the tourists being numbered alphabetically. Others wearing the All Black jersey for the first time that afternoon were Colin Meads, Terry Lineen, Frank McMullen, and Russell Watt.

From Sydney, the team headed some 550 kilometres northwest to the small rural township of Warren, where the 'dirty dirties' (those players not required for the next fixture) were taken on a kangaroo-shooting outing by a group of local farmers. Those who volunteered,

Wilson among them, were roused from their sleep at 4am and soon found themselves roped to the back deck of a truck, which took off across desolate countryside in pursuit of kangaroos. Although plenty were identified (most at a considerable distance from the truck), and dozens — it might have been hundreds — of shots were fired, leaving a maze of spent shells on the tray of the truck, not one kangaroo was felled. The solitary marsupial damaged from that night's activity was a kangaroo that didn't clear the path fast enough and was clipped by the truck!

It was a weird itinerary that the ARU had prepared for the 1957 All Blacks, the internationals featuring as matches three and five, leaving eight encounters still to be played once the test series was through. The final three games were against three of the weakest opponents: Riverina, Victoria, and South Australia.

Television was a mind-boggling treat for the New Zealanders, prompting the New Zealand Press Association (NZPA) reporter with the team to file this item:

> Television which has intrigued the All Blacks since their arrival in Sydney will be carrying the first international to thousands of Sydney homes. Almost a dozen TV cameras will follow the game from start to finish on all three channels operating in the metropolitan area. Since the Sydney Rugby League refused to allow any of its matches to be televised because of the possible effect on the 'gate', rugby has become one of the most popular features of Saturday transmission. Local followers say that the television view especially of lineouts and scrums is even better than being at the ground.

Wilson concluded his preparation for the first test by nonchalantly drop-kicking two goals at training from outside the 22 with bare feet. A news item said teammates gaped as he kicked one with his right foot and then another with his left.

Wilson's heroics didn't finish on the training field. He was a star — some would claim *the* star — as the All Blacks overran the

Wallabies by 25 points to 11 at the Sydney Cricket Ground the next afternoon, scoring four tries to one. That enthusiastic NZPA correspondent identified Whineray and McMullen, who was also making his test debut, as the standout players for the All Blacks. Here's what he wrote of Whineray:

> Playing in his first test, he was magnificent in all phases of play, and on his display must be regarded as one of the best forwards New Zealand has produced in recent years. His lineout work was first class but it was his speed to the loose ball that was his strongest point. By selecting such a young team — the average age is 24 — the New Zealand selectors were obviously looking to the tests against the British Lions in 1959 and South Africa in 1960 and in young Whineray they look like having a winner.

'Great game, Willie,' his coach, Dick Everest, said as he entered the changing room.

'OK, was it?' asked Wilson. 'Frankly, it was all a bit of a blur.'

Because television hadn't stretched to New Zealand in 1957, the rugby faithful had to rely on the viewpoints of commentators and journalists present at the events. And they were unanimous in their praise of the new prop Whineray. Here's what Roving Reporter wrote after the first test:

> I would say unhesitatingly that Wilson Whineray played the best forward game for a newcomer that I have seen in an international since the war. His breaks away from the lineouts, especially the one that led to MacEwan's try, were most astutely judged and were made with a vigour and purpose and a controlled intelligence good enough in any man and wholly remarkable in a boy of 21. I must give Dick Everest credit for bringing out the best in a young man like this. The gingering up which he instituted has proved extremely congenial to a youngster like Whineray.

The *Pink Pages*, Christchurch's Saturday evening sports edition, said:

All hail to Wilson Whineray, newcomer supremo among the All Black forwards. His first test appearance for New Zealand against Australia was the most impressive debut of a young forward since Tiny White skyrocketed to fame in Australia in 1949. Colin Windon, one of Australia's greatest loose forwards, described this All Black pack as the best he had ever seen.

While Wilson was plainly a specialist prop, coach Everest had some difficulty pinpointing Colin Meads's ideal role and during the tour used him variously as a No. 8, flanker and lock. For the two internationals, Meads was played on the side of the scrum with Everest hammering into him the need to contain Australia's dangerous fly-half (and captain) Dr Dick Tooth. Well, 'contain' probably doesn't too accurately describe the coach's instructions to the rangy King Country fellow who was making his test debut.

'He's a threat to us,' Everest told Meads. 'Your job is not only to stop him running, but to unnerve him.'

'How am I going to do that?' asked Meads.

'You're going to hit him with dive tackles.'

'Dive tackles, what the hell are they?'

'Watch, and I'll show you.'

Everest ran and threw himself at a tackle bag. 'See, that's how you do it.'

Meads pondered the directive with suspicion.

'Hmm,' he muttered. 'I'm not sure about that.'

No matter how hard he tried, Meads's feet remained firmly in contact with terra firma, although he sure gave the tackle bag a pounding. Dive-tackling never did become part of his repertoire.

When he entered the dressing room after the first test, Everest said to him, 'You never left the ground once.'

'I know, but I unnerved that bloody first-five of theirs!'

Meads, at 20 the youngest member of the side, might not have collected Tooth with a dive tackle, but he scragged him repeatedly, ripped his jersey, and generally made his afternoon a misery. The good doctor would have worrying recollections for some time afterwards of this All Black flanker coming after him.

The second test was in Brisbane, and the All Blacks again demolished the Wallabies, this time by 22 points to 9, prompting the Australian coach, Barney Walsh, to describe the tourists as the most brilliant team he had ever seen.

The final month of the tour was little more than a flag-flying exercise for the All Blacks as they engaged a succession of outclassed opponents. They scored 18 tries against South West Zone at Grenfell to win 86–0 (with five-point tries the score would have been 122–0). Halfback Alan 'Ponty' Reid captained the team from second-five against Riverina at Wagga Wagga, and tight forwards Tiny Hill and Dennis Young kicked conversions in the tour finale against South Australia, to put them on the tour scoreboard.

Reid captained the team in every Saturday encounter, while Hill, Robin Archer and Ian Clarke had turns at leading the side in some of the midweek romps. Not surprisingly, Wilson, who didn't turn 22 until a couple of weeks after the tour concluded, wasn't burdened with leadership concerns. But in the season ahead he would become New Zealand's youngest test captain since Herb Lilburn in 1929.

There is an offbeat footnote to the triumphant tour of Australia, because the team lost its tag of invincibility three days after returning home. One further challenge remained before the team disbanded: a game against Canterbury at Lancaster Park. Wilson was one of three players appearing against his own province; Dennis Young and Tiny Hill being the others. It was the Cantabs, who had lowered the Springboks' colours the previous year, who triumphed, recording an 11–9 victory.

Three weeks later Wilson would, strangely enough, experience defeat against his own province again, this time as a member of the New Zealand Universities team, Canterbury winning a tight contest, 8–3.

A teammate for the first time was John Graham, then of Auckland

University. They would enjoy each other's company and go on to become lifelong friends.

With its All Blacks back, Canterbury enjoyed a hugely successful season of representative play. The national championship wouldn't be introduced until 1976, but, had it been operating in 1957, Canterbury, based on results against major opponents, would have reigned supreme.

Having established himself in the Canterbury team in 1956, Wilson regarded it as vital to consolidate his place in the front row. It was something he managed with bells on.

At season's end, the *New Zealand Rugby Almanack* named him one of its players of the year, a remarkable achievement for someone so young.

The *Almanack*'s citation read:

> Wilson Whineray is one of the younger generation of players bound to serve New Zealand for many seasons. His studency as an agricultural cadet has taken him to many parts, at each his strong and bustling play as a front row prop carrying him into his adopted union's side. He rightly went into the New Zealand team for the tour of Australia where he played in eight matches including the two internationals.

The first indication that the wise men of the NZRU had Wilson in mind as an All Black captain came when they named him to lead the New Zealand Under-23 team on a 10-match tour of Japan and Hong Kong in February and March 1958. It was phenomenally good fortune for Wilson and his good mate Colin Meads that the NZRU, having despatched them both to Ceylon as Colts three years earlier, should now choose to raise the age restriction on the team to 23. They were both delighted to find themselves eligible again, and, in the light of the progress they had made with the All Blacks in Australia, they were sitters for this assignment.

Japan actually wanted a full-blooded All Black team to tour, not because they rated themselves worthy of such a formidable opponent, but because they knew it would be easier to market the real thing, the All Blacks being adored by rugby followers throughout the land. The NZRU compromised, despatching a team of Juniors, six of whom had been blooded as All Blacks on the tour of Australia — Terry Lineen, Russell Watt, Colin Meads, Rex Pickering, Ack Soper, and Wilson. Others who would subsequently rise to full international status were Pat Walsh, Ross Brown, Kevin Briscoe, Roger Boon, Kevin Barry, John Creighton, and Kel Tremain. Their coach was Jack Sullivan, who would take over the All Blacks later in the year.

As the Juniors moved around Japan, playing games in Tokyo, Fukuoka, Nishinomiya, Osaka and Nagoya, they found the Japanese were promoting them as the All Blacks anyway!

Not surprisingly, Wilson was the star of the trial from which the touring party was chosen. The NZPA report had this to say of him: 'Whineray's touch of real class contrasted with the exuberance-but-no-finesse form of some of the other young forwards e.g. his fielding while on the run of high punts and the way he slammed them back up the sideline.'

The team flew out of Whenuapai on 17 February, returning on 24 March. At least they didn't have to endure the slow-boat-to-China routine that had tested the fortitude of the Colts three years earlier. The players were all given Japanese/English dictionaries.

Thirty thousand fans turned up for the tour opener against All Waseda University in Tokyo, the city where the young New Zealanders met Princess Chichibu, Her Imperial Highness.

The Juniors won their opening game effortlessly, and proceeded to cut a swathe through all opponents. All 10 matches were won by big margins, Whineray's men scoring 88 tries while conceding just eight, although the goal-kicking didn't match the team's try-scoring capabilities.

In the first international against All-Japan, a game won 34–6, they scored 10 tries and converted only two. In the next game they scored 11 tries and converted three.

Captain Whineray was challenged in a manner he hadn't

anticipated, and confessed he feared social ostracism on his return if the Japanese continued to present him with flowers. 'If my hard old front-row mates could see me now,' he said after receiving his fourth bouquet of the tour (a large bunch of carnations and a buttonhole spray) at Osaka, 'they would be sure to scrub me.'

4

FOLLOW THE LEADER

Until Wilson came along, there had never been, in the 55 years the All Blacks had been involved in test-match rugby, a long-term appointment as captain. The longest any one individual had survived as leader was seven tests, that honour belonging to Cliff Porter, who led the 'Invincibles' on their famous 1924–25 expedition to the United Kingdom and France, although ironically because of injuries and selection vagaries he appeared in only one of the five internationals. After missing selection for the tour of South Africa in 1928, he went on to captain the All Blacks in Australia in 1929 and against Great Britain in 1930. Obviously, he was a gifted leader, and in a sense you could argue he was a long-term appointee.

In the early days, tours and test matches were infrequent; indeed, there were several years when the NZRU was not required to field an international team at all. This is in dramatic contrast with the modern professional game, where élite players can make up to 14 test appearances in one calendar year.

In the dozen years after international rugby was revived following the Second World War, the All Blacks remarkably got through no fewer than eight test captains. Fred Allen, who boldly stepped aside as team leader during the traumatic tour of South Africa in 1949, when all four tests were lost, led his country in six internationals. Ron Elvidge was captain in five tests; the same as Bob Stuart, who led the All Blacks on their tour of Britain and France in 1953–54. Essentially, the All Blacks chose a fresh captain for each tour and each series. That was all about to change with the appointment of a certain Wilson Whineray to lead the men in black against the 1958 Australian touring team.

One who was particularly enthusiastic about this selection was Brian O'Brien. He wrote in the *New Zealand Sports Digest* that, since the retirement of Fred Allen after the 1949 tour of South Africa, the All Black captaincy had been anything but a static appointment.

> Indeed, in the eight years since, many different captains have been appointed — Ron Elvidge against Great Britain in 1950, Peter Johnstone in Australia in 1951, Kevin Skinner against Australia in 1952, Bob Stuart on the long tour of the UK and France in 1953–54, Ian Clarke against Australia in 1955, Pat Vincent and Bob Duff against the Springboks in 1956 and Ponty Reid in Australia in 1957.
>
> Wilson Whineray has acceded to the rank of New Zealand captain without first having filled that role at provincial level (although he did captain the New Zealand Juniors to Japan).
>
> In Whineray's favour are his earnest approach to the game, his ability to deliver impressive pre-match dissertations to his colleagues and his polish and sincerity in speechmaking on social occasions.
>
> One critic has written that one thing New Zealand has now after a long lapse is a captain. In Whineray, there is a captain to hand who is sure of his place, who is always to the forefront on the field, who can give a team talk calculated to leave the average coach open-mouthed and who can speak fluently, pleasantly and wisely in official circles.
>
> Whineray has a number of things in common with another well-known All Black front rower in Kevin Skinner. Both achieved distinction in the boxing ring. Whineray was the NZ Universities heavyweight champion and Skinner was national heavyweight champion in 1947.

Although he was only 23, Wilson's appointment appeared a formality after he led his trial team to a resounding 51–20 win in Palmerston

North, then captained North to a 12–6 victory in the inter-island fixture in Dunedin, South also being led by a prop, Mark Irwin.

Wilson had no personal forewarning of his elevation to the leadership, although the newspapers were proclaiming him the captain elect long before the chairman of the NZRU, Cuth Hogg, made the announcement at Carisbrook, at the function that followed the inter-island game. He was standing alongside his good mate Colin Meads when the touring party was named.

'You're the captain, you bugger,' said Meads, shaking Wilson's hand vigorously. 'They couldn't have done better.'

Wilson was prepared for this moment. *If they want me as a leader, I'll deliver.* He would reveal to his good friend John Graham years later that captaincy suited his personality because he always liked to be involved, was prepared to make decisions, related to people around him, and derived satisfaction from plotting campaigns and putting them into execution. 'People think everyone is aspiring to be captain,' he would tell Graham, 'but they aren't. Only a few seek leadership, because it's something that can impact seriously on performance. While a lock, say, only has to concern himself with pushing in the scrum, jumping in the lineout, getting to the next breakdown and making tackles as required, the captain, besides performing his individual duties, has to be aware of the score, the weather, the time remaining, keep in verbal contact with the backline leader about what's working and what's not and sense if the opposition are planning something special.'

Wilson had relocated since 1957. Having completed his studies at Lincoln College, for his fifth and final year as an agricultural student he was employed by the State Advances Corporation in Hamilton, focusing on the financial side of farming. It was akin to working for the Rural Bank. Through the Lands and Survey Department, the Government was purchasing blocks of land and creating subdivisions. One large station would be broken down into half a dozen farms. On behalf of State Advances, Wilson then worked to assist the new landowners with their budgets. For about four months he was seconded to Rotorua, where State Advances was short-staffed. There he immediately made contact with Bill Gray, who was established as the All Blacks' second-five at the time, and with whom Wilson had become good friends on the tour of Australia in 1957. They combined in several successful pig-hunting outings.

Wilson had linked up with the City club in Hamilton, to the delight of the Waikato coach, Bill Corby, and had duly won selection for Waikato. When he took the field against Auckland in the traditional Queen's Birthday fixture, it meant he'd represented four unions in five years. He was in good company, for the Waikato team also featured four other All Blacks who had toured Australia in 1957: brothers Don and Ian Clarke, Ponty Reid, and Rex Pickering. Wilson turned out seven times for Waikato in 1958, without ever tasting defeat. Given that the opponents included Auckland twice and Australia, that was no small achievement.

When you are 23 and the new skipper of the All Blacks, you naturally want everything to go right. And that's exactly what happened at Athletic Park. Not only did the All Blacks overrun the Wallabies, scoring seven tries to one, but the first two tries were scored by … guess who? The new captain, no less! His two touchdowns came within 15 minutes of kick-off. He was beginning to think this captaincy role was a bit of a lark.

Well, in sport you should always enjoy the moment, because you never know what's around the corner. Two weeks later, the Wallabies staged a dramatic form reversal and won the second test in Christchurch. And in his remaining 31 internationals, Wilson would never score another try!

Wilson had become accustomed to having The Boot (Don Clarke) at fullback whenever he took the field for the All Blacks. It was terribly reassuring to have someone who could slam over goals from your own half and drive opponents back with prodigious touch-finders. The Boot demoralized opponents and Wilson was delighted to have him in his team. Then, for the first time since he'd aspired to the All Blacks, Wilson went into a game — that second test at Lancaster Park in Christchurch — without The Boot wearing the No. 1 jersey, injuries having denied both Clarke brothers selection. Their replacements were Lloyd Ashby at fullback, who in what would be his solitary appearance for New Zealand failed to score a point, and Mark Irwin at prop.

The All Blacks scarcely fired a shot. Notwithstanding the urgings of their new captain, they laboured along, managing just three points in 80 minutes. The Wallabies held them to 3-all at half-time, and secured victory with a dazzling individual try by the lightweight winger Alan Morton. It was hard to believe this was the same All Black team that had demolished the Aussies in Wellington — well, the same team minus a brace of Clarkes.

Pertinently, the Clarke brothers were back for the decider in Auckland, a game staged not at Eden Park, which was closed while the new southern grandstand was being constructed, but at Epsom Showgrounds. Coach Jack Sullivan and captain Whineray, aware that an element of complacency had undoubtedly crept into their play in Christchurch, insisted that nothing less than a complete 80-minute performance would be acceptable in the series decider. The All Blacks controlled the game throughout. Clarke's booming boot brilliantly complemented an accomplished forward performance, the home side establishing a decisive 17–3 lead before the Wallabies ran in a last-gasp try. The massive Bledisloe Cup, which didn't have the name Australia inscribed on it many times, remained securely in New Zealand's grasp.

Waikato's representative programme wrapped up in late September, but, before Wilson could pack his boots away for the summer, he was off to Wellington to honour an invitation from the Centurions club, which had enterprisingly brought together a collection of players from the New Zealand Juniors team that had toured Japan to play Wellington.

Wilson saw it as a perfect opportunity to resolve a personal matter. His relationship with Beth had to that point been limited, their romance separated by distance. Letters had heavily outweighed liaisons. With Wilson's rugby and work commitments, and Beth's dedication to the nursing profession, they'd only seen each other about four times in 1957, and 1958 hadn't shaped up much better. So Wilson, who was smitten with the good-looker from Palmerston North, decided it was time to make things happen.

Having first talked with Beth's mother and conveyed his intentions, he invited Beth to Wellington for the Centurions game.

'It's not easy to get away,' she initially protested, 'because I'm working six days a week. I'll have to take leave.'

'I think you should come,' he insisted.

'I'll see what I can arrange,' said Beth.

To Wilson's delight, Beth came to Wellington. To Beth's delight, Wilson proposed. To Wilson's delight, Beth accepted.

It was Beth's first experience of mixing with other players' wives and girlfriends, all of whom were thrilled when the news broke. Suddenly, Beth, who'd lived a quiet, anonymous existence in Palmerston North, was a national celebrity. The All Black captain getting engaged was big news for the Wellington daily newspapers, and Beth found herself splashed across the front page. She began to appreciate why her girlfriends were so excited when Wilson came to town. He certainly had status.

In Wellington that weekend, she was fortunate to have Colin Meads's wife Verna to take her under her wing and guide her through the social protocol, which included a separate dinner for the partners while the players were dining with the Wallabies. The guys eventually linked up with the gals for the social and dance.

The *Rugby Almanack* was lavish in its praise of the Centurions for arranging the end-of-season encounter.

The Centurions club obtained a 'scoop' when arrangements were made to meet Wellington with a side drawn from the under-23 New Zealand team which went to Japan and Hong Kong. The team fielded included seven All Blacks and proved successful by one point. The club is to be congratulated on its initiative in providing the capital city audience with the opportunity of witnessing a side containing many players who could well be the backbone of New Zealand teams for some time to come.

Given that the Centurions team featured Colin Meads, Kel Tremain, Pat Walsh, Ross Brown, Kevin Briscoe, Ack Soper, Rex Pickering, John Creighton, Kevin Barry and the newly engaged Wilson Whineray, it was an astute statement.

It was Grant, the eldest of the Whineray boys, who was suddenly in the headlines in 1958 after performing a heroic surf-rescue. Thanks to their father, all the boys were strong swimmers, and a couple of teenagers attending a Bible class camp could be grateful for that. Grant was holidaying at Waipu Cove, and after a long day had gone to bed. He was roused by an anxious neighbour, informing him that a couple of swimmers were in trouble in the surf.

Grant wasn't prepared to enter the water without a surf-belt on, so he smashed open the door of the Waipu Surf Club to obtain one before plunging into the water. The two teenagers were about 100 metres offshore and in serious difficulties. He first brought in the boy, who had almost no energy left, before returning for the girl.

The Royal Humane Society presented him with a plaque. The citation reads: 'To Grant Whineray, who roused from bed at 10 p.m. on 25 October 1958, rescued Kay Kelly, 16, and Christopher Quarry, 17, who had got into difficulties swimming at Waipu Cove. Mr Whineray donned the belt and swam out approximately 100 yards through heavy seas and darkness to rescue them.'

Wilson and Beth agreed that 1959 would be the ideal time to marry, but the opportunities were scant because of Wilson's rugby commitments. If they didn't tie the knot early, they would have to wait until the conclusion of the rugby season late in September.

Having spent most of the previous four years separated, and having committed to spending the rest of their lives together, they decided sooner was definitely better than later. So the wedding was set for March in the Methodist Church in Palmerston North.

Wilson drove down from Auckland in his mother's Morris Minor with his eldest brother Grant, who was his best man. They arrived a day later than scheduled after running short of petrol near Waiouru. Finding the service station closed, they elected not to tackle the Desert Road on a quarter-tank, instead waiting patiently overnight until they could replenish their tank.

It was a simple, friendly wedding. Beth's bridesmaids were her best friend, Gillian Croll, and her sisters, Anne and Pru. Immediate family aside, most of Wilson's support crew were his fellow students from Lincoln College, plus a handful of rugby mates.

Wilson had told his bride-to-be that their honeymoon destination was Wairakei, in the centre of the North Island. She was delighted, aware that that was where the Tourist Hotel Corporation administered one of New Zealand's finest hotels. After a two-night stay in a motel at Waitarere Beach, on the west coast about 40 kilometres from Palmerston North, the Whinerays headed north in Wilson's mum's trusty Morris Minor.

When they arrived at Wairakei, it wasn't the tourist hotel that Wilson headed for, but the camping ground. They were staying in a cabin lined with bunks. And they were the only ones staying there!

'Interesting,' Beth said to Wilson.

'Nice part of the world,' said Wilson, as he headed for the water pump to fill up the kettle so they could brew a cup of tea.

After a couple of nights' rustic existence in Wairakei, they drove through to a bach at Tapu on the coastal road north of Thames on the Coromandel Peninsula, where they stayed in a motel. Beth began to discover what it was like being married to a rugby player. By the time she woke each morning, Wilson was out running. After all, there was a big season ahead — the British

Lions were coming to challenge the All Blacks.

On the Friday, Wilson announced to his new bride that they were now driving to New Plymouth.

'New Plymouth?' asked Beth, slightly perplexed. New Plymouth wasn't exactly a natural stopover *en route* to Auckland, where they would be setting up their home. In fact, it was almost 400 kilometres out of their way. 'That's a long way from here.'

'Er, yes,' said Wilson. 'The Grammar Old Boys rugby team is competing in an Easter tournament down there and they want me to play.'

'Oh, I see. That'll be nice.'

And away they went to New Plymouth, where Beth watched another game of rugby, met some more players' wives with whom she dined, and had another dance with her new husband.

On the Sunday they motored through to Auckland, where they moved into a flat in Epsom. On the Monday, Wilson was back at work. The previous year, as his rural cadetship drew to a conclusion, he'd approached the management at State Advances, advising them of his intention to study for a commerce degree, asking if he could be posted to a university centre. That narrowed the options to Auckland, Wellington, Christchurch or Dunedin, because at the time Hamilton didn't have a university. Auckland it was, Wilson taking up a position as field appraiser. Although his office was in the city, his territory was well to the north of Auckland, embracing Warkworth and Kaiwaka, coast to coast.

Life was certainly full-on for Wilson in 1959. He attended lectures from 8am to 10am, before tending to his farm-appraising work, then was often back in the lecture room early evening. In addition, he slotted in training sessions a couple of nights each week with Grammar Old Boys, before heading home to spend time with his wife.

Fortunately for Wilson, rugby seasons in the 1950s were not cluttered with Super 12, 14 or 15 championships. The first representative fixture for Auckland in 1959 was, believe it or not, on 1 June, the traditional Queen's Birthday clash against Waikato in Hamilton. Today, by 1 June most leading rugby players have completed an entire Super 14 campaign of up to 15 matches, not to mention warm-up fixtures in January and February!

In the same manner that Waikato had embraced Wilson the previous season, Auckland now spread the welcome mat for the All Black skipper. Auckland's coach was Fred Allen, who didn't waste any time in appointing Wilson captain. Although Fred the Needle, as he would become known, would earn legendary status as a coach, his record entering the 1959 season was extremely modest. There had been 19 wins, 9 losses, and a draw across the previous two seasons; nothing to write home about. Something needed to happen for 'The Needle' in 1959. And WJ Whineray was just the fellow to help turn around Fred's fortunes.

Fred Allen completed a trio of coaches who had all served in the Second World War and would massively influence Wilson's career. The others were Neil McPhail, who'd been Wilson's mentor with Canterbury and with whom Wilson would combine with sensational effect in the United Kingdom and France, and Jack Sullivan, who would guide the All Blacks through until the completion of the 1960 tour of South Africa. They were real men who had experienced life at the sharp end. They were tough but fair, not men you pushed around. They all earned the utmost respect from those who played under them. If you made mistakes or let your team down, you knew you would have to account to them. But when you were successful, they applauded you.

Sullivan was more taciturn than the other two; indeed, McPhail was positively gregarious. But on the long tour of South Africa in 1960, Sullivan often confided in his captain. He told Wilson once that the worst mistakes he had made as a selector were in choosing players who had performed showily against soft opponents, in preference to others who had grafted away against quality markers.

Beware the Flash Harrys, was his message.

One of the ridiculous features of rugby in the 1950s as decreed by the IRB, presumably in their determination to preserve the amateur sanctity of the game, was that replacements were not permitted in international matches. A broken leg, even two broken legs, was no justification for allowing a fresh player onto the field. As a consequence, reserves ceased to be reserves the moment the game commenced. At that point, they changed back into their civvies and took a seat in the grandstand. Although they featured in official team photos, they were not credited with an appearance unless they were part of a starting XV.

This archaic piece of rugby legislation, which the game's administrators would not alter until 1968, would impact drastically on the All Blacks in the opening test of the 1959 series against the British Lions at Carisbrook in Dunedin. The game was no more than 10 minutes old when flanker Brian Finlay suffered a painful leg injury. Barely five minutes later, Peter Jones, another of the loose forward triumvirate, also went down injured. They would both remain on the field, but as virtual passengers.

Wilson pondered the gravity of the situation. The All Blacks were going to have to play virtually three-quarters of the game with only 13 able-bodied players. He called aside Rex Pickering, the solitary surviving loose forward. 'Rex, you're going to have to play off the back of the lineout and also as an open-side flanker. You're going to have to pace yourself.'

He then summoned his tight forwards. 'Listen, guys, we've got a hell of a predicament here. We're two loose forwards down, which means we effectively have no cover defence, so we really need to play the game in their half and keep the ball away from their backs as much as possible.'

The Lions possessed brilliant, speedy backs — individuals like Bev Risman, David Hewitt, Tony O'Reilly and Peter Jackson, some of the classiest footballers ever to visit New Zealand. Benefiting from the absence of any effective cover defence, the Lions scored four tries to establish a 17–9 advantage entering the final quarter. With tries worth only three points, that represented a massive lead in 1959, the equivalent of 25–9 under modern-day scoring. Given that the Lions were playing a depleted opponent, the odds appeared insurmountable for Wilson's men.

But Wilson continued to exhort his team to produce a supreme effort. And in The Boot the All Blacks possessed the ultimate match-winner. Big Don Clarke, weighing in at 16 stone 4 pound (103.5 kilograms), making him the equal heaviest player in the game, banged over a penalty goal from 50 metres to bring the All Blacks closer at 12–17 and another from 45 metres to haul his side up to 15–17 with seven minutes remaining. Refusing to yield to exhaustion, the 13 'surviving' All Blacks maintained pressure on the tourists, who continued to infringe at ruck time, where Otago referee Alan Fleury was severe on them. Two minutes from time, he awarded yet another penalty, this one in close proximity to the posts, and The Boot wasn't going to miss this opportunity.

The All Blacks survived one desperate late surge from the British Lions to win by 18 points to 17, an outcome that would reverberate around the rugby world; not for the result but for the manner in which it was achieved. Outrage, screamed the Fleet Street journalists. Six penalty goals should never defeat four tries. The referee predictably came in for a shellacking, and many questioned why a penalty goal was worth the same number of points as a try. Although there were cries from many quarters for the value of a try to be increased from three points, the IRB — a body that never moved with undue haste, until, almost unbelievably in 1995, virtually overnight it declared the game professional — chose to leave the game's scoring system intact for a further 13 years.

Wilson knew there would be a fuss over the outcome, and he diplomatically deflected questions that came his way in the inquest that followed. He hadn't personally awarded any of the penalties. His sympathy was not for the hapless tourists but for the heroic display by his team, forced to take on Britain's finest with 13 players for the last hour. He was also full of admiration for Clarke's goal-kicking.

He was quoted in *Rugby Greats* as saying, 'There is a tendency to overlook the fact that Clarke's six penalty goals represented one of the great kicking exhibitions of all time. They made silly blunders, and Clarke kicked the goals. I certainly didn't feel happy about winning by six goals to four tries, but they made the mistakes.'

It would be Clarke who would frustrate the Lions when the teams clashed again four weeks later in Wellington. Only this time, it wasn't his goal-kicking that invoked further gnashing of teeth; indeed, he landed just one conversion in the game. A minute from time, he came storming into the backline, fielded a pass from John McCullough, and dived spectacularly across the line for the winning try. A one-point win in Dunedin, a three-point win in Wellington — Wilson's men didn't have much to spare, but they were getting home.

A player who would become a great colleague of Wilson's and win recognition as one of the great All Black forwards made his test debut at Wellington: Kel Tremain. By the time Tremain joined the scene, Don Clarke and Colin Meads had established themselves as individuals of enormous influence, The Boot for all the obvious reasons; Meads in more subtle ways.

'Colin helped me when things were getting touchy in my test debut,' Tremain would later relate. 'Roddy Evans [the Lions lock] was giving me a rough time in the lineouts, pushing at every throw-in. Finally, Colin moved back and said, "Listen, if you don't leave this guy alone, you won't walk off the field!" Evans left me alone from that moment and I settled down to concentrate on the rugby.'

In the third test in Christchurch, the All Blacks crushed the tourists 22–8 and — although the Lions restored some pride with a well-taken, if narrow, victory at Eden Park, when Clarke proved he was mortal by missing a close-range penalty goal a couple of minutes from time — it meant that the All Blacks had completed a decade of action since last losing a test series. That had been against the Springboks, who were looming as the All Blacks' next challenge.

The 1959 season just kept getting better for Wilson, who was enjoying his rugby for Auckland because Fred Allen was using him at No. 8 — a position in which he always fancied himself — the reason being that Auckland had two crash-hot props already functioning well: Snow White, who would go on to create a remarkable record of 196 appearances for the union, and the inimitable Alby Pryor. Pryor had a reputation as a *provocateur*, one he tended to enhance with his raucous wit, and was a much-underestimated footballer. Wilson soon identified him as an individual who could rev a set of forwards up a gear or two at critical moments. He would play an important role when the team got to Invercargill.

As in the two previous seasons, Auckland's record, at the time it embarked on its four-match southern tour, was most unflattering (seven wins, four losses and a draw, one of those losses being to the British Lions) and there were murmurings that Fred Allen's tenure as coach would be under threat if things didn't improve. Auckland and Fred the Needle's good fortune was that the Ranfurly Shield was at stake when the team arrived in Invercargill after a good win over Otago, Southland having prised the 'log' off Taranaki. However, Wilson knew that defeating the southerners on Rugby Park — which in those days had a notoriously gluey surface that had tripped up many visitors — would not be easy.

Wilson's style as a captain was to essentially remain silent in the shakedown to kick-off time, leaving the coach in charge. Fred Allen was a forthright coach, not beyond banging his first on a table to make a point or singling out a hapless individual for personal attack. He didn't need his captain joining in. When Wilson, in his considered, meaningful way, made a contribution it was usually after Fred the Needle had exited the dressing room. Prior to kick-off in Invercargill, he quietly addressed each of his fellow forwards. To each one, he said simply: 'This will be a difficult afternoon — at some stage I may have to call for a supreme effort.'

That moment came about 15 minutes from the finish, after Southland's goal-kicker Lloyd Ashby had landed a third penalty goal, leaving Auckland ahead by a solitary point, 10–9. As the next lineout was forming, Wilson moved quietly from forward to forward. 'Supreme effort,' he said, squeezing each player by the arm. To Alby Pryor, he added a rider: 'This is where I need you, Alby.'

Southland threw everything at Auckland over the next 10 minutes, but the challenger's defence remained resolute, and a late try to Paul Little saw the Ranfurly Shield on the move again. Back in Auckland, the players were fêted as heroes and Fred Allen's future as coach was secure. 'No doubt about it,' he admitted years later, 'if we hadn't won the shield, I was a goner.' He forthrightly declared he would remain Auckland's coach for as long as the shield was retained. Despite a brief blip the next season, the 'log' would hold permanent residency in Auckland until 1963. That's when Fred finally stepped aside.

5

FRUSTRATION ON THE HIGH VELDT

There's nothing as daunting as a full-scale rugby tour of South Africa. Modern-day players wouldn't appreciate this as they zap in and zap out for international contests. The longest a present-day player would be likely to spend in the republic, rare British Lions tours excepted, is three weeks. Contrast that with the 1949 tourists, who were four months in South Africa and had to endure boat travel to and from New Zealand, extending their expedition to more than six months.

At least the 1960 touring party that Wilson captained had the luxury of flying, albeit far more laboriously than players enjoy these days. A 2010 All Black boards a jumbo jet in Sydney and doesn't disembark until it touches down in Johannesburg some 14 hours later. In 1960, Wilson's team, after playing a series of warm-up fixtures in Australia, flew from Perth to Cocos Islands, and on to Mauritius, before eventually landing in Johannesburg. There they had to contend with high altitude, long domestic journeys, formidable opponents, never-ending injuries, and South African referees.

Wilson's team's 1949 predecessors returned traumatized after being whitewashed in the test series. Although the All Blacks had since won a home series against the mighty men in green, those heading to South Africa in 1960 knew the challenge confronting them was of monumental proportions.

Tom Pearce was appointed manager, and Jack Sullivan coach; the one as garrulous as the other was reserved. Together, Tom and Wilson would equip the All Blacks with a pair of orators who would enthral audiences with their speeches, stories, quotations and occasional poetry.

The All Blacks played five matches in Australia *en route* to South Africa, including two double-headers. The opening game against Queensland (played in Sydney) produced a gem for trivia buffs, for the All Blacks' first try was scored by an Australian, Eddie Stapleton. This came about because, with two players injured and the New Zealanders required to field two separate XVs, a couple of local personalities were recruited as honorary All Blacks. Stapleton, who played 16 tests for the Wallabies in the 1950s, was one; Maurie Graham, who would become a prominent administrator, the other. They played at wing and fullback, respectively.

The All Blacks played another double-header at Orange, before taking on Western Australia in Perth, winning all the matches by wide margins. They then winged their way to the republic on a South African Airways DC-7B aircraft.

The seating allocation was conducted in a novel manner. The team's biggest players were placed up front in business class, while the small blokes, mostly the backs, were relegated to the back few rows of the plane. One of the 'little buggers', as he referred to himself, was Adrian Clarke, a five-eighth from Auckland. He was not related to Don and Ian Clarke, but was the son of Vernon Clarke, who was for many years the official photographer for the NZRU. During the flight Adrian fell into conversation with a South African woman sitting across the aisle from him.

'My niece would love to meet your players and get some autographs,' she told Clarke.

'Well, I'm sure that won't be a problem,' said Clarke, imagining the niece to be aged about 10 or 11.

'She'll be at the airport to meet me — perhaps we can manage something there?'

'No problem.'

Well, there was a problem, because at Jan Smuts Airport in Johannesburg some 7,000 to 8,000 people — by far the biggest crowd ever to welcome a sporting team to South Africa — packed the concourse. Wilson would tell author AC 'Ace' Parker that the reception given to his players was the most moving thing he had ever experienced. Because of the bedlam at the airport, Clarke didn't link up with his travelling companion. The niece who wanted some autographs passed completely from his mind until, a few days later, he fielded a call from the woman.

'Remember me?' she asked Clarke.

'Certainly,' replied Clarke politely. 'Your niece wants some autographs.'

'Yes, do you think that is possible?'

'I'm sure it is,' said Clarke, wondering when would be the best time to accommodate a young enthusiast. 'Tell me, how old is your niece?'

'Oh, she's 20, and she was recently crowned Miss South Africa.'

Clarke gulped. 'Oh, really . . . um . . . er . . . well, do you think she might like to come to the dance on Saturday night after the first game?'

'I'm sure she would. Listen, her name's Moya [Meaker] — why don't I get her to give you a call and you can make the arrangements?'

Clarke couldn't believe his good fortune. It was only the first week of the tour and he was about to escort Miss South Africa to the team's first social function.

The opening encounter, which was won handsomely by the All Blacks, didn't involve Clarke. His main focus that day was obviously going to be on his glamorous partner, but, when she arrived at the hall where the dance was being held, Clarke found to his dismay that she was an inch and a half taller than him.

'Look,' he said, 'I'd feel a bit stupid dancing with you, being such a little bloke as I am.'

'Nonsense,' said Moya. 'I'll take my shoes off.'

And for the opening couple of dances, Moya got around the floor comfortably in bare feet. A photograph of Clarke and Moya dancing duly appeared in Ace Parker's book *The All Blacks Juggernaut in South Africa*. They appear the same height, with the photo conveniently not showing Moya's bare feet.

The evening deteriorated for Clarke, who was soon cut out by one of the taller members of the touring party. 'Life can sometimes be very cruel for us short blokes,' he quipped to his teammates later.

On the other side of the height ledger was Don Clarke, whose phenomenal exploits as a goal-kicker, combined with his massive presence — at 16 stone 8 pound (105.5 kilograms) he was the second-heaviest member of the side — understandably made him the team's star celebrity. Aware of his popularity, he packed 15 right boots in his luggage for the tour. He knew that locals were always trying to souvenir his boots, so he was always hiding some and asking teammates to look after others. Wilson quite often had a couple of DB Clarke's right boots stowed away in his suitcase.

Notwithstanding these precautions, Clarke managed to arrive at Newlands for the Western Province match minus his kicking boot, because he'd forgotten where he'd hidden it. The boot he borrowed from a teammate was ill-fitting, and disintegrated when he let fly with a booming touch-finder during the game. Wilson was about 10 metres in front of him and ducked as the remains of the boot flew narrowly over his head like an Exocet missile!

Manager Tom Pearce arrived in South Africa with a reputation as something of a firebrand, but he controlled himself well in the early stages of the tour.

However, criticisms of his management style from some of the more sensational newspapers began to ruffle him.

Pearce brought some of it upon himself by vetoing cocktail parties, and even severely trimming barbecues (*braaivleis*, as the South Africans know them). 'I am against civic cocktail parties,' he declared, 'because the players stuff themselves with savouries which are not good for them. I am a great believer in rugby men having proper meals and eating plain, wholesome food. While appreciating the kind intentions behind all the invitations, we cannot accept all of them. We are here to play rugby and primarily to meet the rugby people of your country.'

While that made sense, he also said he was not enamoured with the South African *braaivleis*. By mutual arrangement with the South African Rugby Board, he decreed that the All Blacks would attend only three official functions on the entire tour. Some of his rulings were obviously misinterpreted by some journalists, who became extremely critical of him. He in turn became sensitive to criticism, whereas his phlegmatic assistant Jack Sullivan would have shrugged and offered a 'No comment'.

Things reached boiling point at a golf course, where several of the players were enjoying a day off when a journalist and photographer from *Die Transvaaler* arrived.

Pearce saw red. 'That's the paper that's been writing all that bloody tripe,' he roared, and took off after them, chasing them off the golf course.

The next day Wilson called Meads aside. 'I want you to make a speech on behalf of the team, reassuring Tom that he's doing a great job and that we're all behind him.'

Meads gulped. 'You're the captain — why don't you make the speech?'

'Because he likes you.'

At the next team meeting, Meads delivered a heartfelt speech. 'Don't let the bloody media get you down,' he said. 'We know there's a hell of a lot of pressure on you — and while it's on you, it's not on us. You're doing a grand job as manager. You have our full support.'

It worked. The manager settled down, and there were no further major issues between him and the media.

One of Pearce's finest moments would come at Vereeniging, an industrial township on the high veldt where Afrikaans was obviously the preferred language and where the All Blacks acclimatized at the start of the tour. It began to irk manager Pearce that too great a percentage of speeches in the presence of the All Blacks were being delivered in Afrikaans without being translated.

'I'll put a stop to this,' he told his senior players, and went off to prepare a speech that would leave the locals gobsmacked.

'Righto, fellows,' he told his troops, as he prepared to respond to a speech at a civic reception in Vereeniging, 'I'm going to address them in Maori, only I can't speak Maori. But they won't know that, so it's important you guys laugh and applaud at appropriate moments.'

'OK, Tom, go for it,' said Wilson, bemused at what might follow.

Manager Pearce was summoned to the podium after the local mayor had again burbled on in Afrikaans without giving the New Zealanders the courtesy of a translation.

'Oamaru, Timaru, Waipukurau,' boomed out Tom. And away he went. He rattled off a good two dozen Maori place-names, pausing occasionally for appropriate reaction from his players. Te Kuiti got a mention — to Meads's delight — and so did Waikaremoana, Ruatoria, Matamata and Waipapakauri.

He stepped down to rapturous applause from his players but to more subdued clapping from the men of Vereeniging, who were beginning to appreciate that speaking in your native tongue wasn't such a good thing to do.

At the conclusion of his ingenious speech, Pearce said to his audience, 'And now I will translate, a courtesy you do not extend to us.'

It stopped all the nonsense. From that moment, no officials addressed All Black functions in Afrikaans, or, if they did slip in a few phrases, they courteously conveyed to their visitors in English what those words meant.

A fortnight out from the first test, the All Blacks took on Boland at Wellington, in Western Cape Province, a significant contest because three Springboks constituted the entire Boland front row. Chris Koch and Piet du Toit were the props, and Bertus van der Merwe the hooker. Another Springbok, Butch Lochner, was at No. 8. Although the Boland backs were unrated, obviously the forwards were going to severely test the tourists.

And that they did. It soon became apparent that Wilson was having trouble containing Du Toit, whose habit of pushing inwards at an angle was contrary to the laws. (This activity would bring Wilson and Du Toit into violent conflict in the internationals.) Such was the pressure from the Boland pack that All Black hooker Ron Hemi was jack-knifed at one scrum and tore his rib ligaments. The injury was so severe it necessitated a replacement (Roger Boon) being summoned from New Zealand. For the remainder of the Boland game, Nev MacEwan moved from lock into the front row, with Mark Irwin and Wilson taking turns at hooker.

It was typical of Wilson that he should shrug himself free of the traumas unfolding in the front row to score the first try. Positioning himself at the back of a lineout, he gathered the throw-in and crashed through the defence to score.

Fortunately, Boland didn't possess backs of the quality of its forwards, and the All Blacks, not without moments of anxiety, eventually pulled away to win by 16 points.

The Afrikaans weekly newspaper *Die Landstem* published an explosive article the week following the Boland game, in which it claimed that the All Black captain was heard to say that if Piet du

Toit was included in the Springbok team for the first test and used methods they considered illegal — notably his habit of pushing inwards at an angle — the All Blacks would use their fists.

The article angered manager Pearce, who in a statement said that the story was 'absolutely without foundation'. He added, 'We consider this article is a direct attempt to cause dissension between the players of New Zealand and South Africa. We have not instructed and we will not instruct our players to use illegal tactics.'

Pearce was so incensed about the whole affair that he asked the South African Rugby Board to withdraw travel privileges from the writer of the article, but Dr Danie Craven, on behalf of the board, said it could not place such restrictions on a journalist whose expenses were met by his newspaper.

A victory in the first test was regarded as essential if Whineray's men were to become the first New Zealand team to claim a series on South African soil. Unfortunately, the venue for the series opener was Ellis Park in Johannesburg, 6,500 feet above sea level. These days, New Zealand teams prepare for fixtures in Johannesburg by either staying at sea level and flying in 24 hours before kick-off or by basing themselves for at least a week in the rarefied air. Players relocating themselves at more than 6,000 feet above sea level are at their most vulnerable two to four days after first exposing their bodies, and particularly their lungs, to the extreme altitude. That is the mistake the 1960 All Blacks made. They chose not to move into their Johannesburg hotel until 48 hours before kick-off.

Wilson's team took a 13–0 drubbing from the Springboks, and although he was, as always, extremely diplomatic in his post-match comments, acknowledging that the Springboks had comprehensively outplayed his team, he would many years later attribute his team's dismal performance to the altitude factor. The All Blacks found their minds and their bodies were reacting slowly to happenings, and against a super-sharp South African side that spelt disaster.

Although most of the critics had predicted an All Black win, based on their demolition of the strong Northern Transvaal team the weekend before, when Wilson stood down because of a rare injury (a sprained thumb, the media reported) the tourists were never in the game. And Don Clarke had an afternoon to forget. Not only did he not score any points — the first time in his test career he had drawn a blank — the flying Springbok winger Hennie van Zyl also twice eluded him to score tries.

This was the All Blacks' first encounter with Martin Pelser, who had won renown on two counts: his uncompromising play, and the fact he possessed only one eye. By the end of the series, Meads and company would acknowledge him as the toughest player they had ever encountered. Meads and Tremain agreed that at lineouts one would jump while the other took care of Pelser. The theory was impeccable, but Pelser wasn't a player to be trifled with. The first time Tremain shoved him, he turned around and whacked him. 'Hey, Colin, I think you better go back and deal with him,' said Tremain. 'I'll do the jumping for a while.' At the next South African throw-in, Meads laid into Pelser, then beat a hasty retreat. 'You wouldn't believe it,' he said later. 'The bugger came round our side of the ruck offside, pulled me out and hit me! Kel and I gave up at that stage!' Meads said he played against Pelser five times and never did work out which was his good eye.

It was a sombre touring party that made the gruelling 1,100-kilometre trek to Kitwe in Northern Rhodesia, from where they were able to unwind during a visit to Victoria Falls, one of the great natural attractions on Earth. It was as well they were based there for only four days, because by the time they returned to Johannesburg, political events in the Belgian Congo, across the nearby Northern Rhodesia border, were about to burst into full fury.

After the game against the Northern Rhodesian XV, which the All Blacks battled to win by four points (leading journalist Terry McLean unkindly labelling it one of the worst performances ever), the teams socialized over a drink or two. It afforded an opportunity for Wilson to get to know one of the props he'd packed down against that afternoon, Eden Holton, who'd kicked all his team's points. He was a distinctive fellow, standing 6 foot 2 inches tall and wearing a handlebar moustache. (The other prop, incidentally, was Andy Macdonald, who would not only achieve greatness as a Springbok but international fame for surviving a confrontation with a lion.) Wilson and Eden Holton got on famously over several beers, finally shaking hands and agreeing to meet up again in Salisbury four days later, Holton having been selected to represent the Rhodesian national side in the Saturday game against the tourists.

On the eve of the Salisbury game, Wilson was comfortably in bed and about to turn out the light when there came a knock on his door. He opened it to find Holton standing there.

'Hello,' said Wilson, 'nice to see you again, Eden. Can I help you?'

'Yes — do you know where the Rhodesian team is staying? I've just driven seven hours from Kitwe and no one seems to know where my team is.'

'I'm sorry,' said Wilson, 'I have no idea.'

'Then I've got a problem. Where the hell am I going to sleep tonight?'

'Well, we can't have you destitute,' said Wilson. 'Wait here a minute and I'll see if I can bunk down in Colin Meads's room.'

Meads was only too happy to accommodate his good friend, so the All Black skipper magnanimously offered up his warm bed to the opposition front-rower.

'See you in the morning,' said Wilson as he headed for Meads's room.

'You're a great mate,' said Eden.

It was to Holton's advantage that Wilson wasn't playing the next day, but it still demonstrated the wonderful camaraderie that existed among rugby players in those far off, truly amateur days. In this seriously professional era, Holton would never have advanced beyond the hotel reception, let alone got to knock on the All Black captain's door.

A fortnight out from the second test, the All Blacks took on the Junior Springboks in Durban, and, because injuries were becoming a major concern, Wilson took the field at No. 8, an opportunity he relished. The All Blacks had been accused of neglecting their backs, but in this game they cut loose and scored some delightful tries.

At sea level in Cape Town, where their lungs functioned normally, the All Blacks levelled the series with a well-taken 11–3 victory in the second test. Meads, operating at No. 8, scored the only try, the balance of the points coming from Clarke's boot. If the All Blacks had cashed in all their opportunities, they could have won by 20 points.

The clash between Wilson and Piet du Toit, who possessed a frenetic desire to buckle the front row, was reignited. Not only did Du Toit test the All Black forwards' patience, the front-row shenanigans frustrated the referee, who gave a warning. 'Pull the scrum down again and I'll give a penalty,' said Michael Slabber, who was obviously having trouble identifying the villain.

The next scrum was duly pulled down, not by Du Toit but by a defiant Wilson, who promptly protested to the referee about the fearful behaviour of his opponent. Du Toit, who spoke gutteral English — Afrikaans being his natural tongue — barked at Wilson: 'What da hell you doing, man?'

'Well, you bloody started it!' responded Wilson.

During the game against Western Transvaal at Potchefstroom, the crowd reacted with hostility at some of the referee's decisions and began throwing bottles on to the field, knocking the ball over as Clarke was preparing a penalty goal attempt from his own half. The unflappable Clarke waited several minutes until order was restored, then promptly slammed the ball straight between the uprights. Wilson would observe later that this was a classic illustration of Clarke's wonderful temperament.

So the All Blacks advanced to Bloemfontein with the series all tied up. Amazingly, after 80 action-packed minutes there, nothing was changed. These two mighty sides were still locked together. However, seven minutes before fulltime, the prospect of the All Blacks extracting anything from the third test appeared remote, as the Springboks were leading 11–3. Spectators were starting to filter out of the ground. The All Black captain hadn't given up, though, and, when his team was awarded a penalty some 15 metres inside its own half, he took a quick tap and rushed at the nearest South African player, Pelser, forcing him to infringe. The referee promptly marched the South Africans back 10 metres.

This time, Wilson signalled to the goalposts. 'We'll take a shot,' he said, summoning The Boot forward. Clarke didn't disappoint, finding the posts with a booming kick.

Reg Sweet would write in his book, *Springbok and Silver Fern*, that Wilson's decisiveness saved the test for the All Blacks. 'It will always be clear that Whineray's decision to abandon what had become accepted All Black policy and to commit himself to out-and-out attack from a most unpromising position was the move which saved the third test of 1960 when it seemed so decisively lost.'

After Clarke's prodigious goal, only five points separated the teams. A converted try would keep the series alive. Another penalty went to the All Blacks, but this time Wilson opted for a tap-kick, knowing three points wasn't enough. It led to an attacking lineout from which Tremain broke away, setting up a ruck. Halfback Kevin Briscoe, in his haste to feed the line, threw the ball along the ground, missing Steve Nesbit and instead finding centre Kevin Laidlaw. He drew the fullback and kicked through for winger Frank McMullen, who sprinted through to score a metre in from touch.

That made it 11–9. Everything hung on The Boot's conversion from the sideline.

'Good luck,' said Wilson, as he handed him the ball.

'Don't worry,' said Clarke, who at that moment appeared to be the coolest person of the 56,000 inside Bloemfontein Stadium.

Big Don's brother, Ian, was running touch that afternoon — as happened in those days — and the New Zealanders swear he had the flag up the instant the ball left Don's boot!

'Gosh,' said Wilson as he came forward to congratulate his fullback, 'you didn't even look to see if it had gone over.'

'I didn't need to, Willie,' he said. 'The moment it left my foot I knew it was a goal.'

A photo in the local paper the next morning showed Clarke turning away with the ball not halfway to the goalposts.

Wilson had more to celebrate than just the heroic on-field comeback while in Bloemfontein. On the eve of the international, he received a phone call from Whangarei and was told his wife Beth had given birth to a son. She had been staying with her mother in the north.

Wilson matured as a leader on the tour of South Africa, a development observed by John Graham, who was able to make comparisons with the rookie 23-year-old who'd led the team to Australia two years earlier. Graham — who concedes that whenever he personally captained teams he was a regular yapper — was enormously impressed with Wilson's constant calmness. If something was not functioning properly with his team, Wilson would ask a dignified but meaningful question; in fact, Graham came to understand that Wilson's way of dealing with problems or challenging situations was to ask questions.

When Wilson's main adversary, Piet du Toit, was causing mayhem in the scrums, Wilson posed a question of the referee. 'Tens of thousands have paid good money to come and watch this game — are you going to allow one player to stuff up the game for them?'

If it was something involving Graham, Wilson would quietly inquire, 'You OK, DJ?' or 'What's going on out there, DJ?'

When one of the wingers was having difficulty finding his lineout targets, Wilson asked, with more than a tinge of irony, 'Would you like to come and join the lineout for a while?'

One aspect of the leadership that never sat comfortably with Wilson was that traditionally the All Black captain was allocated a single room while all the other players shared. 'Wilson hated that,' noted Graham, 'because he was such a naturally personable fellow. He hated being isolated from his team, although he appreciated that as captain it wasn't wise to over-fraternize with his players. When he could, he re-jigged the rooming arrangements so he could share with Colin Meads, Kel Tremain or me.'

A discussion developed in a hotel lift during the tour about the speed of falling objects, possibly even the lift, should the cable snap. One player, who claimed a university degree, asserted that everything fell with the acceleration of gravity. 'That's Galileo's law of gravitation,' he declared solemnly. Another team member asked if a full beer can and an empty can were simultaneously released, would they strike the ground together.

'Yes,' said the academic.

The equality of falling speeds was quietly regarded with suspicion by many, if not all, of the others present. And the claim was openly challenged, resulting in bets being placed. Experiments were conducted in hotel rooms with players standing on their beds and releasing two cans. However, the simultaneous release was questionable, and the distance of fall too short to establish the true situation.

Back in Auckland, Scott Whineray, then lecturing in physics, received a letter from his brother Wilson, expecting it to provide a valuable insight into the Springbok test series and his experiences in South Africa. Instead, it asked him to explain the phenomenon of differently weighted objects falling to earth.

'Wilson wanted an explanation,' recalls Scott, 'which I gave him. It was that the drag force on falling objects increases with velocity, therefore eventually reaching terminal speed when the weight down equals the drag force up.

'Therefore, the heavier can — the full one — will hit the ground first. If a full can and an empty can were dropped from the fourth

Fourteen-year-old Wilson clears the ball efficiently from halfback for the Auckland Grammar School First XV in 1950.
WHINERAY COLLECTION

New Zealand Juniors to Japan 1958. Back row: Mark Whitta, Ray Cossey, Howard Prain, Pat Walsh, Kevin Briscoe, Eddie Thompson. Third row: John Creighton, Barry Dineen, Russell Watt, Terry Lineen, Rob Morris, Derek Johnstone, Roger Boon. Second row: Kevin Barry, Roger Green, Colin Meads, Kel Tremain, Rex Pickering, Alan Rowlands. Front row: Alan Hayes, Ross Brown (vice-captain), Jack Sullivan (coach), Wilson Whineray (captain), Geoff Brown (manager), Don Davison, Ack Soper.
VERNON CLARKE PHOTO

Teammates on the 1955 New Zealand Colts tour of Ceylon (now Sri Lanka), from left: The captain Ack Soper, Brian Frederikson, Wilson, and Roger Boon.
WHINERAY COLLECTION

The Colts team that played and beat Combined Colombo Clubs at Colombo in 1955. Extreme right in the middle row is 19-year-old Colin Meads. Two along from him is Wilson, aged 20.
WHINERAY COLLECTION

A teenage Wilson roughing it above the snow-line at Lewis Pass, Canterbury, during a deer-hunting expedition in the 1950s.
WHINERAY COLLECTION

Wilson scores in the corner for Canterbury in a Ranfurly Shield defence against Southland at Lancaster Park in 1956.
WHINERAY COLLECTION

Rival scrummagers Wilson, 21, and Piet du Toit, 20, clash for the first time during the Springboks' game against New Zealand Universities in Wellington in 1956. They would become deadly rivals in South Africa four years later.
WHINERAY COLLECTION

Wilson with Springbok No. 8 Jan Pickard following the classic tour game against New Zealand Universities in Wellington in 1956, a game in which the Springboks were sensationally beaten.
WHINERAY COLLECTION

The Whineray family in 1957 after Wilson's elevation to All Black status.
Back row: Wilson, Mum Ida, Murray, Dad Harry. Front row: Bruce, Scott, Grant.
FAIRFAX MEDIA

Wilson (wearing No. 23) has flanker Don McIntosh in support against New South Wales in Sydney in 1957.
WHINERAY COLLECTION

Wilson mingles with a bunch of backs during the 1957 All Blacks' tour of Australia. From left. Frank McMullen, Terry Lineen and Bill Gray, with Pat Walsh in behind.
WHINERAY COLLECTION

Less than 15 minutes into his career as All Black test captain, Wilson scores a try against the Wallabies at Athletic Park, Wellington, 1958.
WHINERAY COLLECTION

Trouble in the form of the All Black skipper looming for Wallabies fullback Terry Curley during the 1958 series at the Epsom Showgrounds in Auckland.
FAIRFAX MEDIA

Wilson in conversation with Bob Davidson, who would captain the 1957–58 Wallabies on their tour of Great Britain, and Ian Clarke in Australia in 1957.
WHINERAY COLLECTION

Wilson meeting the premier of South Australia at Adelaide during the All Blacks' tour of Australia in 1957. At right is manager Bill Craddock.
WHINERAY COLLECTION

One aspect of touring Japan in 1958 that Wilson, as the New Zealand Juniors' captain, wasn't altogether happy with was receiving bouquets of flowers!
WHINERAY COLLECTION

That's one super-slim captain — Wilson involved in the coin toss before one of the New Zealand Juniors' matches in Japan in 1958.
WHINERAY COLLECTION

Being an accomplished horseman undoubtedly qualified Wilson to try his luck on an elephant in Ceylon in 1955.
WHINERAY COLLECTION

A cluster of All Blacks making like golfers before preparing to play the British Lions in 1959. From left: Des Webb, Kevin Briscoe, Ian Clarke, Jack Sullivan (manager), Dick Everest (coach), Don Clarke, Nev MacEwan, Ralph Caulton, and Wilson.

NZ RUGBY MUSEUM

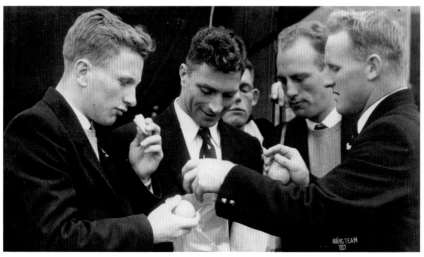

Snack time for this group of All Blacks in Australia in 1957. From left: Russell Watt, Frank McAtamney, Rex Pickering, and Wilson.

WHINERAY COLLECTION

Wilson marries his charming bride, Beth, in Palmerston North in 1959.
WHINERAY COLLECTION

Wilson, captain of Auckland, holds the Ranfurly Shield aloft after his team's triumph over Southland in Invercargill in 1959.
WHINERAY COLLECTION

Wilson talking to Don Clarke, hero of the 1960 series.

Wilson marks the opening game of the 1960 All Blacks' tour of South Africa with a try against Northern Universities at Potchefstroom.
WHINERAY COLLECTION

Wilson and French captain François Moncla lead their teams on to Eden Park for the opening test of the 1961 series. Following Wilson out are Des Connor and Nev MacEwan.
NZ RUGBY MUSEUM

Wilson and Beth cut a dashing couple after he had received the Order of the British Empire in 1962.

Ah, yes, the delightful days of amateurism when rivals socialized together. Here, Wilson, Kel Tremain, Kevin Briscoe and Colin Meads share a few beers with Wallaby great John Thornett, centre, in Australia in 1962.
WHINERAY COLLECTION

Wilson in club action for Grammar Old Boys against Otahuhu at Eden Park in 1967.
WHINERAY COLLECTION

floor of a hotel, when the heavy one hit the ground, the light one would be about a floor behind. From 20 floors, the light one would be perhaps five floors behind.'

By the time his reply reached the All Black captain in South Africa, the resourceful players who were sceptical of the academic's claims had conducted the experiment themselves by dropping two cans from the top floor of their hotel. And, yes, the heavy can did indeed reach the ground first. No locals were injured or property damaged during the execution of this experiment!

Port Elizabeth rivals Wellington as the windiest rugby city on Earth, and, true to form, the wind was piping through Boet Erasmus Stadium for the all-important fourth test. Wilson desperately wanted to win the toss and play into the elements in the first half, but he called wrong, and Avril Malan, the Springbok skipper, almost gleefully announced that the All Blacks could take the wind.

When it was 3-all at half-time, the All Blacks knew they were in trouble. They were desperately unlucky to have a try by Frank McMullen disallowed by the referee Ralph Burmeister, who claimed a South African player had hold of him when he crawled across the goal-line after being ankle-tapped.

McMullen would reveal in *Rugby Greats* two decades later that he believed he had just scored the try of a lifetime. 'But to my horror, Mr Burmeister, who arrived on the scene a couple of seconds late, gave a penalty for rabbiting. In the heat of the moment I abused him and it needed Wilson Whineray to quieten me down and apologise.'

With the All Blacks managing no more than a penalty goal by Clarke, it meant the test, series and world crown went to the Springboks.

McMullen was one who was critical of Jack Sullivan's coaching methods in South Africa, claiming he was too staid in his approach, and, because of Clarke's omnipresence, virtually commanded the All

Blacks to play 50-metre rugby. After the first test defeat, a cluster of players, including McMullen, approached Sullivan, pleading for a more enterprising approach, which was trialled in the Junior Springboks game, where five tries were scored. But pretty soon, the All Blacks reverted to type.

As Ace Parker reported: 'What appears to have happened is that back play has become so neglected an art in New Zealand that the players lack confidence. In the national set-up they are regarded as a mere appendage to the forwards. The 1955 Lions backline behind this All Black pack would have run up cricket scores in almost every game.'

Sullivan concerned himself more with team strategy than individual skills — throughout the 1960 tour he would merely observe while Wilson organized the training sessions — and sometimes displayed surprising naïveté.

Back in 1959 the selectors had named Ralph Caulton and Tuppy Diack as wingers for the second test against the British Lions in Wellington, notwithstanding the fact that both were specialist left wingers. Perplexed, because neither wanted to move to a position with which he was unfamiliar, both attempted to take station on the left wing at the first training session.

Sullivan asked them what was going on.

'We're both specialist left wingers,' one of them explained.

Sullivan pondered the situation for a moment, before focusing on Diack.

'You played for New Zealand Universities, didn't you?'

'Yes,' answered Diack, unsure where the question was leading.

'Well then, Ron Jarden always played on the left wing, so you must have played on the right wing.'

'Yes, but—' Diack didn't get to explain that it was the only occasion in his entire career in which he'd finished up on the right wing, and he didn't like the experience.

'You're on the right wing.'

It was bad enough that Diack had to make his test debut out of position — sadly, he would never represent his country again — but what made it even more gruelling was that all the play went left on that occasion, Diack watching from afar as Caulton scored two tries.

A similar situation occurred in South Africa prior to the third test, when Sullivan and his fellow selectors named both Dick Conway and John Graham to play in Bloemfontein. Both expected to operate off the back of the lineout. As in Wellington the previous year, two players found themselves getting in each other's way at training. They agreed the coach should resolve the problem.

'Which one of us will play off the back of the lineout?' Sullivan was asked.

Sullivan paused for a moment.

'Whichever one of you arrives at the lineout last.'

Yeah, right!

Caulton, who would return from the matches in Australia and South Africa as the equal top try-scorer, was appointed weigh-master for the tour. There was nothing sophisticated about the methods used to establish an individual's weight in 1960. They simply stepped on to a set of scales and the 'weigh-master' noted down their weight. A half-century on, Caulton reveals that many times he was tempted by bribery. 'Some players wanted to be heavier, others wanted to be lighter,' he says. 'On long tours like that, it was easy to over-eat and put on weight. My role as weigh-master extended to issuing dietary cautions!'

The All Blacks and the Springboks fraternized well, and particularly at the conclusion of the series in Port Elizabeth. One player they couldn't share a beer with was Martin Pelser, because he didn't drink. In the wee hours of Sunday morning following the final test, Colin Meads took himself off to the room he was sharing with Kel Tremain. Next morning, he noticed there was a strange person sleeping on the settee. Who could that be? Closer inspection revealed it to be Pelser. Meads confessed later that many dark thoughts crossed his mind about what he could do to the individual who'd caused both of them such angst throughout the series. In the event, he woke him and offered him a cup of tea.

Much was written, during the 1960 tour and subsequently, about the niggling that went on in the internationals between the front rows, and in particular between Wilson and his volatile opponent, Du Toit. Countless scrums were disrupted by Du Toit, who persisted in boring in, a tactic which the All Blacks found disruptive, but which the South African referees either didn't detect or were reluctant to penalize. The considerable number of media, almost none of whom had put their heads anywhere near a front row, even at club level, concluded that what was going on was representative of Du Toit's superior strength.

Paul Dobson, an extremely fair critic, would write in his excellent book, *Rugby's Greatest Rivalry*, that Du Toit's scrummaging was 'significant and reduced the All Black front row to the ordinary, to the frustration of Wilson Whineray against whom he packed'.

If the Springbok front-rowers, Du Toit in particular, were so superior, how come the All Blacks won 13 tight-heads (strikes against the feed) to six during the four-test series? The New Zealand hooker Dennis Young claimed five tight-heads in the first test, four in the second, one in the third, and three in the fourth. Not then, not now, do sets of forwards secure tight-heads if their scrum is inferior and under pressure.

The fact is, Wilson found Du Toit's antics nothing short of a pain in the arse. Nothing that went on in the front row influenced the outcome of the series. Wilson's attitude to scrummaging had never changed from the moment he first packed down in the front row. For him, the scrum was a means of re-starting play. He wanted the ball fed quickly and hooked quickly, so his team could get on with the important business of attempting to score tries. Grinding down an opponent through power-scrummaging was never something that either impressed or appealed to the All Black captain. Given that

Wilson scored 50 first-class tries in his career, it would be hard to argue against his philosophy. Du Toit scored about five. The reason for the lack of precision about Du Toit's record is that it appears no one in South Africa is in possession of that information. He scored three tries in total in all his outings for the Springboks, none in tests, and no one can find any record of him scoring for Boland or Western Province.

Four months after they'd flown out of Auckland, the All Blacks departed for home. (This was more than a week after playing the final test, because, with time to kill before their flight took off from Jan Smuts Airport, they played an extra game against a Transvaal XV in Johannesburg.) With a new baby awaiting him, Wilson was anxious to get home, but fate would extend the tour by several days. When their flight landed for refuelling at Cocos Island, they were advised there would be a delay because of a technical fault. Many hours later, they heard that the 'fault' was an engine that couldn't be risked. A replacement would have to be flown out from Sydney.

Situated in the middle of the Indian Ocean about halfway between Australia and Sri Lanka, Cocos Island, an Australian territory comprising two atolls and 27 coral islands, enjoys a tropical climate and miles of gorgeous beaches. Before anyone slipped into their togs, the players were warned against swimming because of the presence of stonefish, which could prove fatal if you had the misfortune to stand on them.

So what to do? The male members of the Qantas staff based there provided the answer: a game of cricket. Being Aussies, they were into their cricket big-time, and challenged their unexpected visitors to a test match on the surprisingly well-prepared pitch. Many kegs of beer were wagered on the outcome.

Kel Tremain was appointed selector-coach of the All Black team — many would claim he appointed himself — and was excited about unleashing the rare cricketing talent he had available. Ron Hemi had played Plunket Shield cricket as a batsman for Auckland, Roger

Urbahn had represented Taranaki, and, oh joy of joys, Don Clarke was a fiery fast-bowler who had not only played in the same Auckland team as Hemi, but, at his peak, had certainly interested the New Zealand cricket selectors. Wilson had played for the Auckland Grammar First XI and believed he could contribute tellingly, but Tremain was in an outrageously bullish mood and felt it was important the All Black captain should know what it felt like to miss selection.

There's no such thing as sweet sportsmanship when New Zealand and Australia front up in any sports contest, and nor was there on Cocos Island in 1960. Don Clarke powered in from what seemed like 70 metres to deliver his thunderbolts, causing mayhem among the Qantas batsmen. Hemi scored a packet of runs, and the All Blacks waltzed away with the contest — and the kegs.

Finally, after the All Blacks had spent two nights sleeping in makeshift accommodation — no great hardship given the climate — the new engine was attached and the plane resumed its journey. In Sydney, they transferred to an Air New Zealand flight that transported them through to Auckland, where at Whenuapai Airport Wilson finally got to meet, and hold, his three-week-old son, James.

If Beth believed she would have Wilson to herself for the remaining weekends of the year, she was to be disappointed. Auckland still had three Ranfurly Shield defences stacked up and, as if the leading players hadn't had enough for one year, a special charity fixture had been arranged for Athletic Park in Wellington at the beginning of October between the All Blacks and the Rest of New Zealand.

When Auckland's astute coach, Fred Allen, realized his captain Wilson would be overseas on national duty for the greater portion of the domestic season, he considered it appropriate to appoint a fresh leader for 1960. Not without some apprehension, he broached the issue with Wilson, who supported him 100 per cent. 'It makes complete sense,' Wilson said to him.

And so Fred Allen inducted Bob Graham as Auckland's new skipper, an appointment that would prove such a resounding success that Graham — John Graham's brother — would continue to lead the blue-and-whites through until the mid-1960s.

While Wilson was in South Africa, the Ranfurly Shield spent 11 unscheduled days in the north, to coach Allen's dismay. North Auckland, prepared by a cagey campaigner in Ted Griffin, had prised the 'log' away from the holders with a quality performance at Eden Park. However, in a re-match in the Whangarei mud the following week, Auckland managed to reclaim the prized trophy.

Coach Allen drafted Wilson straight back into his team for the final three challenges of the season, against Wellington, Taranaki and Canterbury. The first two were dealt with comfortably, leaving Auckland and Canterbury, which had its All Black forwards — John Graham, Dennis Young, and Hugh Burry — back in the side, to present a worthy climax to the season.

A key member of the Auckland line-up was flanker Waka Nathan, who hadn't been considered for the All Black tour of South Africa because of that country's apartheid policy, the NZRU having accepted the South African Rugby Board's conditional invitation. Nathan made a tour of Tonga and Samoa with the New Zealand Maori side instead.

Such was the interest in this midweek encounter, with tens of thousands converging on Eden Park, that Auckland's city roads became gridlocked. This so seriously delayed the Auckland team's bus that the kick-off was put back 30 minutes. While this probably caused a certain disgruntlement among many of the spectators, it was a game worth waiting for, one of shield rugby's true classics.

Canterbury, which had been in awesome form, made most of the running and led 18–14 as the last scrum packed down with time virtually up. It was a Canterbury feed and, given that Dennis Young — acknowledged as the best striking hooker in New Zealand if not in the world — was hooking, it was dollars to doughnuts that the scrum would be won.

But the Auckland pack produced a mighty heave and almost

unbelievably claimed a tight-head. Halfback Des Connor passed the ball left to Mac Herewini, who put in a 'wipers' kick — a popular ploy with the Auckland team — that found vacant territory between the Canterbury halfback and fullback. The ball sat up sweetly for Waka Nathan, who had made an art form out of chasing his Otahuhu clubmate Herewini's kicks, and suddenly the goal-line was at his mercy.

Wilson, close behind, shouted 'Behind the posts, Waka!', which was Nathan's intention anyway. 'It was not the fact we needed the converted try that made me run towards the posts,' Nathan would explain later. 'It was just the fact there wasn't a player in sight. We had completely stunned them.'

The try was converted by Mike Cormack, giving Auckland the lead, 19–18. The photo of Nathan grounding the ball behind the goalposts, with Wilson, in jersey No. 8, throwing his arms in the air in exaltation, is one that has decorated countless rugby publications ever since.

The shield was not quite Auckland's yet, although the fans were celebrating as though it was all over. There was sufficient time on the clock for the referee to permit a re-start. Canterbury's only chance was to re-gather the ball from the kick-off and create something before it went dead. Wilson wasn't having any of that. As Henderson's kick wafted towards the Auckland players, Wilson thrust himself forward. 'Mine!' he demanded. He fielded ball, swivelled around, and let fly with the heartiest punt he could manage, putting the ball several dozen rows back in the grandstand. The shield was now well and truly secure for Auckland.

One player who didn't share in this treasured moment was Kel Tremain, who had been operating off the side of the Auckland scrum. During the second half, Tremain was rather daringly holding down Canterbury's 'iron man', 33-year-old Tiny Hill, in the lineouts.

'Do that again and you'll be filled in,' warned Hill.

'Just try, Grandad,' said Tremain, full of bravado.

Following the next lineout, Tremain exited the field on a stretcher, regaining consciousness in the dressing room just in time to hear the crowd erupt when Nathan scored.

The concussion kept Tremain out of the season finale in Wellington, a contest in which the All Blacks rounded out a long, demanding season by crushing the Rest of New Zealand 20 points to 8. Tremain's place on the side of the scrum was taken by John Graham.

6

A VALUABLE FRENCH LESSON

The late Sir Terry McLean named his book about the 1963–64 tour of Great Britain and France after a classic rugby move and also made it the focus of the book's introduction.

> Willie Away, they called it. The word would pass quietly from captain to halfback, who would do no more than take stance to inform all ranks of what was intended. The lineout would form in the normal way. Everything would look straightforward, normal, usual, until as the three-quarter made his throw, the ball sailed higher and faster than it did for the straightforward, normal, usual throws to Numbers 2 or 3 or 5.
>
> As the ball left the three-quarter's arm, all aspects of the straightforward, the normal, the usual departed. Galvanic energy possessed various players. The Number 4 began running along the back of the lineout. The halfback of the day kept pace with him. Other forwards, 2, 3 and 5, tailed after him. Number 6 or Number 7 tensed and poised and made ready to spring into the air to touch, tap or grab and pass the ball down into the arms of the first runner. And within seconds, the whole pack was shambling in his wake into the open field, ready for a pass if the opportunity offered, ready, too, to dive and drive with head and shoulders if he was tackled and brought to ground.
>
> When it was perfectly done, the manoeuvre compelled both the midfield and the forward defence of the opposing side to close in

upon the ball-carrier and so offered the chance of a swift strike, one way or the other, through the bemused and bewildered defence. Even when it was imperfectly done, the manoeuvre frightened seven bells out of someone or other because of the power, almost, you might say, the ferocity with which it was delivered.

This was 'Willie Away', a favourite ploy of the 1963–64 All Blacks team while they were on tour of the British Isles, France and British Columbia. The name came from the captain, Wilson James Whineray, who was the principal instrument in it.

The Willie Away move — which would remain a potent attacking weapon of the All Blacks for more than three decades and enshrine the name of its leading performer — had its origins on the first tour of New Zealand ever undertaken by France, in 1961.

That '61 French team, captained by François Moncla, and featuring any number of gifted individuals who would achieve greatness in the game — players like Pierre Albaladejo, brothers Guy and André Boniface, and Michel Crauste — certainly didn't set the world on fire. Of the 13 matches it played, seven, including all three internationals, were lost. Moncla's men also came off second-best against Waikato, North Auckland, New Zealand Maoris, and South Canterbury.

Although the French returned home with an extremely disappointing record, and have never since been listed among the distinguished touring teams to New Zealand, they were in some respects an extremely potent force and left a lasting impression on many of their opponents, in particular a certain All Black captain and his Australian-born halfback.

The All Black line-up in 1961 featured for the first time Des Connor, a gifted halfback who while based in Brisbane had made 10 test appearances for the Wallabies, including the 1958 series against the All Blacks. He then relocated to Auckland, where he was gratefully snapped up by Fred Allen and became a vital member of the Auckland Ranfurly Shield team.

As an aside, Connor, who had moved to New Zealand to take up a teaching position, credits Wilson's shrewd guidance for his progression from All Black triallist to test player in 1961. Connor featured at halfback in Wilson's trial team in Palmerston North. 'Wilson said to me if I was going to progress I would need to attract the selectors' attention in the first half,' Connor recalled. 'Well, after 20 minutes nothing much had happened, whereupon Wilson turned to me and said, "Time to have a go." So I did, getting through almost to the goal-line and creating a try. That would do until the second half, Wilson assured me. Twenty minutes from time he encouraged me to have another go. This time I scored the try myself! That experience illustrated the sort of guy Wilson was.'

Wilson and Connor related to each other superbly in matters tactical. They enjoyed bouncing tactical manoeuvres off each other, assessing opponents' strengths and weaknesses and plotting fresh moves. They found they had a wealth of material to work on after the All Blacks had come from behind at half-time to defeat the French in the first test of the '61 series at Eden Park. The 13–6 scoreline didn't reflect how frequently the tourists had placed the All Blacks under pressure by surging powerfully around the back of lineouts. These tactics had led directly to two dropped goals by Albaladejo, who had arrived in New Zealand sporting the nickname of M'sieur L'Drop.

What impressed Wilson and Connor about the French ploy was that it was hellishly difficult to stop. The assaults, always launched off the rear of the lineout, committed an alarming number of defenders in midfield, because the French kept rolling away from any point of impact. Fortunately for the All Blacks, the French never embellished this clever tactic. Their main option was to continue rolling forward *ad nauseum* until they either scored a try or the opposition conceded a penalty. The solitary variation came when, after creating a platform out from the opposition goalposts, they would fire the ball back to Albaladejo to drop a goal.

Most observers interpreted the tactic as something totally

appropriate to the French game, given their strong, mobile forwards and propensity for dropping goals. Connor and Wilson, however, saw it as something that could be tellingly adapted to the All Black game. They would refine their thinking after the series against France.

The French never had an opportunity to implement raids off the back of the lineout in the second international in Wellington, because a hurricane-force wind, which almost caused the cancellation of the fixture, made it impossible for either side to throw deeper than about two in the lineout. The All Blacks eased home 5–3, thanks to a freakish conversion from Clarke, who launched his kick from near touch straight across the field, parallel to the goal-line. Clarke himself believed the conversion was impossible. 'I simply kicked out along the twenty-five and left the rest to the wind [which was blowing at around 80 kilometres per hour],' he explained later. 'To my astonishment, it went over. I take no credit for that kick — it was a fluke. And it won a test!'

Wilson's All Blacks overran the French in the final test in Christchurch to complete a satisfactory international season. The 32 points they scored — which would equate to 52 today — demonstrated the All Blacks' superiority. At one stage of the final test, All Black centre Paul Little was crudely high-tackled. Colin Meads was not impressed and was about to deliver retribution when Wilson dragged him away. A few minutes later, Meads scored a try.

'There,' said Wilson, 'that hurts them more than you belting them.' Meads could but agree.

The disappointing French would not appreciate it, but they would leave New Zealand rugby a valuable legacy. And that was because of the insightfulness of Messrs Connor and Whineray. At what in modern parlance would be regarded as 'brainstorming sessions', they analysed France's concept — and expanded upon it.

The potency of the move, as exploited by the French, was in the number of defenders it committed in midfield. Connor and Wilson reasoned that, with the opposition defenders so focused on the midfield surge, they would be extremely vulnerable if suddenly play was switched away from that fulcrum, left or right, with, say, the fullback chiming in.

So was born the Willie Away movement. Willie was the natural codename, because 'Willie' Whineray was the individual whom Auckland, and subsequently New Zealand, used as the central character in the move. He was the one who peeled back from the front of the lineout, collecting tap-downs from Bob Graham with Auckland and Kel Tremain (and subsequently Brian Lochore, who would become the move's finest exponent) with the All Blacks, before rampaging around the rear of the lineout with the purpose of causing as much consternation and confusion as possible among the opposition defence.

In the 1960s, when it was introduced, opposing backlines stood up flat, not having to be back 10 metres as they do now. 'Willie' mostly targeted the second-five and, although he usually made physical contact close to the advantage line — because of the element of surprise, plus the fact his teammates were surging behind him, rather like a human tsunami — the move invariably made serious inroads into enemy territory.

It was launched at lineouts no further out than 30 metres from the opposition goal-line. And to coax the enemy into complacency, the jumper used for the Willie Away would not be targeted for four or five lineouts leading up to the move.

Paul Little and Don McKay — two other Aucklanders who had played in the series against the French and had witnessed at first hand the damage the French tactic was capable of causing — were enthusiastic supporters of the Willie Away when Connor and Wilson first explained it. Auckland coach Fred Allen bought into it, although he insisted it be well practised before being implemented in a match. It was first used successfully by Auckland in the Ranfurly Shield defence against Hawke's Bay in late 1961, producing the winning try for Waka Nathan.

Auckland had exclusive rights to the Willie Away for two seasons, until the All Blacks developed it on their tour of Britain and France late in 1963. It would be used with devastating effect on that tour, but of course the publicity that subsequently accrued meant opponents domestically and internationally eventually became aware of it. Not that that made it any easier to defend, but the initial element of surprise was lost. Testimony to the greatness and effectiveness of the move is that it was still being used by teams, including the All Blacks, three decades on.

Few families in New Zealand would be able to claim two brothers who captained national sporting teams in the same year, but that was the Whinerays' boast in 1961. Around the same time that Wilson was leading the All Blacks against France, his elder brother Bruce was captaining the New Zealand hockey team in a test against Japan. Bruce, a fullback, had toured Australia earlier in 1961 under the captaincy of John Smith. When Smith didn't play, Bruce led the team; and when Smith was unavailable for the test against Japan back home, Bruce led the New Zealand team on to the field.

The 1961 season was a hugely successful one for Wilson. His All Black team disposed of France, he led North to a crushing 25–3 victory in the inter-island game, his team won the main North Island trial 33–9, and Auckland survived a further eight challenges for the Ranfurly Shield.

Although Wilson was a natural leader, the more he captained the All Blacks the better leader he became. He would say that by the time he finally stepped aside from the international scene at the conclusion of the 1965 season, there wasn't anything that might confront him on the rugby field for which he wasn't prepared.

Being a captain in the 1960s bore greater responsibilities than apply today. For instance, because the players remained on the field at half-time sucking oranges, while their coaches and managers sat nervously in the grandstand, it was the captain who had to deliver tactical directions for the second half. These days, Graham Henry,

Steve Hansen and Wayne Smith command the attention of the All Blacks during the 10-minute break in the sanctity of the dressing room, while they review the opening 40 minutes and provide guidance for the second half. That wasn't how it worked in the 1960s. The tactical scheming for the second 40 minutes was entirely in the hands of the captain. This was something at which Wilson demonstrated great acumen. John Graham says he had a deft 'feel' for the game, and his half-time directions were always appropriate.

Wilson rounded out the 1961 season with a couple of memorable encounters — memorable for entirely different reasons.

The first incident occurred during North Auckland's challenge for the Ranfurly Shield at Eden Park, a game that marked the final appearance for his union of Peter Jones, the rampaging No. 8 who on this ground had scored the epic try in 1956 to clinch the All Blacks' first series win over the Springboks. Late in the game, Jones embarked on a most remarkable diagonal run. He was so hyped-up that he punched every opponent he approached. Tracking him were Barry Thomas and Wilson, who couldn't believe what they were seeing. As they converged on him, both knew there was only one way to stop Jones's personal demolition derby — they both struck him. Jones went down in a heap, stunned. He recovered soon enough, and at the after-match function came and apologized to Messrs Thomas and Whineray, saying he'd deserved what he got. But that didn't stop the *New Zealand Truth* lambasting the Auckland team for its 'brutal' tactics.

A photo of the incident showed Thomas's clenched fist zeroing in on Jones's jaw, although Thomas would argue to this day that it wasn't his punch that flattened Jones.

The second notable occasion for Wilson involved him turning out for the Centurions against Wellington, the uniqueness of this contest being that those who represented the Centurions were literally centurions: individuals who had appeared in more than 100 first-class fixtures.

The starting XV was Bob Scott (then aged 40), Lyn Russell, Ross Smith, Pat Walsh, Ross Brown, Robin Archer, Ponty Reid, Don McIntosh, Tiny Hill, Colin Meads, Albie Pryor, Snow White, Dennis Young, Ivan Vodanovich, and Wilson Whineray.

The final memorable moment of the year involved the principal of the Howard Morrison Quartet, which at the time was wowing New Zealand audiences at concerts around the country. Besides being a singer with a million-dollar voice, Morrison was also an enthusiastic and accomplished rugby player; a midfielder with the Waikite club in Rotorua, he had once appeared in a trial for Hawke's Bay. It may be apocryphal, but the story goes that Morrison's father (who had played for the New Zealand Maori team) attended the trial and, after observing his son's performance, said, 'Stick to singing, son!'

Anyway, Howard, who was an enormous fan of the All Blacks, never turned down invitations to play for selected teams, and, when a young player from the Waitemata club in Auckland tragically died and a benefit game was arranged at Huapai, Howard turned up. And so did Wilson. They were in the same XV, as was Adrian Clarke, the effervescent Auckland five-eighth who'd made his mark on the All Black tour of South Africa in 1960.

It might have been a low-key benefit game, but Clarke insisted on organizing a few elaborate moves. It's the way he was. If the French hadn't inspired the Willie Away move, Clarke would have invented it. He described a complex scissors-move that he and Morrison would unleash on their unsuspecting opponents at an appropriate moment.

'Righto, Howard!' Clarke called as the game was unfolding. 'We'll give that a move a go.'

Out came the ball. Clarke ran one way, Morrison ran another, and — *ker-thunk* — they crashed straight into each other. Howard thought he'd broken his nose as he lay stunned on the ground. Clarke recovered first.

'Sorry about that, Howard — we'll get it right next time.'

'You can stuff your fancy bloody moves,' said Howard. 'Just pass me the ball!'

The All Blacks undertook a 10-match tour of Australia in 1962, and while it was unfolding Wilson was named in the Queen's Birthday Honours List, being awarded the Most Honourable Order of the British Empire (OBE) for his services to rugby, famously becoming the only All Black captain to be so honoured while his career was still in progress. He received the award from the Governor-General, Sir Bernard Fergusson, at a ceremony in Auckland. It was becoming a special year for the Whinerays, because in February their second child, Kristen, had been born.

You would think his colleagues would ensure that someone so gloriously decorated would not be allowed to complete the two-month jaunt through Australia without scoring a few points. Yet the record books would reveal that although the team amassed 91 tries and 426 points in 10 outings, the only one of the 25 players who failed to score a solitary point was the captain! Even Dennis Young — the hooker who once famously dived triumphantly across the 22 in a club fixture, thinking he'd scored his very first try — got on the board with a conversion.

The All Blacks indulged in a couple of outrageously one-sided scoring sprees, beating Northern New South Wales at Quirindi 103–0 (with five-point tries, the score would have been 147–0) and South Australia at Adelaide 77–0.

One of the reasons Wilson remained scoreless related to a Sunday incident outside a pub following the first test in Brisbane. Former All Black 'Rusty' Page — a distinguished individual who had commanded the 2nd New Zealand Expeditionary Force's 26th Battalion during the Second World War, winning the Distinguished Service Order and rising to the rank of brigadier — had invited the All Blacks to go cruising on a luxury yacht. Wilson, ever the considerate one, suggested the players should take along some beer, so they called at a hotel *en route* to the marina. Some of the players needed to relieve themselves out the back of the hotel. A curious Wilson was peering into a ramp, down which beer kegs were rolled to the cellar, when Kevin Briscoe, the regularly mischievous Taranakian, gave him a shove from behind. Wilson, in seeking to protect himself as he fell forward into the ramp, jagged his hand on a hook, lacerating it nastily. There was much blood and Wilson finished up with a gaping wound that would sideline him through until the second test, rendering him unavailable for the 103–0 romp at Quirindi, when 22 tries were scored.

Remarkably, it would be one of only two occasions in his eight-year, 77-match international career that he was unavailable for selection because of injury. The other was after he fractured his thumb playing against Boland in South Africa in 1960, an injury he kept secret.

One Friday night during the tour, Wilson was invited to appear on a television sports show along with league superstar Reg Gasnier. Afterwards, they got chatting.

'Now come on, Wilson, tell me,' begged Gasnier, 'how much do you guys really get paid?'

'Nothing, Reg.'

'Come on, what's in the blazer pocket when you put it on?'

'Absolutely nothing, Reg, we are the last of the great amateurs.'

'Bloody hell!'

Intriguingly, two months after the All Blacks completed their free-scoring sweep through Australia, the Wallabies undertook a full-scale tour of New Zealand. Like the French the previous year, they would play 13 games and, exactly like the French, would win just six. However, they would cause the All Blacks a good deal of angst in the opening two internationals at Wellington and Dunedin, which produced modest scorelines of 9-all and 3-0, prompting the national selectors (Neil McPhail, Jack Finlay and Ron Bush) to take some drastic measures.

Following the draw in Wellington, in what became known as the Night of the Long Knives, they dropped Colin Meads, Kel Tremain, Dennis Young and Ian Clarke. You had to be brave to drop players of that stature, especially the mighty Pinetree, but the selectors decided it was time to convince tight forwards they should be tight forwards, not auxiliary loose forwards.

Alex Veysey would write in Meads's biography that Meads and Tremain were sour at their demotion. 'We snarled and snapped a lot,' he quoted Meads as saying. 'It was very hurtful to be dropped at that stage as established players. But looking back on it, a bit of a shake can bring you back to reality. Strangely enough, that was the beginning of a fantastic era for New Zealand rugby and if dropping us contributed to it, then I guess it was worthwhile.'

Wilson, the only player of his era other than fellow prop Kenaray never to suffer the indignity of being dropped, was one who believed the mighty Pinetree became a better player for the experience. He told Veysey that from that moment Meads's priorities changed.

'He became a lock in every sense, not least of all in spirit,' Whineray said. 'Now he had the temperament of a lock; he saw the value of his performance not as he would be judged but how the team played. It wasn't quite like St Paul on the road to Damascus being blinded by a flash of light. But it was an awakening of decision. You know, "I'd better start being a good lock or I'll be knocked off by, say, my brother Stan [his replacement for the Dunedin test]." His priorities changed. He exerted pressure on the opposition at all times; he won our ball and made it hard for them to win their ball; he kept a ruck going forward; he'd make the tackle, he'd thicken up a passing rush; he'd hit the ruck squarer rather than rolling that yard too far; when he saw he was finished on the run, he set up the ruck.

'He was running more cleverly in the total team sense and the rest of the forwards were homing in on him with the confidence of that organised ruck being on. I have seen Piney lose a round but never beaten, always in at the end, plugging on and on.'

When the All Blacks exhibited little improvement in the second international of the home series in 1962, winning by a solitary Don Clarke penalty goal to nil, the selectors restored Meads and Young to the playing XV, but not Tremain or Ian Clarke.

The All Blacks produced a better brand of rugby in the final test at Eden Park to make it four victories and a draw from five internationals against their Bledisloe Cup brothers. While the continued unbeaten sequence at test level was satisfying, the rugby produced wasn't of a quality to thrust fear into the hearts of the Home Nations who they would be engaging in pursuit of a Grand Slam the following year.

Still, there's nothing like being dropped to focus the mind, and for Meads, Tremain, Young and Clarke the tribulations of 1962 would pay handsome dividends. All four would win selection on, and become major contributors to, the 1963–64 tour of Great Britain and France.

Before then, however, Wilson would hand the Ranfurly Shield across to Wellington, which, on a wet, stormy afternoon at Eden Park, outgunned a surprisingly lifeless Auckland team. Four days earlier, Auckland, in hanging on for a draw against Hawke's Bay, had created a new shield record of 25 consecutive defences. But that massive effort came at a cost, and the shield moved on.

In the dressing room after the loss to Wellington, Mac Herewini came up to Fred Allen. 'Don't worry, coach,' he said, aware that Auckland was scheduled to play Wellington in Wellington a fortnight later, 'we'll get it back for you.'

'Mackie, I don't want the blessed thing back — it creates too much pressure.'

Any anguish the immediate return of the prized log to Auckland would have created was averted seven days later when Wellington lost the shield to Taranaki at its first defence.

Fred the Needle explained how Auckland had managed to create the shield record. His team had aimed to wear down the opposition until it had control. 'Most teams began to fizzle after about 20 minutes, after which we would run the ball from anywhere. We had plenty of moves which we would practise 10 or 15 times until they became automatic. All the moves were basic and simple and well-rehearsed.'

Allen admitted that the further they went as the shield-holder, the more challenging life became. He said he often told lies to help get his players fired up. As on the famous occasion in 1960 when Nathan's last-gasp try denied Canterbury's challenge. While the Auckland players were getting changed leading up to kick-off, Allen stormed in. 'Those bastards!' he exploded, bringing startled looks from the Auckland players. 'The Canterbury guys are next-door having a photo taken with the Ranfurly Shield for tomorrow morning's paper. That's how bloody confident they are!'

The Canterbury players, in fact, were doing exactly what their Auckland counterparts were doing — preparing themselves quietly for the contest ahead. The Ranfurly Shield was nowhere near their dressing room, and nor were any photographers!

Wilson would write insightfully of the Ranfurly Shield era in *100 Years of Auckland Rugby*, published in 1983. Here are some of his recollections:

> The truly great sides that perform outstandingly well at international or provincial level tend to develop a unique style of play that for a while leaves other sides behind. In 1959 and 1960 there came together a number of extraordinarily gifted footballers, each blessed with a wide range of individual skills and each nurturing an idea that they may not have been able to put into words of how they would like to play rugby.
>
> Enter the catalysts, Fred Allen and John Simpson, to harmonise the rich and separate identities in their charge. Fred holds a special place in the minds of all those who have played in his team — tough, autocratic, outspoken, blunt on occasions and always very demanding. Players were pushed to the outer boundaries of their ability. In a sense, Fred had a truly professional approach — do all you can and play as well as you can. Fred went on to achieve well-

earned national and international honours as a coach, which topped an outstanding playing career. He was, and always will be, the flame around which the players hovered.

John Simpson was tough too, a feature of his own great ability as a player. John had to be tough on his forwards as we generally were disadvantaged with weight and height, and had to find a little more in ourselves than we thought we had.

Bob Graham and I ended up in a strange situation regarding captaining, which given different circumstances and people may have proved awkward, but in fact was beneficial, at least as far as I was concerned. I captained the side that won the shield in Southland, Bob took over whilst the All Blacks were away in 1960 and carried on throughout the entire era.

It was my great privilege to play under Bob, who was an outstanding, competitive, match-winning skipper. We all respected Bob a great deal and hoped he might have obtained national honours, a recognition he richly deserved.

The unique style of play was an amalgam of well-drilled pattern rugby, rapid switches in direction of attack following breakdowns, speed at all times to minimise the weight disadvantage at forward, utilisation of our running forwards where possible to support back attacks and precise lineout calling, throwing and variations to offset the height disadvantage we generally faced.

Following the 1961 French tour, their peel at lineout was copied and refined to become Willie Away. The move was practised and practised, always badly and never used until time was running out in a game against Hawke's Bay. Bob, in desperation, called the move, it worked perfectly and after a slashing cut by Herewini, Nathan walked over for the try. Final score: 5–3. The play was used more often after this happy result.

Did the backs contribute more than the forwards overall, or vice versa? Nobody knows and who cares! The shield sides were nearer to 15-man rugby than any other teams I played in.

With the record behind us, we weren't sorry to see the shield go. It had dominated us for four winters and at the end we had simply run out of steam. The strain of successive challenges from teams trained to a peak for one special game proved too much in the end.

We meet together on occasions to renew friendships, share a drink or two and rekindle old memories. Fred has mellowed a little but still has the eyes that blaze on occasions. The lads sing the old bawdy songs, everyone talks at once and nobody listens. Bob may say a few words before he's shouted down, Alby will say something in Maori and Barry Thomas will say nothing at all. But thoughts and words keep returning to those golden winters when the Auckland Rugby Union put teams on the field that played wonderful rugby, rewrote the record books and produced the 'shield era'.

7

NEWPORT AND BEYOND

Unlike today, when the élite rugby players of New Zealand, Australia and South Africa play against each other and in Britain annually, back in Wilson's era, rugby expeditions to Great Britain and France came around only once every decade. They were events of epic proportions that involved an immense amount of planning. The tour of 1963–64, for which Wilson was named captain, Frank Kilby manager and Neil McPhail coach, involved no fewer than 36 matches in six countries and occupied four full months, from late October to late February. The 30 players toured as amateurs, receiving 10 shillings (about $1) a day for out-of-pocket expenses. Kilby and McPhail represented the total extent of the team's management. There were no assistant anythings, no doctor, no physiotherapist, no trainers, and certainly no media liaison officers. It was a challenge, but, for most, it became the experience of a lifetime.

The All Blacks had been in the United Kingdom just two days in October 1963 when Peter West of BBC television interviewed Wilson. The interview was progressing smoothly if unspectacularly when West suddenly asked, 'Will you regard defeat on this tour as a disaster?'

Wilson, now in his sixth year as All Black captain, took his time to answer. 'The world,' he assured West and his legion of viewers, 'will still go on, the sun will still shine, if we get beaten.'

He could little have suspected that 10 days later — after just the third of the 36 matches his players would undertake in their massive trek through England, Ireland, Scotland, Wales, and France, and on the way home Canada — they would be coming to terms with defeat. The sun didn't shine the next day, as it turned out, but that was because the All Blacks were in the depths of Wales where that golden object in the sky can be mightily elusive through much of autumn and almost all of winter.

The sun may have remained hidden behind the clouds, figuratively, for weeks, probably months, afterwards had Wilson himself not been such a forceful, inspirational leader. Losing to Newport as Wilson's team did could have been a crippling event. A decade on, the next All Black team to the United Kingdom, led by Ian Kirkpatrick, would fail to recover from its loss to Llanelli in almost identical circumstances. Kirkpatrick's team would return a failure, and Kirkpatrick, who merited legendary status as a player, would relinquish the captaincy. Wilson's team, on the other hand, would return in triumph with the captain lauded as the greatest All Black leader ever, an accolade that remains with him to this day.

So much of the success of the 1963–64 team related to events in the 24 hours following Newport's unexpected but deserved 3–0 victory. Their points came from a wobbly John Uzzell dropped goal that crept over the crossbar, and, while many have regarded the Newport victory, on a typically bleak Welsh afternoon, as fortuitous, Wilson knew that his team had been outplayed in the loose, that rookie Earle Kirton had floundered at first-five, and that if the 3–0 scoreline flattered either team, the one it flattered was the All Blacks.

Wilson didn't dwell on the painful setback. Some coaches and captains have been known to lock their teams in the dressing room and harangue them for their shortcomings on the pitch. Instead, Wilson ordered all 15 players into the Newport dressing room to offer congratulations and share in the celebrations of this historic victory. That evening, the All Blacks attended the social function that always accompanied tour matches. Sir Terry McLean, in his wonderful book *Willie Away,* wrote that the Welshmen were in transports of joy, but of a defensive rather than an expressive character.

> You had the impression they were all tightly wound in defensive coils, ready instantly to unwind and spring at any New Zealander who tempered his praise of Newport by remarking on the pitch, or the rain, or the referee, or the crowd, or any other symbol visible or invisible which might have brought about defeat. But neither rain nor referee nor any other thing was mentioned by the All Blacks. The Welsh remained amazed.

Wilson reserved his comments, appropriately, for the team meeting the next day. Confronting his players, he asked them if they wanted to be remembered as an ordinary team. 'I'm demanding you take stock and commit yourselves,' he said, 'so we can go through this tour never playing or feeling like this again.'

John Graham, who'd run touch at Newport, recalls it as a seminal moment in the tour. 'By the time of the '63 tour, Wilson had added wisdom to the already fine qualities he'd demonstrated in South Africa three years earlier. He was now the complete skipper, and he demonstrated these qualities in the wake of the Newport disaster. Significantly, the team never lost another game.'

Wilson would argue that the fixture that followed Newport, against Neath and Aberavon at Port Talbot, was the most critical of the entire tour. It was a foul day with rain bucketing down, reducing the contest pretty much to a mud scramble. Late in the first spell Pat Walsh was injured and, with no replacements permitted, John Graham had to deputize at centre.

Like Newport before them, the Neath and Aberavon forwards took the game to the New Zealanders, and, when the visitors trailed 3–6 with only 25 minutes remaining, the prospect of back-to-back disasters loomed large for the tourists. Would they ever recover from successive setbacks? With Wilson calling for a supreme effort, the All Blacks managed late tries by Paul Little and Ken Gray to escape with an 11–6 victory.

It was a relieved All Black captain who soaked in the hot bath afterwards. In the bath next to him was John Graham.

'Nearly,' was Wilson's solitary comment about the day's tribulations.

Nearly was good enough. The tour was back on track, the All Blacks having responded in the face of adversity. Wilson would not have to deliver any more rallying speeches.

The British had first twigged to Wilson's exceptional qualities when, in the first week of the tour, he had addressed the distinguished gathering at the traditional Sportsmen's Club luncheon. The Savoy Hotel was packed with famous rugby players, cricketers, tennis players, jockeys and administrators. 'You who have been out in the middle,' Wilson told them, 'will know the sort of problems we All Blacks are going to face during our tour.'

Terry McLean records in *Willie Away* that, as Wilson sat down, the Englishman next to him said, 'By gad, this fellow's good.'

No individual had greater affection and admiration for Wilson than Colin Meads, who was massively influenced by the man he would come to call 'Skip'. Terry McLean would write of the relationship in the *Rothmans Rugby Yearbook* many years later:

> All consideration of Meads as a man of rugby should begin at the point of his leaving school at the age of 15 — a shy, withdrawn, introverted boy. From his early appearance in first-class rugby at the age of 18 to the time when he encountered, and was most profoundly influenced by, Wilson Whineray . . . it was the attraction of opposites which turned Meads and Whineray into blood brothers. Whineray could be extremely sensitive but outwardly he was humorous, extroverted

and educated; and Meads could see none of those things in himself. So he gave himself to Whineray and as 'Skip' directed things — the term is still used between them — so Meads obeyed.

On the long, wearying flight from New Zealand, Wilson and Pinetree sat alongside each other. When the plane was a couple of hours out from Los Angeles the hostess handed out landing cards, which each individual had to complete. Meads, concentrating hard, worked his way methodically through the boxes until he came to the last three, politically loaded questions which caused a furrowing of his brow.

The first one questioned whether the traveller had ever indulged in subversive behaviour.

'Hey, Skip, what the hell does "subversive" mean?'

Wilson looked across at his colleague. 'Colin, it means getting into trouble. Just tick the "no" box.'

'But I belong to the King Country rugby team and we get into a hell of a lot of trouble.'

'Yes, but that's not subversive. Just tick the "no" box.'

Meads did as he was directed and moved to the next question: Do you associate with known communists?

'What'll I tick here, Skip?'

'Just tick "no" again.'

'But how do I know I haven't associated with communists?'

'Colin, there are no communists in Te Kuiti. Just tick the "no" box.'

'But I might have associated with a communist without knowing it.'

'The immigration people at Los Angeles will believe you if you tick "no", I promise you.'

The final question asked if the individual completing the form had any intentions of overthrowing the US Government.

'Don't ask,' said Wilson, 'just tick the "no" box.'

It's rumoured that one member of the touring party, in response to that same final question, wrote 'Solitary purpose of visit' and was apparently detained by immigration officials.

The opening match of the tour, against Oxford University, afforded three of the more scholarly members of the side — John Graham, Chris Laidlaw (who would become a Rhodes Scholar and study at Oxford), and Wilson — a rare and wonderful opportunity to spend an evening in the confines of this august establishment, the history of which dates back to the 12th century. The trio had journeyed up early from Bournemouth, where the All Blacks had run off their jetlag, and were met at the railway station. They were wined and dined in one of the colleges. Their Oxford hosts said they always extended an invitation to visiting international teams, but never before had their hospitality been taken up. Messrs Graham, Laidlaw and Whineray, who found the experience uplifting, failed to comprehend why.

A couple of days later, the Oxford University rugby players presented no difficulties for the All Blacks, who won handsomely. This represented the first occasion in which Meads, Whineray, and newcomer Brian Lochore had appeared in the same starting XV for their country. They would all go on to be knighted. Given that they are the only three New Zealanders to be knighted for services to rugby, it's truly remarkable that they all featured in the same team, in the same scrum, at the same time.

The All Blacks were several times accommodated in central London for matches at Twickenham and for games that could be easily reached by train. On each occasion their place of residence was the posh Park Lane Hotel, close to Piccadilly Circus. If it wasn't five-star, it was no more than a half a star removed, all of which took some adjusting to for humble Kiwi lads, especially those from small rural towns.

After training on their first day in London, in the lead-up to the London Counties fixture, the players poured into the dining room — a separate area having been blocked off for them — in search of lunch. As most had events planned for the afternoon, they were wanting something, anything, quick. They soon discovered the Park Lane didn't do quick luncheon service. Park Royal dining was a leisurely experience. Much grumbling emanated from the players. Wilson, who not only captained the All Blacks but represented them in matters of negotiation, approached the *maître d'*.

'There is a problem, sir?' asked the *maître d'*.

'No problem, but time is important to many of the players,' replied Wilson, in his most diplomatic voice. 'Is there a way we can speed up the process?'

'No problem, Mr Whineray — we'll attend to that immediately. How would it be if we offered them a condensed menu with limited choice? That will certainly speed up the process.'

'Excellent.'

Lunch the next day was certainly speedier, but still there were grumbles from the players. The problem now was the main choices on offer: *filet mignon* and *coq au vin*. Superbly prepared and presented, they were a tad high-brow as luncheon options for the New Zealanders, most of whom would have settled for a pasta dish or sandwiches.

Again, Wilson approached the *maître d'*.

'There is a problem again, Mr Whineray?'

'The players feel the mains on offer, while of high quality, are a little richer than they would prefer at lunchtime.'

'I understand perfectly. What would they prefer?'

'I'll sound them out and let you know,' said the captain.

The players were almost unanimous on their requirements. They nominated mince, sausages, beef and roast potatoes.

Again Wilson confronted the *maître d'*.

'I have the preferences,' he said.

'Excellent, and what might they be?'

'Mince, sausages, beef and roast potatoes.'

A look of horror spread across the face of the *maître d'*.

'We can do miracles, I'm sure, Mr Whineray.'

The players didn't exactly get their mince and sausages, but the mince stew with carrots that was served the following day sent most of them away satisfied!

On the journey across to Britain, a group comprising some of the 'senior' survivors of the 1960 South African campaign — John Graham, Ralph Caulton and Wilson, plus coach Neil McPhail — had discussed strategies and goals for the tour ahead. It was generally conceded that the selection policy in South Africa had been faulty, that the team had been obsessed with wanting to win every game. There had been no rotation policy, and the touring party soon evolved an 'us and them' mentality.

They decided that this time their chief objective should be to win the five internationals against Ireland, Wales, England, Scotland and France, plus the Barbarians game, and that team selection in the remaining fixtures should be alternated. All players, when fit, should be given the opportunity to participate fully in the tour. It was a policy that would operate handsomely, although one hapless individual who would miss out on his share of games after the setback against Newport was Earle Kirton. But he would survive the experience and return four years later as the All Blacks' test first-five.

The first indication that McPhail's men might be something special came in the team's first outing at Twickenham against London Counties. Well, some might argue the first true indication of the team's worthiness came in the resolute, second-spell fight-back against Neath and Aberavon immediately following the Newport setback, when defeat could have plunged the team into an uncontrollable tailspin. But that was about gutsing out a victory in the face of adversity. What the London Counties game at Twickenham demonstrated was that this All Black team possessed footballers of exciting talent capable of dissecting a quality opponent.

London Counties was expected to test the tourists, but the All Blacks chose this occasion to unleash a performance of sublime quality. Their performance inspired Uel Titley of *The Times*, the senior pro of the Fleet Street rugby correspondents, to quote Shakespeare in his match report. 'And gentlemen of England now abed,' he wrote, 'shall think themselves accurs'd they were not here.' And Terry McLean, the most senior of the New Zealand writers, proclaimed that, of all the games of rugby he had ever seen, this one 'counts as my heart's desire'.

The All Blacks won 27–0, seven tries to none, with Waka Nathan — the 'Black Panther' as the French would dub him — in imperious form. He scored a brace of tries as the All Blacks cut loose in the second half.

Colin Meads had been warned by coach McPhail about the threat posed by the London Counties lock he was opposing, Scottish international Michael Campbell-Lamerton.

'You reckon you're the best lock,' said McPhail. 'Well, they tell me this fellow is. What are you going to do about it?'

What Meads did about it was to push and shove his opposite number mercilessly for fully half an hour before Campbell-Lamerton, a disciplined, and heroic, army officer who had served in the Korean War and risen to the rank of colonel, finally retaliated and shoved Meads.

'Do that again and I'll knock your head off,' warned Meads, in mock outrage.

Not only did Campbell-Lamerton not do it again, shortly afterwards he left the field with a mysterious ailment. When he returned, he opted to jump at six in the lineout, well away from Meads.

Meads reported back to McPhail. 'I don't know who advised you about Campbell-Lamerton,' he said, 'but he ain't tough.'

Campbell-Lamerton would captain the British Lions to New

Zealand in 1966 and become Meads's bunny. They would clash on five occasions — four test matches and a provincial contest in Wanganui — with Meads on the winning side every time.

If the 'oil' about Campbell-Lamerton was astray, the next tip-off would turn out to be alarmingly accurate. On the train journey from London to Cambridge, Wilson got into conversation with a couple of the British journalists, Uel Titley and JBG Thomas.

'Do you know anything about any of these Cambridge University players we're up against?' he asked.

'Yes, the young fly-half Mike Gibson is uncommonly good,' one of them advised. 'You'll need to watch him closely.'

In his team talk prior to kick-off, Wilson turned to the flankers of the day, Kel Tremain and Keith Nelson. 'You'll need to keep a close eye on the 18-year-old playing at first-five,' he warned. 'They say he's very dangerous.'

'Right, Skip,' replied Tremain, in a laconic way that suggested he was thinking the skipper should concentrate on the front row and leave precocious teenage backs to him.

In the first move of the game, Cambridge worked the ball to Gibson, who stepped Tremain, leaving him sprawling. He was finally brought down only metres from the goal-line.

'I told you to bloody watch him!' Wilson barked at Tremain.

'He won't do that again.'

Not 10 minutes later, Gibson effected another dazzling break, leaving Tremain in a heap again. This time, the All Black defence was so shredded that Gibson scored a fabulous try. As the All Blacks sauntered behind the goal-line for the conversion, Tremain said to Wilson, 'Christ, this kid's good.'

To Tremain's credit, Gibson, who would go on to achieve legendary status with Ireland and the British Lions — Wilson would label him the finest back he ever opposed — didn't get past him again that afternoon, but he sure left a lasting impression.

If it sounds like Gibson was the standout performer at Cambridge, he was, quite remarkably, upstaged by a front-rower — the All Black captain, no less. Gibson would confess to Wilson after his majestic career finally came to a conclusion almost two decades later that he believed he never played the perfect game.

Well, Wilson came awfully close to perfection against Cambridge at Grange Road, turning in a colossal performance. He made slashing breaks, he bumped off opponents, he tackled heroically, and he created two of his team's four tries. His *pièce de résistance* came after he broke away down the left touchline, in front of the packed grandstand. As the cover defence advanced upon him, he sighted his winger Malcolm Dick, whose marker had gone walkabout, far away on the opposite side of the field, waving frantically. With remarkable skill, Wilson, a natural right-footer, let fly across-field with a raking left-footed punt that sat up perfectly for Dick, who gathered and scored behind the posts. That a prop should accomplish such feats left many in the crowd, and not a few in the press box, spellbound.

When reminded of this performance many, many years later and asked if he considered it his finest in the black jersey, he nonchalantly tossed it away. 'No, that was a frothy kind of game against a modest opponent,' he replied. 'The performances I drew greatest satisfaction from were the tense, tight ones against formidable opponents when maybe one tactical manoeuvre represented the difference between defeat and victory. Those were the occasions when you went to the dressing room purring.'

Full-scale tours of Britain and France, of the sort Wilson's men undertook, involved a huge amount of down-time, in hotels, at airports and railway stations, and on lengthy coach and train journeys. One way in which Wilson helped break the monotony was by playing euchre. Early on, a euchre school was created, comprising coach Neil McPhail, Don Clarke, John Graham, Ian MacRae, Terry McLean and Wilson — and sometimes Pat Walsh. They would engage in furious games of six-handed euchre, the arguments from which could be heard throughout the carriage or coach in which they were travelling.

Modest sums of money were usually at stake, but bragging rights from the latest contest mattered far more than any financial gain.

♣

As if Wilson didn't have enough to focus upon, as leader on this four-month quest of New Zealand's finest footballers, he sat three of his Bachelor of Commerce papers while on tour. Fortunately, there was a well-established procedure in place for overseas students sitting papers in the UK; otherwise, there would have been little point in his attending lectures back in Auckland throughout 1963. Having cleared it all with the University of Auckland, he sat one paper in London (at London University) and two in Cardiff (at South Monmouthshire University).

After he completed the first paper, which was awaiting him in a sealed envelope in Cardiff, the exam observer, who just happened to be a rugby enthusiast, inquired if Wilson would be back in about 10 days' time.

'Well, yes, as a matter of fact, I will be,' replied Wilson.

'How are you planning to get through to Abertillery for the game that day?'

'I hadn't thought that through yet,' said Wilson.

'Then would you like me to drive you through?'

'That would be wonderful.'

So through the marvellous network that binds rugby players worldwide — it certainly did in those truly amateur days and hopefully continues today — Wilson was chauffeured from Cardiff to Ebbw Vale for the midweek encounter, but not without a stopover for lunch at the school where his driver taught. Word that the famous All Black captain was coming to their school for lunch ensured a full turnout and the serving of a meal to be remembered.

On the eve of the Cardiff match, news was received that President John Kennedy had been assassinated in Dallas, Texas. The All Blacks, like most people in Wales, were shocked. The two teams observed a minute's silence before kick-off the following afternoon. When the next Kennedy brother was assassinated, Wilson would be resident in America.

The All Blacks made it through to the opening international against Ireland in Dublin — the 14th match of the tour — with only Newport listed in the debit column. There had been a couple of tight encounters, but the All Blacks always managed to come out on the right side. They knew the Irish would be tough, simply because they were the Irish. What Irish teams may have lacked in flair, they more than compensated for in passion and sheer physical commitment — as the All Blacks of 1963 were to discover at Lansdowne Road.

Pinetree Meads's opponent was a tough one, a certain Willie John McBride from Ballymena. Down Under no one messed with Pinetree; in the Five Nations, McBride commanded the same respect. Now here were these two titans of rugby opposing each other. Applying shrewd Irish cunning, McBride determined he would get his retaliation in first. The game wasn't a quarter old when Meads felt the wrath of his famous opponent. Like a boxer KO'd, he hit the canvas, and hit it hard. Meads was somewhere between Thursday and Tuesday when Wilson tended to him.

'For Gawd's sake, get up,' said Wilson. 'Don't let him know you're hurt.'

'I don't know that I can get up,' replied Meads, in roughly the same state a member of the public would be if they'd just been run over by a bus.

'Of course you can. Come on. Here, grab my arm.'

With a fair portion of the galaxy still dominating his vision, Meads walked slowly to the next lineout, Wilson at his shoulder, steadying him.

'What about McBride?' asked Meads.

'Leave that to me,' replied Wilson.

During the next several lineouts — remembering that Meads was always a commanding figure at lineouts — he was anonymous as he sought to regain his composure. Intriguingly, while he was quietly putting himself back into the game, someone did to McBride what McBride had done to him. Who could that have been?

The All Blacks escaped with a 6–5 win, managing no more than a try by Tremain and a penalty goal by Clarke, and hung on for grim death as the Irish threw everything — kitchen sink included — at them over the final 16 minutes. It wasn't a pretty win, it certainly wasn't a convincing win, but by God it was a win. The All Blacks were an immensely relieved lot as they sipped on their Guinnesses that evening.

Four days later the All Blacks had to contend with Munster at Limerick. There's something about the men of Munster. To say they play above their weight is a gross understatement. Buoyed by their home fans, they give 300 per cent, especially against All Black touring teams, and 1963 was no exception. The All Blacks were fortunate to escape with a 6–3 win. Neither Wilson nor Meads played in this game, but when his players commented favourably upon the performance given by the referee, Ray Williams from Ulster, Wilson that evening arranged to meet him and coerced Pinetree into joining him.

'Come on, we're going to have a drink with the referee,' he said, 'to see how strong a character he is.'

Meads and Wilson sat with Williams by a roaring fire, shared several drinks together, and found him to be an absolutely delightful person. A week later they selected him, from a panel of three, to referee the Welsh test. He so impressed the tourists with his calm handling of all situations that they also chose him to control the Scottish and French tests. Wilson would, upon retirement in 1965, nominate Williams and Australian Roger Vanderfield as the two best referees he had played under.

By the time the All Blacks reached Cardiff a fortnight later, seeking revenge for what the Welsh had done to their predecessors (and to the teams of 1905 and 1935), Whineray's men had strung together 14 straight victories since the calamity against Newport.

On many occasions — the exact number probably exceeded a thousand — the All Blacks were warned, 'Wait until you get to Wales'. They were aware the Welsh selectors had been studying their play and, like the Irish, they knew the 15 men outfitted in scarlet would take immense inspiration from the 60,000 fans crammed into Cardiff Arms Park.

Pat Walsh, one of the senior members of the All Black backline, had suffered a serious injury and hadn't played since the fourth match of the tour, meaning that Mac Herewini, who'd been named as a reserve, was thus the only Maori apart from Waka Nathan involved in the Welsh international.

Nathan, a gifted entertainer on the guitar, didn't do hakas. Mackie Herewini, with some reluctance, did. He was prepared, he said, in the interests of the team, to lead the haka, the 'Ka Mate' version that was in vogue in those days, against the Welsh. What's more, to make it appear more authentic, he would wear a flax skirt that had been presented to the team. Manager Frank Kilby gave it his seal of approval. After the All Blacks ran on to the Arms Park, Wilson made sure he was in close proximity to Herewini.

'After the singing,' Wilson explained to Herewini, 'when I say "go", you launch into the haka.'

'Righto, Skip,' said Herewini.

Herewini seemed fine while 'God Defend New Zealand' was ringing out, but when nearly 60,000 Welshmen, every single one of whom seemed to have a cherished voice, gave 'Land of Our Fathers' their all, he became traumatized.

'Righto, Mac,' said Wilson, after the lilting tones of the Welsh anthem subsided.

There was no movement. Cameras were panning in on the All Blacks ready to record the haka.

'Are you all right, Mac?' asked Wilson.

'I don't think I can do it.'

Sixty thousand Welshmen — well, maybe it was 59,500

Welshmen and 500 Kiwis — had fallen silent.

'Come on, Mac — you'll be fine,' said Wilson, who was desperately trying to remember if he knew all the words, because the terrible realization was coming to him that he might have to lead the haka himself. Rangi Whineray at the ready!

To Wilson's undying relief, Herewini suddenly said, 'I'm all right now.' And proceeded to lead the haka with great aplomb.

Wilson had more important things to concentrate on than the haka — like a fired-up Welsh team that he knew was preparing to throw everything at them. The one individual who scared the Welsh — there was no doubt about that — was Don Clarke. Wilson decided it would strike an important psychological blow for the All Blacks if The Boot was unleashed upon them early in the game. The test was only minutes old when the All Blacks received a penalty near halfway and 5 metres in from touch.

'How's it look?' asked Wilson.

'I can land it,' declared Clarke.

'Have a go then,' said Wilson.

It was a monstrous kick by 1963 standards, but Clarke struck it so beautifully that the distance was no problem and it slammed into the left upright. When Wales's clearing kick failed to find touch, Clarke fielded that and let fly with a left-footed drop-kick from 45 metres that cannoned into the right upright.

No points were scored, but Wilson knew that psychologically Clarke had plunged two daggers into the opposition. What the Welsh didn't know, and nor did Wilson, was that in attempting the first massive kick, Clarke had strained his right groin muscle. For the remainder of the game, all his touch-finders were despatched with the left foot.

Although the All Blacks managed only one penalty goal (by Clarke) and one dropped goal (by Bruce Watt), they deserved their victory. They were the stronger team, and the Welsh, who failed to score, never seriously threatened their line.

Deserving winners they might have been, but they weren't cheered from the field. Oh no, they were booed — thanks to that man Colin Meads, who in the final five minutes had got himself embroiled in an ugly incident involving the Welsh scrum-half and captain, Clive Rowlands.

Rowlands had got up Meads's nostril by yakking incessantly throughout the game, but that wasn't a factor in what unfolded when Meads pursued an up-and-under from his halfback Kevin Briscoe that was fielded by Rowlands. In Pinetree lingo, Meads 'kneed him in the arse'. Fifty-nine thousand, five hundred Welshmen saw it differently. They all swore blindly that Meads had callously kneed their representative in the spine. Rowlands lay on the ground writhing in pain. The booing rose to a crescendo.

Meads saw it as a Hollywood, one that almost merited an Oscar given Rowlands' facial expressions. The referee certainly didn't see it as an act of brutality, even though he penalized Meads, but that was for him being offside. Rowlands exited the Arms Park on a stretcher. While this was happening, with the hills alive with the sound of booing, Tremain said to Meads, 'Don't stand near us!'

In the dressing room afterwards, Meads, not quite believing the way the Welsh crowd had turned on him, declared he had better go next-door and see how the Welsh halfback was faring. As he stepped out of the door, Rowlands' wife spied him. 'There's the dirty bastard!' she hollered.

Meads fixed his gaze firmly on the concrete floor as he made his way steadfastly through to the Welsh changing room, where Rowlands still bore a pained expression, although he appeared well recovered from the agonies that had necessitated his removal from the field horizontally.

A dance followed the test dinner that evening, and Meads was amazed to discover Rowlands rocking and rolling. 'There's nothing wrong with you, you bugger!' he told him. Rowlands just smiled.

Some time after midnight Wilson accompanied Meads on the

walk back to the Angel Hotel, where the All Blacks were quartered in Cardiff. A few hundred metres from the hotel, they became aware of a group of inebriated individuals on the opposite side of the road. 'Meads, you dirty so-and-so. Come over here!' barked out one of them.

Meads was prepared to confront them.

Wilson placed a hand on his arm. 'Don't you lower yourself to their standard,' the captain advised. 'We're going home.' And they did.

For several of their matches in Wales, including the international, the All Blacks were quartered at the Seabank Hotel at Porthcawl, which is as close to Cardiff as Pukekohe is to Auckland, Paraparaumu to Wellington, and Momona Airport to Dunedin. It wasn't a logical arrangement geographically, but it did allow the All Blacks to have their space and to be away from the maddened throng. And when it comes to rugby in Wales, the throng can be absolutely overwhelming.

Cricketer Fred Trueman, England's fiery fast bowler, was at the peak of his powers when the All Blacks were touring, which inspired some of the All Blacks to roll their arms over at the Seabank — indoors. The long, wide corridors led to the All Blacks creating a 'pitch' on which the bowlers endeavoured to emulate Trueman. Mind you, they weren't releasing the same projectiles Trueman's victims were facing a few hundred kilometres down the road at The Oval. In the corridors of the Porthcawl Hotel, the All Black batsmen were facing oranges!

It so happened that where the first cricket one-dayer began to unfold was right outside captain Wilson's room. It wasn't long before he opened his door to determine what was going on.

'What the hell are you guys up to?' he asked. 'Oh, cricket. Great, mind if I join you?'

The protracted tours that All Black teams undertook up until the 1970s no longer exist, which may or may not be a good thing.

But tours lasting four months, such as the tour that Wilson's team endured, were brilliant for developing team camaraderie and bonding. One of the weekly highlights, staged on Sundays — always a travel-free day back then — were court sessions.

Kevin 'Monkey' Briscoe of Taranaki was the team's judge, a role at which he was a natural. A short bloke, he used to borrow one of his teammates' red dressing-gowns and march in like one of the seven dwarfs, the gown trailing behind him. Briscoe developed a hilarious partnership with Pat Walsh, another naturally funny person, who became his Clerk of Court. They were merciless at identifying blunders involving teammates, managers and journalists. Defence 'lawyers' didn't stand a chance. Anyone charged simply had to cough up with a cash donation towards the team fund.

On one of their many visits to London, the All Blacks attended the Houses of Parliament, where they partook of afternoon tea. Wilson spied a wig sitting on one of the judge's desks at about the same time that Monkey did. Briscoe couldn't take his eyes off it.

'Pinch that and there will be a row,' Wilson warned Briscoe. 'First with me, and then with the judiciary.'

Briscoe shrugged. 'Don't worry, Skip,' he replied.

Two weeks later at the All Blacks' court session, Briscoe entered resplendent not only in his red dressing-gown but wearing a dinkum judge's wig. At the conclusion of the session, Wilson asked Briscoe if the wig was the same one they had sighted at the Houses of Parliament. Briscoe assured him it wasn't.

'Are you telling the truth?'

'I am indeed.'

Wilson, being the honourable person he is, accepted Briscoe's answer, but would tell you that to this day he harbours his suspicions!

A highlight of the team's court sessions was often the singing, not of the massed choir variety for which the Welsh are famous, but solo offerings, often with guitar accompaniment from Waka Nathan, and sometimes even from Wilson, cued in by the team's music master, Pat Walsh. At the start of the tour all the players were told to memorize at least one song — pop, classical or traditional, it mattered not — which they would be required to sing at team sessions whenever Walsh called their name. A handful of the players were possessed of uncommonly good voices, most got by, and a few, like the Taranaki hooker John Major, were tone deaf and couldn't sing to save themselves. After a few bars, the chorus would normally come in behind the individual, usually to that player's immense relief. Major was so unbelievably bad that he was usually left babbling along solo, because his indescribable voice was such a priceless source of entertainment.

One of the finest voices belonged to the captain. Wilson's brother, Scott, was a talented musician who probably could have made a career as a pianist. Wilson knew his way around a piano keyboard well enough, and could strum ukeleles and guitars adequately, but his finest moments musically came when he was induced to sing. He had two favourites: 'Scottish Soldier', the song made famous by Ian McKellar, which he delivered with great gusto, and 'I Talk to the Trees' from *Paint Your Wagon*.

Wilson gave many renditions of 'Scottish Soldier' over the years, but the one he would treasure most fondly occurred around midnight one evening in the house bar of a hotel the All Blacks were staying at in Christchurch. Wilson and his mates had played their game, done the dinner and social thing, and were preparing to relax over a quiet drink or three before retiring for the night.

It was drawn to Wilson's attention that the fellow with the Scottish accent at the bar was none other than Ian McKellar, he of 'Scottish Soldier' fame.

'Don't tell me!' said Wilson.

'Would you like to meet him?'

'Yes, I would, but I'm not sure he wants to meet me.'

'Of course he would.'

After the introductions were completed and Wilson's reputation for singing McKellar's song established, there was only one thing for it: a duet.

It was a rousing version that deserved a greater audience than the half-dozen who were in the house bar at the time. It was an occasion to treasure for the All Black skipper.

Much is made these days of the raucous behaviour of intoxicated rugby and league players in the wake of team celebrations. The same dangers existed in the 'sixties, and occasionally an individual would get out of hand. But the 1963–64 All Blacks had the best possible leader. Always, at the conclusion of the court sessions, Wilson would issue a warning note. 'That's it, boys,' he would say. 'No clowning around in public now, no pinching waitresses' bottoms. Remember, you're representing your country.'

In the four months the team was at large in Great Britain, France and Canada, there was not one unseemly incident that spilled over into the public arena. Ralph Caulton, many decades on, would say that Wilson brought sophistication and decorum to the All Blacks, and that the behavioural standards he set permeated right through the team.

'Another of his great qualities,' Caulton recalls, 'was that players identified him and used him as a counsellor. He was always available to sit down and talk to the players. He stood up for the players. If we had a problem, we'd take it to Wilson and he'd talk to management.'

Wilson had acquired the nickname of Noddy prior to 1963, the title being confirmed on the tour of the United Kingdom and France. It came about because of Wilson's extraordinary capacity for nodding off on the team bus *en route* to matches. While many of his teammates were wide awake and galvanized for action, some chattering away nervously, Wilson blissfully dozed off. It was apparently a nervous manifestation; whatever, it ensured he arrived at the match venue in a nicely relaxed state.

The All Blacks, the management in particular, were always receiving invitations to some activity or other. Many had to be declined, but often when the pressure was off the reply would be in the affirmative. One such invitation taken up by Wilson was to appear on the BBC 4 radio programme 'Desert Island Discs', a programme created by Roy Plomley and hosted by him since the 1940s. Wilson happily journeyed down to London for the interview, where he was told he would have to reveal half a dozen discs he would take with him to his imaginary desert island retreat, along with one book and one *objet d'art*.

The book he declared he would be reading as he lay in his desert island hammock was *A History of the English-speaking Peoples* by Winston Churchill, the *objet d'art* would be a landscape by one of the leading New Zealand artists of the 19th century, and the music he said he preferred ranged right across the spectrum, from opera sung by José Carreras to Frank Sinatra, to country music, to the Welsh choir, the Treorchy Male Voice Choir. Wilson told Plomley that his musical preferences related to the mood he was in.

Speaking of the Treorchy choir, one Sunday while the All Blacks were quartered at Porthcawl they were told if they stayed around they would be in for a treat, for the choristers were coming to their hotel to practise. Most of the golfers sacrificed the musical offering for fresh-air activity, but Wilson hung in and told the sporty ones when they returned that they had missed one of the great experiences of the tour.

McLean would write in *Willie Away* that, by the end of the tour, it was dollars to doughnuts that at least one newspaper each day would refer to Whineray as the finest prop in the world. Bert Toft, in *The Observer*, classed him as the world's best prop and the world's worst packer, a fascinating contradiction in terms.

McLean wrote that Whineray emerged as, without any question, the best loosehead prop in 'the whole wide world'.

> His abilities at fielding, kicking and passing were quite staggering.
> He picked up the ball on the dead run like a man trained for nothing

else, and with his running he combined a barge which was by far the most fearsome in the team and which made him by far the hardest man in the team to bring down, or even check.

In a nutshell, Whineray in a strenuous, tight, competitive match with little between the teams was a splendid forward, the more valuable because of his abilities as a leader. In a match where the strenuousness tailed off or in which, from one cause or another, it was possible to run the ball a good deal, he was what the British critics said — the world's best.

8

FOR HE'S A JOLLY GOOD FELLOW

Christmas 1963 arrived four days after the Welsh test. For New Zealanders, of course, Christmas is an event that falls in the thick of summer, when a swim is a desirable option once the luncheon excesses have worn off. But in the United Kingdom, Christmas is a winter experience, occasionally celebrated poetically with snow falling. Snow didn't fall on 25 December 1963, but in London, where the All Blacks were based, it was seriously cold. Winter was all about. At the opposite end of the Earth from families and loved ones it could have been a desolate occasion for the All Blacks, but the Rugby Union of England had arranged for all the players to be privately hosted on Christmas Day. Wilson and Colin Meads became the guests of New Zealand's High Commissioner to the United Kingdom, Tom McDonald. They shared turkey and Christmas pudding and wine with Tom and his family in what was a most memorable occasion.

Wilson was totally relaxed, but Pinetree, who was rarely fazed by anything, was slightly on edge, as he had been ever since Wilson had told him he was going to captain the All Blacks — for the only time on tour — in the Boxing Day encounter against Combined Services at Twickenham. Leading the All Blacks and making on-field decisions didn't bother Meads one iota. What troubled him was having to deliver the speech at the function that followed the game.

'I said to Wilson, "I'm not going to make the speech — you can".'

'He said, "Yes, you are." It was alright for him. He was a natural when it came to speaking, an orator, to be honest. It didn't matter whether he was addressing the Queen, Members of Parliament, businessmen or rugby players, he took it all in his stride and always made a fantastic speech.

'But this boy from Te Kuiti wasn't at home in front of a microphone — not in those days, anyway. And it was obvious that the audience at the after-match function would be overflowing with colonels, commanders and admirals, which I found more than a little bit daunting.'

While Meads was leading the All Blacks to a comfortable victory, scoring a try in the process, Wilson was hob-nobbing in the President's Box, high above, and far removed from, the immaculate turf of Twickenham.

He'd finished up there at the invitation of Sir George Augustus 'Gus' Walker, a distinguished serviceman who'd played two rugby internationals for England in 1939, lost his right arm when a Lancaster bomber exploded, and was now Inspector-General of the RAF. Sir Gus had had a handwritten note delivered to the All Black captain requesting his company in the official box. Wilson considered it would be inappropriate to decline.

In conversation with Sir Gus, Wilson let it be known that he'd received a letter from his old Auckland Grammar School Third Form room-mate, Sir Kenneth Hayr, who having received a double knighthood for his wartime heroics was now a flying officer at Leconfield military air base in the north of England. Sir Kenneth had suggested that while the All Blacks were based at Ilkley in Yorkshire for the North-Eastern Counties game, they might like to spend a day at Leconfield, where they could train, have lunch and be entertained by a flying display.

'Would you like to do that?' asked Sir Gus.

'Yes, we would,' replied Wilson.

'Then tell Sir Kenneth to organize it. Tell him not to let the request come anywhere near my desk — I might have trouble justifying burning off a few thousand litres of jet fuel to entertain a rugby team!'

The Leconfield experience represented one of the great events of the tour for many of the players, some of whom got to position themselves in fighter jets. If Sir Kenneth had had his way, Wilson would have been taken aloft in one of the two-seater training planes, but Sir Gus wouldn't authorize it, reminding Sir Kenneth — on several occasions — that civilians simply were not allowed aboard military aircraft.

Sir Gus, an accomplished referee, would become president of the Rugby Union of England in 1965–66. Sir Kenneth, as Assistant Chief of Air Staff Operations, would go on to become Deputy Chief of the Defence Staff (Commitments) at the Ministry of Defence. Upon his retirement he returned to New Zealand, but continued to split his time between the United Kingdom and New Zealand in order to indulge his love of flying by performing displays in various vintage aircraft. It was in such an aircraft, a De Havilland Vampire, that he was killed during the 2001 Biggin Hill air pageant.

After the narrow squeaks against Ireland and Wales, the All Blacks were relieved to put England away by 14 points to nil, a commanding scoreline; indeed, it represented the heaviest loss ever suffered by England in 54 years of playing at Twickenham. Wilson created the first try, for Ralph Caulton, by bumping the England fullback and captain John Wilcox back several metres, and Meads scored the second, between the posts, after a sensational interception 80 metres up-field by Caulton.

Nick Drake-Lee led the English front row and, as his team's fortunes began to subside, he urged them on, to the amusement of the All Blacks, with the classic line 'More fire in the mauls, chaps!' Wilson, in similar circumstances, would have used more basic terminology, something like 'Come on, you bastards — get stuck in!'

England appeared on the verge of scoring a try after fly-half Phil Horrocks-Taylor stepped John Graham and swept on to attack. But he ran too far, and in delaying his pass found not a teammate but Caulton. The flying winger linked with Graham, who redeemed himself, he felt, by putting Meads across for the try.

Graham hadn't been in the dressing room 30 seconds when he was reminded of the fact that coach McPhail recalled everything that had happened in a match.

'You missed him,' he said to Graham, referring to Horrocks-Taylor's burst.

'But we scored a brilliant try out of it.'

'You missed him!'

Graham was about to prolong the discussion, when McPhail, breaking into a broad smile, said, 'But you played well.'

Brian Lochore made his test debut in this game, thanks to a chance encounter with Wilson on the morning of the match. Lochore, who'd played the midweeker against Llanelli, was one of the 'dirty dirties' for the Twickenham international — that is, a player simply not required for this game. He was rooming with Keith Nelson, who had been practising with the test squad after Waka Nathan had sustained a jaw injury in the midweek game at Llanelli. Lochore had picked up a cold, and decided that a game of squash on the Saturday morning would help run it out of his system. He was at the lift door holding his sports bag when Wilson came along.

'Where are you going?'

'For a game of squash.'

'I think you should go back to your room — we might need you.'

Puzzled by this sudden development, Lochore returned to his room where Nelson was on the phone talking to his parents back in Auckland, telling them he would almost certainly be playing against England because it had been confirmed that Nathan had a broken jaw. When Nelson finished his call, he asked Lochore what he was doing back.

'I ran into Wilson and he told me to wait here.'

About 15 minutes later the phone rang, and it was team manager Frank Kilby.

'That you, Brian?'

'Yes.'

'You're playing this afternoon.'

'I've got a bit of flu.'

'You'll rise above that.'

Lochore finished the call and turned to Nelson to give him the obviously disappointing news.

'I'm playing against England this afternoon.'

Lochore would turn in a massive performance and launch a stellar international career that would extend to 24 test appearances. But he has often wondered how things might have developed if he'd not encountered Wilson at the lift.

'This was just after breakfast time, and the game at Twickenham was starting at two o'clock. If I'd headed off for my squash game, no one would have known where to get hold of me.'

Traditionally, All Black teams touring the United Kingdom are hosted by the ruling monarch. But because Her Majesty Queen Elizabeth II was heavily pregnant (with Prince Edward), she was unable to fulfil that duty. However, Wilson and his players did get to meet the Queen Mother at Clarence House and the Duke of Edinburgh at Buckingham Palace. The Duke enjoyed the New Zealanders' company so richly — indulging in conversations about hunting, sailing and horse-riding — that he was late for his next appointment and virtually had to be dragged away by his aide-de-camp.

Another classic example of Wilson's special leadership qualities came the Saturday following the England international, when the All Blacks found themselves embroiled in a desperately tough encounter with North-Eastern Counties at Harrogate. The home side was 11–0 in front after eight minutes and still up 11–3 at half-time.

During the half-time break, Wilson didn't round on any of the players, although goodness knows several of them deserved a strum-up given the way they'd been playing. He quietly spelt out his requirements. 'Chaps,' he said, 'I'd like us to get one try in the first five minutes after half-time.'

His players had the message. A penalty goal after three minutes, a converted try after eight minutes, and a dropped goal after 15 minutes put them ahead. Wilson hadn't put the stopwatch on it; he knew what his players were capable of and was content when they eked out another victory.

In the match preceding the Scottish international, the All Blacks took on North of Scotland at Aberdeen, notable for the fact that Wilson, after 16 appearances at prop, turned out at No. 8. While he was accomplished in the position, having played a couple of seasons there for Auckland, it's fair to say his presence in the No. 8 jersey 'pissed off' the team's loosies. Wasn't there anything at which their mighty leader might be ever so slightly deficient?

When Wilson's men came to the Scottish international at Murrayfield, a Grand Slam (which none of their predecessors had achieved) was still a possibility. The 1905 Originals had lost to Wales; the 1924 Invincibles didn't play Scotland (because of a dispute over the proceeds from the match); and both the 1935 and 1953 teams had lost to Wales.

The All Blacks' greatest concern about the Scots was their power-scrummaging, and in particular their renowned ability to screw the scrum on the opposition put-in. Meads and Graham worked painstakingly to develop a counter, coming up with an effective solution which they perfected against the 'dirt-trackers' in training. 'We crabbed with them every time they went to screw the scrum,' explained Meads afterwards, 'and it neutralized what they were attempting. It made for some weird scrums which moved around all over the place, but it denied the Scots a tactic they expected would give them an important advantage over us.'

Notwithstanding their ingenuity at scrum-time, the All Blacks' Grand Slam aspirations went west at Murrayfield. Although they kept the doughty Scots scoreless, they failed to score any points themselves. Clarke went close with several penalty attempts, including one from 55 metres, but none raised the flags. In 107 years of All Black test rugby, this remains as the only occasion when the final scoreline read nil-all.

By the time of the Scottish international, Wilson considered he had an excellent working relationship with Ray Williams, the referee from Ulster. So he was a little surprised when Williams called Meads out and led him across to the touchline to discuss an unsavoury incident. Wilson went across to join them.

'I don't want you here, captain.'

'If you're going to talk to a team member, I want to hear what you're saying,' said Wilson.

'I don't want you here — go away.'

'Are you correct in law?'

The referee gave Wilson his best 'be-told' frown.

Because of the relationship he'd developed with this referee, Wilson retreated, confident nothing alarming would happen. And it didn't. Meads received a stern talking-to and soon resumed his place on the field. Four years later, after another incident against Scotland on the same ground, Meads would be sent from the field.

The South-Eastern Counties match at Bournemouth was, so far as on-field achievements go, memorable for almost nothing. Captain of the day John Graham had wanted the All Blacks to wrap up their English encounters in style and had given licence to his players to attack at every opportunity. But against a well-organized opponent, superbly captained by DG Perry, who had distinguished himself on England's tour of New Zealand earlier in 1963, and with former Wallaby 'Chilla' Wilson causing mayhem among the All Black backs, the tourists were extremely fortunate to scrape home 9–6.

No, the Bournemouth game merits mention for the unusual behaviour that followed the contest, and, in particular, for a remarkable piece of improvisation by the All Black captain. Problems arose when South-Eastern Counties officials ruled that the players' wives and partners were not welcome at the official dinner that followed the game. This was common practice around international fixtures in the 1960s. Only blokes attended official dinners; women became involved at the dances that followed.

For some reason, the South-Eastern Counties players decided to take a stand against their officials' sexist attitude. They boycotted the dinner, meaning only the All Blacks and local rugby officials were in attendance. As a consequence, with so many empty chairs, the traditional speeches were virtually irrelevant.

Old customs die hard, however, and after a local dignitary had proposed the toast to the All Blacks, Wilson was invited to reply. He decided, with that talent that belongs to born leaders, to retrieve the situation with something utterly impromptu. He quoted, without notes, the closing lines of Tennyson's famous poem, 'Ulysses':

> 'Tis not too late to seek a newer world.
> Push off, and sitting well in order smite
> The sounding furrows; for my purpose holds
> To sail beyond the sunset, and the baths
> Of all the western stars, until I die.
> It may be that the gulfs will wash us down:
> It may be we shall touch the Happy Isles,
> And see the great Achilles, who we knew,
> Tho' much is taken, much abides; and tho'
> We are not now that strength which in old days
> Moved earth and heaven; that which we are, we are;
> One equal temper of heroic hearts,
> Made weak by time and fate, but strong in will
> To strive, to seek, to find, and not to yield.

On that classical note, the All Blacks wound up their three-month sweep through the Home Unions and headed for France. They would return to make one farewell appearance in the United Kingdom, against the Barbarians at Cardiff, before flying out — and what a triumphant occasion that would become for Wilson.

But first there were challenges aplenty in France, including a novel one for Wilson. After 20 outings on tour, and notwithstanding his massive contribution as a captain and player, he had failed to score a point, a shortcoming that hadn't gone unnoticed by individuals such as Meads and Tremain.

'On the board yet, Skip?' Tremain delighted in asking him.

Having failed to register a point on the previous tour of Australia, Wilson, although mindful that there were far more important issues at stake than his personal record, sensed that an opportunity might soon arrive to get himself 'on the board'.

That wasn't at Toulouse, where the All Blacks, even with a surfeit of ball, found themselves in trouble against France B. Into the second half, Wilson approached winger Ralph Caulton.

'We're giving you guys plenty of ball,' he said. 'Why aren't we scoring tries?'

'Leave it to us, Skip,' replied Caulton.

What Caulton might more accurately have said was: 'Leave it to me.' With 20 minutes remaining and his team sweating on a three-point lead, Caulton scored a classic winger's try, bamboozling the France B fullback by running at him and then around him, to make the game safe.

The midweeker prior to the French international, against South-West France at Bordeaux, became a romp for the tourists and finally provided Wilson with the opportunity to break his 'duck', albeit in unusual circumstances. Amid a phase of confused, broken play about 35 metres out from the South-West France goalposts, the home team fullback inadvertently passed the ball to the All Black captain. Wilson didn't waste breath saying 'Thank you' or even *Merci beaucoup*; he simply swivelled around and let fly with a drop-kick that sailed sweetly through the uprights.

'Goal!' declared the referee, Monsieur Marie.

'Offside — he was blatantly offside, referee!' protested one of the players. But it wasn't a Frenchman doing the complaining — it was an All Black!

'You can't award that,' declared another All Black. 'He was definitely offside.'

The referee, plainly bemused that New Zealand players and not Frenchmen were challenging his ruling, held firm.

'It eez a goal, I 'ave awarded it.'

At that, Monsieur Marie moved across to Monsieur Whineray and placed his arm around his shoulders. 'I am surprised,' he said, 'that your teammates would react like that.'

'Me, too,' replied Wilson, although unlike the referee he knew exactly why his players were protesting. He also knew he had been patently offside, but, if the referee was satisfied with the outcome, so was he. The captain permitted himself a smirk, knowing he would no longer have to suffer his teammates' jibes for having not scored.

The All Blacks had been defeated on their previous visit to Colombes Stadium in Paris a decade earlier, and there was a resolve among the tourists not to let that happen again. Besides, they had now gone 28 matches without defeat. Wilson knew it was paramount not to allow the French players' volatility to spill over, and he knew that could easily happen if the players, and their fans, became over-emotional. Although there were several potentially ugly incidents, Wilson's calming attitude, and the presence of another placid individual in referee Ray Williams, meant the game ran its course without any regrettable happenings.

Meads was to endure a regrettable happening of his own, however. Late in the game, with his team comfortably ahead 12–3, the All Blacks surged on to attack, Meads receiving a pass from Wilson no more than a dozen metres from the goal-line. The solitary individual blocking his path was the smallest player in the French team, winger Jean Gachassin. Meads had Caulton unmarked outside him, but the pint-sized defender didn't represent a challenge, surely. Pinetree decided to go it alone. 'I didn't think he was capable of stopping me,' he would say later, 'but this little bloke skipped aside and swung on the tail of my jersey. I dragged him four or five yards, and then he put the anchor out and pulled me back.' The try-scoring opportunity was lost.

Wilson was not amused, and nor was Caulton. And coach McPhail gave Pinetree a dressing-down back in the changing room, accusing him of greediness. Furthermore, Meads had to endure Gachassin's exaggerated wit at the dinner that evening. Whenever he caught Meads's eye, he held up his arm and flexed his muscle. He was reminding him that Goliath had been well slain by David that afternoon.

The Paris test represented the only occasion during Wilson's term as All Black captain that he relieved Don Clarke of the goal-kicking duties. The Boot's confidence as a goal-kicker had waned throughout the tour, and his percentage of success had diminished alarmingly. In the two lead-up matches in France, he had added the conversions to only two of the 10 tries scored and not managed any penalty goals at all; indeed, at Bordeaux he so badly hooked a long-range penalty attempt that the ball finished up going into touch near the corner flag. Some among the crowd applauded, obviously believing that that was what he had set out to achieve! Anyway, after Clarke had missed several kicks at goal against France, Wilson tossed the ball to Mac Herewini, who promptly goaled his first attempt.

The occasion that sealed the greatness of Wilson as a player and a leader was the Barbarians game at Cardiff Arms Park. It started out as something of a festive occasion, with the Baabaas' line-up featuring four internationals from England, four from Wales, three from Ireland, and one from Scotland, plus uncapped players from the British Army and Penarth in Wales — and an All Black. Yes, an All Black.

The Barbarians committee had approached the New Zealand management, inquiring if they would be prepared to make one player available. Wilson was in on the discussion, and the unanimous choice was Ian Clarke, at 32 a survivor of the previous tour of the United Kingdom a decade earlier.

Although he hadn't been able to break into the test XV, with Ken Gray and Wilson having the prop positions firmly sewn up, 'Chutney', as he was known to his fellow players, had been a major contributor on tour, and a guest appearance for the Barbarians would be a fitting reward for a footballer who had contributed massively to the All Black cause.

After 40 minutes of the tour finale, at which point the All Blacks led 6–3, it seemed as though Chutney might well emerge as the game's star personality, he having audaciously drop-kicked a goal from a mark from almost 45 metres. When he asked the referee to direct the touch judges to the goalposts, many in the crowd laughed. Well, their laughter turned to shrieks of delight when the goal found its target.

The players laughed, too. At the next scrum, Wilson felt obliged to say something. 'Listen, Chutney,' he said: 'I don't mind you kicking goals, but do me a favour — get that big grin off your face, will you?'

What happened thereafter, and which is now firmly etched in the game's folklore, is probably best described by New Zealand's greatest rugby writer, who was in the press box that afternoon: Sir Terry ('TP') McLean.

Here's how TP conveyed the fabulousness of the afternoon to the readers of the *New Zealand Herald*:

> Shakespeare talked of gentlemen of England still abed, who could

regret that they were not present at one of the great battles that was military history.

In rugby history there will assuredly be for a generation or more to come gentlemen of New Zealand still abed who will regret they were not present at Cardiff Arms Park on Saturday when Wilson Whineray's All Blacks brought their tour to an end by defeating the Barbarians by the smashing score of 36 to 3.

The regret will be justified. This was a moment of sporting time to treasure for the rest of one's life. A crowd of 58,500, sympathetic to begin with, became so generously partisan towards the New Zealanders that, with time running out, they were spontaneously singing 'Now is the hour' in lament at the end of the tour.

Just before the end they were paying Whineray the greatest personal tribute any rugby man has had by singing 'For he's a jolly good fellow' to celebrate the try he had just scored to end the tour.

But most of all and this is the part that will remain longest in the memory of one who has had the good fortune to see close to 150 matches by All Black teams, the match will live in the memory because of the quality of the rugby played by the New Zealanders.

So it was when as the grand climax of his career and of the tour, too, Whineray scored the last try. Again, there was a breakdown in the Baabaas backline, again a galvanic movement as the All Blacks instantly regrouped and pressed forward and again perfect passing and backing up.

Paul Little and John Graham were the main figures this time and Whineray began his bolt 20 yards from the goal-line, Ralph Caulton on his inside, Colin Meads outside him.

Amid the fantastic noise, Whineray passed. Or so it seemed. His arms moved out towards Meads. Coincidentally, he sidestepped the other way. It was the dummy pass to end all dummy passes. Hook, line and sinker, Mick Flynn bought it. Whineray, so it seemed, slackened to a trot as he carried the few more yards to the posts. It was a perfect movement with a perfect ending.

They sang to him then. The All Blacks crowded upon him. The television camera picked him out, at halfway, hands on his knees, bald head gleaming, waving now and again in response to the noise.

They sang again. 'Whineray, Whineray, Whineray!' The mood

carried over. At the celebratory dinner, Brigadier Glyn Hughes, president of the Barbarians, said that when the crowd chanted, 'More, more, more!' all that the Barbarians could think of was 'Yeah, yeah, yeah!' There never had been such a thing before. There never could be again.

JBG Thomas was equally ecstatic in the *Western Mail*:

> In all my travels I have never seen a full New Zealand side in such a gay, rampant mood — so effective, so well together, so ready to run the ball.
>
> Never before has Cardiff Arms Park echoed to such a musical accolade for any player, Welsh or otherwise. It was Whineray the Great, the man who symbolises all that is good in rugby football, who inspired this special performance and he fully deserved the tribute, rare and sincere, paid to him.

Wilson admitted later he had every intention of delivering the final pass to Meads. 'I knew there was a player coming from my right at speed and I was going to pass, I really was. I was concentrating on getting my timing right, and I was in the act of passing when I realized the defender was committed to Pinetree. The ball stuck in my hands and suddenly there was this wide open space between me and the goalposts. I was able to amble over. The crowd was amazingly happy — it was film script stuff!'

Meads, having copped a barrage of criticism for costing the All Blacks a late try against France by holding on, couldn't resist the opportunity to have a wee dig. 'And you reckon I'm a greedy bugger!' he said to his skip.

With such a player at hand, Brigadier Hughes wasn't going to allow this opportunity to pass. At the celebratory dinner that evening he invited Wilson to become an honorary member of the Barbarians club. Brigadier Hughes said that the All Black pack was one of the greatest of all time, and Whineray one of the greatest captains of all time. Wilson was only the 10th player in 75 years to be so honoured.

Richard Evans, in his book *Whineray's All Blacks*, described Wilson as a man of character and principle. 'He is one of the most straightforward people I have ever met. He was also amazingly frank on occasions when speaking of various incidents and problems that cropped up from time to time — a frankness that typified his whole outlook on life. He will, without doubt, go down in sporting history as one of the greatest captains of all time.'

Evans managed a breakfast interview with Wilson before the tourists flew out. In response to a question as to why the All Blacks didn't produce more of the dazzling, attacking rugby that highlighted the Barbarians game, Wilson pinpointed injuries to the team's second-fives (or inside-centres, as the Brits referred to them), Pat Walsh and Derek Arnold, as a major problem.

'Weakness in this one vital position has been the biggest barrier to our aspirations to greatness,' he told Evans. 'But for this, we might really have been remembered as a great side.'

Evans spoke glowingly of Wilson's relationship with the UK media — a relationship which, as many touring team captains and managers since would testify, had the capacity to place almost unbearable strains upon their teams. He wrote:

> Whineray made it quite clear from the moment he arrived what he expected of us, and we made it equally plain what we wanted from him. It can be summed up in one word — co-operation. By speaking quite freely, on the mutual understanding it was all off the record unless specific permission was asked to quote him on a certain point, Whineray ensured two things: One was that reporters could verify the facts and consequently give the public a more accurate report; the other was that with the press kept regularly informed, opinions expressed on any single aspect of the tour would be both informed and balanced. In this way, Whineray, with his masterful flair for public relations, ensured that the All Blacks' image would be fairly represented.

The following tribute to Wilson appeared in *L'Équipe,* the internationally regarded sports newspaper published daily out of Paris:

It is impossible not to notice his presence on a rugby field when he is surrounded by men in black. He is not the tallest. Physically, he is not the strongest. When he wears headgear over his fair hair, already somewhat thin, the force which his face reveals is even more obvious. When people mention the All Blacks they speak more often of Don Clarke than of this outstanding prop.

Wilson James Whineray has never accomplished deeds comparable to those of the giant fullback but he has commanded the respect of the best forwards in the world. He is a man who knows his duty and neglects none of his responsibilities as a prop. If in the course of the game he gets the chance to appear in the open, he takes it with speed and determination, at the same time demonstrating his tremendous skill.

A movement does not end with him; on the contrary, it penetrates even further. When he passes to a teammate at a critical moment, you may be sure the ball will not go astray. Wilson James Whineray is in this sense the prototype of today's prop.

He is respected by everyone. An opponent is not an enemy. As a reward for his brilliant services to sport, he received the OBE from the Queen. And seldom was a distinction of this kind better greeted in New Zealand.

There are some players who are born to lead. Wilson Whineray is one of these. From the stands you can scarcely hear the sound of his voice, but it seems that everything is made clear just as you saw him give the order. He was captain in South Africa in 1960, he is still captain in Europe. This did not prevent him from sitting two exams at Cardiff University during his stay in Wales.

He constitutes a fine example. Our British colleagues take delight in praising his amiability. He replies to all the questions relating to the most diverse subjects pertinently if not humorously without departing from the quiet manner which is his character. He is as curious of the life of a country as of the secrets of the scrum or of the lineout in which he is a specialist. Wilson Whineray has done much for the popularity of the 1963–64 All Blacks.

Terry McLean would write of the All Black skipper in *Willie Away* that though Whineray on that tour was 28, mentally he had the maturity of a man of at least 40.

> His intelligence could be reckoned from the fact that during the
> tour he passed the Bookkeeping II unit of the B. Com degree. The
> odd thing about Whineray was that he seemed incapable of losing
> his temper. He could speak with a deadly purpose, but there was no
> violent explosion of name-calling, no expletives; rather was there
> couched, within the strong and direct statement, an appeal to the
> intelligence of the man concerned to improve himself for one purpose
> only — the good of the team.

Acclaim for Wilson's team wasn't unanimous. Although there was
tempered criticism at odd moments during the tour, directed mostly
at the team's lack of daring, startling condemnation of the side came
a decade on when one of the team's emerging stars, Chris Laidlaw,
appeared outspokenly in print in his book, *Mud In Your Eye.*

He claimed a deep crevasse existed between the senior and junior
members of the touring party.

> As one of a number of young players first selected in 1963, I sensed
> immediately the sharp division between the young and old, the raw
> and the experienced elements of the team, In 1963, Whineray, Meads,
> Tremain, Young, the Clarkes, Graham and one or two others were
> clearly a separate society, and the in-betweens and the youngsters were
> continuously reminded of this division. The senior players ate, drank,
> played cards and went sightseeing together. They offered little in the
> way of advice or encouragement to the others. They were blatantly
> impervious to the plight of any player whose game was faltering. It
> was a case of sink or swim.

Laidlaw went to bat for his Otago mate Earle Kirton, who became
largely surplus to requirements after his display in the loss to
Newport.

> The crucifixion of Kirton following the Newport match was a
> direct result of seniors passing the buck. Whineray, Meads, Briscoe
> and co played so abominably badly that day that they had no one

but themselves to blame. Kirton was nevertheless, as the new boy, a convenient scapegoat as he had played no better than any of his fellows. While the press cudgelled his career into a four-year limbo, the 'senior' clique remained silent, unwilling to lift an eyebrow in Kirton's defence.

While acknowledging the team's exceptional achievement in winning 32 of its 34 matches in the United Kingdom and France across four months, Laidlaw argued that the backs were grossly under-utilized. He directed his wrath at the captain.

> It was perhaps a shame that most of the backs on that tour were too young or inexperienced to realise they were being done a disservice. Whineray would rarely issue any tactical instruction to his backs, but would occasionally be heard to bark at the offending lieutenants behind: 'For God's sake, get it [the ball] in front of us' [the forwards]. Faced with this attitude any sense of daring was well and truly nipped in the bud.
>
> But Whineray knew how to win matches and understood very well that he had been uncommonly lucky to have emerged at a time when the finest imaginable group of forwards seemed to appear from everywhere.
>
> I can't help thinking that the management and Whineray were guilty of neglect [of the young backs] in several cases and almost criminal neglect in the case of Earle Kirton. If Whineray failed in any respect on that tour, then it was in maintaining communication with all his players. Perhaps he was too much a man's man and not enough a boy's man.

Laidlaw's book certainly provoked plenty of discussion, and that in itself isn't a bad thing, because too many rugby books for sure have been nothing more than promotional publications for the great game of rugby.

John Graham is one who strenuously refutes Laidlaw's argument. 'I never forgave him for what he wrote in his book,' he says. 'It wasn't a case of Wilson making personal decisions contrary to team policy.

Collectively, we discussed how we should play and, because opposition backlines were always so flat — eyeball to eyeball — we determined it was more prudent in the crunch games to be conservative. The thing was, the British teams wanted us to take all the risks.'

The chief reason the All Blacks of 1963–64 played less expansively than individuals like Laidlaw wanted were rugby's constraining laws of the time. There being no limit on the depth of the lineout meant that the No. 8 could position himself in midfield to frustrate opposition attacks. Backs could stand up much flatter than now, and side-row forwards could follow the scrum-ball through.

The laws of the day permitted defensively minded teams to frustrate the hell out of enterprising opponents. Teams possessing powerful sets of forwards, like the All Blacks, weren't encouraged to go for all-out attack when they knew they could methodically work their way up-field via the touchline as a safer option. It wasn't until the late 1960s that the law limiting kicking into touch from the 22 was introduced.

Members of the IRB had assembled in London at the time of the All Blacks' game against England and were guests at Twickenham. The game they witnessed represented pretty much all that was wrong with rugby at the time, with back play being strangled and both teams monotonously progressing from lineout to lineout via the touchline.

Within days, new laws were announced to apply universally. No. 8s were no longer free to terrorize midfielders; they were constrained. And greater space was created between the backlines. The laws came into effect in New Zealand at the start of the 1964 season.

9

THE GRADUATE

After 11 consecutive seasons of representative rugby, seven of them as an All Black, Wilson chose to make sacrifices in 1964. As a father of two young children — James was four and Kristen two — and with a Bachelor of Commerce degree needing to be completed, he decided to prioritize issues. He would take a year off rugby. It was a gamble, he knew, because once you relinquish your position in a national team, there are no guarantees you are going to reclaim it, and he definitely wanted to play against the Springboks in 1965, although he confessed to Beth that he wouldn't regard it as the end of the world if the selectors decided they didn't want him back.

Before his enforced sabbatical, however, there was one rugby invitation he wasn't prepared to cast aside: he, along with Colin Meads, Don Clarke, Kevin Briscoe and Kel Tremain, flew to South Africa in May to participate in the South African Rugby Football Board's three 75th jubilee matches.

Uniquely, the organizers matched the international forwards (chosen from the four Home Unions, plus Australia and New Zealand) with Springbok backs, and vice versa, which made for wonderful camaraderie and some spectacular rugby.

Wilson, who captained his team in two of the three matches, completed a distinguished front row with former Lions captain Ronnie Dawson and Wallaby legend John Thornett, a player with whom he had developed a close relationship. The line-up of overseas celebrities also included Mike Campbell-Lamerton, who had the enlightening experience of locking the scrum with Pinetree Meads, who would be his adversary when he captained the British Lions to New Zealand in 1966.

Campbell-Lamerton came from a far more conservative rugby background than Meads and struggled to foot it in training with the New Zealand forwards, who were accustomed to running with the ball, while Campbell-Lamerton was essentially along for the set pieces.

'Come on, Mike — this move's for you,' the New Zealanders would call, encouraging him to make like a loose forward, a role with which he was totally unfamiliar. After initial alarm, he admitted he came to enjoy the Down Under style.

That Wilson had spent a year working for Dominion Breweries — as assistant to the general manager — was a bonus for the New Zealanders, because it provided him with a valuable connection with South African Breweries who ensured the Kiwis didn't go thirsty during their visit.

Prior to the second match in Port Elizabeth, Meads, Tremain and Briscoe decided to borrow one of the international team's courtesy cars and visit a pub up the coast. 'Take one of the South African players along for the outing,' suggested Wilson, ever the diplomat, whereupon an invitation was extended to Hannes Marais, at 22 one of the emerging stars of South African rugby, a delightful fellow who would go on to become a distinguished Springbok captain.

It was an enlightening afternoon. To New Zealanders, most pubs offer a public bar and a private bar, and to most individuals it doesn't matter which one you drink at, except that the prices are higher in the private bar. But the two bars the rugby outlaws encountered at the pub outside Port Elizabeth that afternoon were most distinctive: one was for whites only, the other for blacks. The mischievous All Blacks decided they would sample both, which left a certain South African rugby player feeling decidedly uncomfortable, given the apartheid laws under which the country operated at the time. Poor Hannes felt a hell of a lot more uncomfortable when the All Blacks delivered him back to his hotel in a serious state of intoxication. His career wasn't impeded, because the New Zealanders managed to ferry him safely to his hotel room without his team manager, a certain Danie Craven, or any other team official being aware of anything untoward!

The jubilee celebrations came to a climax at Newlands in Cape Town when the team Wilson captained, featuring Meads (but not Clarke and Briscoe, who were in the opposition, or Tremain, who was injured) careered away from Abe Malan's team 44–24 before a crowd of 30,000. Wilson scored two tries, and it was recorded that 'the Willie Away was used time and again from lineouts'.

Back home, Wilson spent the winter being a diligent husband and father while attending university lectures that led to him satisfactorily completing his degree. He was capped at a ceremony at the Auckland Town Hall early in 1965.

As he had an eye on the Springbok series, he maintained his fitness levels and allowed himself one domestic outing — for the Barbarians against Auckland at Eden Park. It was a star-studded line-up the Baabaas assembled, including Wallaby greats John Thornett and Ken Catchpole, along with Tremain, John Graham (who that winter had captained the All Blacks against the Wallabies in Wilson's absence), Dennis Young, Peter Jones, and an emerging Fergie McCormick. Not surprisingly, the Barbarians won the game.

Wilson had monitored the All Blacks' fortunes against the '64 Wallabies closely, mindful that if they performed heroically he could find it difficult to win his place back, his replacement for the series being another Aucklander, Barry 'Bear' Thomas.

The All Blacks won the first two internationals comfortably enough, being led from No. 8 by Graham, but, for the finale at

Athletic Park in Wellington, the selectors switched Graham to flanker and boldly decided to give Pinetree Meads a crack at No. 8. Meads always reckoned he had a future in the position, and would tell anyone prepared to listen that he was an infinitely superior No. 8 to Wilson, who'd appeared there intermittently for his country on overseas tours.

The experiment proved an abject failure, the All Blacks losing to the Wallabies by a then-record margin of 20 points to 5. Wilson wasn't going to allow this opportunity to pass. He sent Meads a telegram saying: *And you thought I was a bloody awful No. 8!*

What it did establish once and for all was that Meads's place in the All Black scrum was at lock! Which is where he would perform heroically for another seven years.

If Wilson was to impress the selectors and reclaim his place for the series against the Springboks in 1965, he needed to be fit, seriously fit. Now, in those days Wilson lived at Waikumete in West Auckland, close to the Waitakere Ranges where legendary athletics coach Arthur Lydiard had conditioned such famous runners as Peter Snell and Murray Halberg.

Wilson linked up with Malcolm Dick, who lived not far away, and, starting in late January, they put in an hour's strenuous run twice a week, busting themselves on the steep inclines. Wilson had long since concluded that heavy players like himself needed to get their stamina work out of the way early in the year. And pounding the roads of the Waitakeres certainly achieved that.

If anyone had any doubts that Wilson was ready for a return to international action, they were well and truly dispelled when his New Zealand XV destroyed The Rest by 40 points to 8 in the final trial, scoring nine tries to one.

The Springbok tour, like its predecessor nine years earlier, was a huge sporting event for New Zealand, although significantly by 1965 there was a greater awareness of South Africa's apartheid system, which had denied Maori the opportunity to tour with Wilson's team in 1960 and, indeed, with the teams of 1928 and 1949. Protests on a comparatively minor scale had made the 1960 All Blacks aware that not everyone in the land approved of them despatching a racially selected side, and those protests would escalate in 1965, with the All Blacks scheduled to tour the republic again in two years' time.

Wilson was mightily relieved when Neil McPhail made contact and confirmed that he and his fellow All Black selectors, Fred Allen and Les George, wanted him to captain the All Blacks in the upcoming series. The selectors would demonstrate great loyalty and use the same eight forwards for all four test matches. Given the abrasive nature of the contests against the great old foe, this was truly remarkable, because the IRB wouldn't allow replacements until later in the 1960s. It meant Wilson, Ken Gray, Bruce McLeod, the Meads brothers — Colin and Stan — Kel Tremain, Dick Conway, and Brian Lochore each came through 240 minutes of test action unscathed, and victorious.

The South Africans, who rarely experience inclement weather at home, were unlucky to encounter a particularly wet winter. For the tests they had to endure a 60-kph cold southerly in Wellington, slushy mud at Carisbrook in Dunedin, and a greasy surface with muddy patches in Christchurch.

The All Blacks were clearly superior in the forwards, and took victories at Wellington and Dunedin. After establishing a commanding 16 points to 5 lead by half-time in the third test at Lancaster Park in Christchurch, they were gloriously on target to whitewash the tourists and take revenge for 1949.

A humble Wilson would initially hold himself responsible for what unfolded in the second half. He would say in *Rugby Greats* that he erred in not delivering any specific instructions to his troops during the interval. 'It's not often you are ahead of the Springboks at half-time by a score like sixteen-five,' he explained. 'I gave no instructions for the second spell. Since then, fifty per cent have told me I should have closed the game up and fifty per cent have told me I should have run the ball. In the event, I trod a middle path — and we lost.'

Wilson subsequently watched a film of that test and realized that the Springboks achieved their winning advantage because the backs missed several crucial tackles in the second half. John Gainsford, a midfielder of legendary status, was just the player to capitalize on missed tackles. He scored two tries in the game and created another for one of his wingers. A late penalty goal, amazingly kicked out of the mud by the Springboks' giant lock 'Tiny' Naude, gave the tourists a stunning victory by 19 points to 16 and the opportunity to square the series.

Between the first and second tests, Wilson was able to celebrate another success against the tourists, being part of the Auckland team that edged out the Springboks by 15 points to 14, a contest in which the second spell was effectively played at 14-a-side after Dawie de Villiers, the South African captain, and Tony Davies, the Auckland fullback, collided, knocking each other out. With replacements still not permitted in international fixtures, De Villiers was unable to continue, while a groggy Davies played on but was virtually a passenger. Later in the tour, New Zealand Universities would complete its match against the tourists with 12 men. It would still take the IRB another three years before they gave the seal of approval to replacements.

The perfect conditions the Springboks ostensibly required to produce their finest form existed for the decider at Eden Park, but instead of being inspired to greatness, the South Africans suffered their greatest test defeat ever, losing by 3 points to 20. The All Blacks, in rampant mood, scored five tries, the Springboks none.

Of the 13 tries the All Blacks scored in the series, the one that ranks as the least memorable, certainly the least spectacular, is the one that at the time gave Wilson the most satisfaction, because it came from a move the All Black forwards had been practising diligently.

The move was for implementing at a scrum close to the enemy line. The No. 8 — in this instance Lochore — would pack in an unorthodox way, not between the two locks but between the blindside flanker and the left-hand lock, bringing him half a metre closer to the ball. With the move 'on', the halfback would feed the ball more quickly and the front-rowers would slightly spin the scrum — all designed to give the loose forwards a flying start. Applied five minutes into the Eden Park test, it produced a try to Dick Conway and left Wilson purring. To the multitude in the grandstands, it was a scrambling, fortuitous try; to the All Blacks' brains trust, it was a masterpiece, something they'd crafted in training and in the heat of battle carried out to perfection, giving the All Blacks a massive psychological boost in the opening minutes of this crunch international.

Wilson had announced before the fourth test that he was stepping down from international rugby, so the victory at Eden Park allowed him to retire in the nicest way possible, with a series victory against the Springboks. He was able to exit the All Black scene having achieved virtually everything possible. There were no World Cups in the 1960s, it's true, and his team had come up short in South Africa, but otherwise his international record was smothered in glory, with series wins against Australia, the British Lions, France, England and South Africa, plus the triumphant sweep through Great Britain and France.

His record (for the All Blacks, Canterbury, Auckland and New Zealand Universities) against the Springboks, who when he first engaged them in 1956 were deemed almost invincible, was pretty special, too: seven wins, three losses and a draw. Not many New Zealand rugby players prior to the 1990s finished on the right side of the ledger against the Springboks.

Wilson missed only three tests in eight years, from debut to retirement, and they were the three in 1964 when he stepped aside to concentrate on his studies. Altogether, he made 77 appearances for his country, in 69 of which he was the captain, and on only eight occasions was he on the losing side. However, Wilson's wonderful final year hadn't finished. There would be one further highlight —

Auckland's winning of the Ranfurly Shield from Taranaki in New Plymouth. Taranaki, superbly guided by JJ Stewart, had been in possession of the prized 'log' for two full years.

Neil McPhail, who had been a wonderful servant for New Zealand rugby and developed a great working relationship with Wilson, also stepped down after the Springbok series. His successor, not surprisingly, was Fred Allen, who after a slow start had fashioned an enviable record with Auckland. McPhail would tell Peter Devlin, in an interview for the *8 O'Clock*, that there had never been a better loosehead prop than Wilson. 'He proved to everyone, which is now accepted fact, that he was also one of the great captains,' said McPhail. 'His players had complete faith in him — they would have died for him. As a prop, he met them all and, remember, he began his front row education against some of those tough men in the 1956 Springbok team. He went on to scrum against all the rugby-playing nations and I don't think he was ever beaten. Not that "Willie" was the strongest prop in the game, but he had the ability to out-think bigger, stronger men and I don't think I ever saw our front row upset.'

Throughout his sporting career, Wilson encountered individuals who were superstitious. Some players would insist on pulling one sock on ahead of the other, some commanded a particular seat or hook in the dressing room, others seemingly wore the same pair of underpants dozens of times. Even Pinetree Meads had one foible: he insisted on being the last player to run out on to the field. Wilson wouldn't have a bar of superstitions, telling John Graham one day when the topic was under discussion that he only believed in the real world. Someone — it may have been Graham — brilliantly described him as a practising pragmatist.

In the run-up to the 1966 season, Fred Allen contacted Wilson to discuss with him the appointment of his successor as captain. Most pundits were nominating Kel Tremain or Colin Meads, but Wilson proffered the opinion that Brian Lochore would be an ideal choice on several counts: he was certain of selection, he possessed charismatic qualities, and he was still young, whereas Tremain and Meads were entering the twilight stages of their careers. Allen plumped for Lochore and the rest, as they say, is history.

Wilson merited a special accolade after his massive contribution to All Black rugby and it came late in 1965, when he won the New Zealand Sportsman of the Year trophy, by a record number of points since the award's inauguration in 1949. The votes he received were only seven short of the maximum. Runner-up was the conqueror of Cook Strait, swimmer Keith Hancox, ahead of champion motorcyclist Hugh Anderson, athlete Peter Snell, and cricketers John Reid and Vic Pollard.

In December of 1965, around the time Wilson and Beth's third child was born — a girl they named Susan — he received a letter from the New Zealand Rugby Union.

Dear Wilson

Council have asked me to thank you for the great services you have given to rugby football over the past 10 seasons. Your contribution has been a tremendous one to our national game and in the future I am sure you will look back with pride on your achievements. My council have also asked me to convey to you its congratulations on your being elected Sportsman of the Year, an honour richly deserved.

George Geddes
Secretary, NZRU

It would be two more years, by which time he was 32, before Wilson finally drop-kicked his rugby boots into the no-longer-required heap. There would still be a few more highlights before Wilson the rugby player became Wilson the scholar and businessman.

One such event occurred in 1966 when the Wilson Whineray XV, including 11 All Blacks, was chosen to play a North Otago XV to celebrate the opening of Centennial Park in Oamaru. Wilson's team — which included Colin Meads, Brian Lochore, Malcolm Dick, Dick Conway, and Bruce McLeod — proved much too strong for the locals, running in 14 tries without conceding any. Interestingly, at second-five for the North Otago XV was Terry Mehrtens, whose son Andrew (who wasn't born until 1973) would go on to become a celebrated All Black.

Wilson allowed Auckland selector-coach Bob Sorenson to talk him into making a one-game representative comeback in 1966 after injuries seriously depleted the Auckland squad. It was for the Ranfurly Shield defence against Waikato, but Wilson couldn't prevent the Mooloo men waltzing off with the prized trophy. Wilson did manage to celebrate his 240th — and what was presumed to be his final — first-class outing (the first had been for Wairarapa 13 years prior) by scoring Auckland's only try. He would actually sneak in one additional appearance six years on, at the grand old age of 37, for the Barbarians!

In 1967, Wilson confined his rugby activities to club play, bowing out on a triumphant note when his beloved Grammar club team, after qualifying only fifth, nosed out the much-vaunted Ponsonby team — which featured All Blacks Malcolm Dick, Ron Rangi, and Keith Nelson — to claim the Gallaher Shield for the first time in 14 years. There were no semi-finals or finals in those days, the winner being the team that completed the championship round with most points. And that, to the amazement of many, was Grammar. The team didn't have a lot to spare — indeed, successive matches were won 11–9, 11–8 and 11–6 — but demonstrated a resoluteness that brought it through.

As his rugby career began winding down, Wilson was naturally giving plenty of thought to his future. A business colleague had suggested in 1965 that he should apply for a Harkness Scholarship — two of which were awarded to New Zealanders annually — to allow him to

Manager Frank Kilby, captain Wilson, and coach Neil McPhail are first down the steps as the 1963–64 All Blacks arrive in London at the start of their epic 34-match tour of the UK and France.

WHINERAY COLLECTION

Waka Nathan in menacing form during the epic Barbarians contest at Cardiff in 1964.
The Baabaas player in front of Wilson is winger Stuart Watkins.

After eight consecutive years representing the All Blacks, Wilson chose to give rugby a miss in 1964 to further his studies, but he would be back for the Springbok series in 1965.
FAIRFAX MEDIA

A training run with a difference for the All Blacks, along the promenade at Eastbourne in 1963. From left: John Graham, Keith Nelson, Malcolm Dick, Dennis Young, and Jules Le Lievre.
WHINERAY COLLECTION

Sir Kenneth Hayr, recipient of a double knighthood who had schooled at Auckland Grammar with Wilson, in conversaton with Mac Herewini and Waka Nathan during the All Blacks' visit in 1964 to the Leconfield military air base where he was the flying officer.
WHINERAY COLLECTION

Together they guided the 1963–64 All Blacks through the four-month tour of Britain and France with great distinction —Wilson, the captain, and Neil McPhail, the coach.
WHINERAY COLLECTION

Wilson's talents extended beyond the rugby field on the 1963–64 tour of the UK, as he demonstrates by strumming a guitar. Bill Davis is dealing with a ukelele, while Dennis Young busies himself with letter-writing.

Four successive captains of All Black tours of Great Britain, from left: Cliff Porter (1924–25), Jack Manchester (1935–36), Bob Stuart (1953-54), and Wilson (1963–64).
WHINERAY COLLECTION

Wilson shaking hands with Springbok captain Dawie de Villiers at a parliamentary reception in 1965.
NZ RUGBY MUSEUM

Lonsdale's cartoon in the Auckland Star *following the All Blacks' triumphant tour of Britain.*

WHINERAY COLLECTION

Wilson chats with the referee he gave the highest rating to during the 1963–64 tour of Britain and France — Welshman Alan Williams.

FAIRFAX MEDIA

Some of the greatest forwards of all time present in this scene from the Springbok series of 1965. All Blacks, from left, are Colin Meads, Stan Meads, Wilson, and Kel Tremain. Springboks, from left, are Andy Macdonald, Sakkie van Zyl, Frik du Preez, and Jan Ellis.
WHINERAY COLLECTION

Wilson in conversation with the Field Marshall Bernard Montgomery, who famously commanded Allied Forces during the Second World War, in the dressing room before the England test at Twickenham in 1964.
WHINERAY COLLECTION

Wilson receives his trophy after being named New Zealand Sportsman of the Year in 1965.
FAIRFAX MEDIA

Wilson chaired off Eden Park at the conclusion of his illustrious international career following the series win over the 1965 Springboks.
WHINERAY COLLECTION

The five Whineray boys all spruced up in the 1960s. From left: Murray, Bruce, Scott, Wilson, and Grant.
WHINERAY COLLECTION

Beth with James and Kristen around the time Wilson was pulling the pin on his playing career in the 1960s.

With two-year-old son James on his shoulders, Wilson talks to members of the Osaka Medical School team on their tour of New Zealand in the 1960s.
FAIRFAX MEDIA

Back home from Harvard in 1969 — Wilson and Beth with Susan, and, in front, Kristen and James.
FAIRFAX MEDIA

Wilson takes up his position as chairman of the New Zealand Wool Board in 1973.
FAIRFAX MEDIA

Wilson and Beth pose with Nelson Mandela during one of the several International Advisory Board meetings Wilson attended in Cape Town.
WHINERAY COLLECTION

Wilson proudly receives his 'cap' after being inducted into the International Rugby Hall of Fame in 2007.
WHINERAY COLLECTION

Wilson with another iconic New Zealander, Sir Edmund Hillary, and Lady Hillary.
WHINERAY COLLECTION

pursue a business degree at Harvard University in America. Initially sceptical, he warmed to the idea and made appropriate inquiries, but realized because of his rugby commitments in 1965 it was an inappropriate time to be pursuing such a venture. He was relieved when the Harkness Fellowship representatives in New Zealand assured him that delaying his application 12 months would not prejudice his prospects of success.

So in 1966, his celebrated All Black career completed, he made application for a Harkness Scholarship, still not completely convinced he was a serious contender. To his pleasant surprise, early in 1967 he was summoned to Wellington for an interview.

The interviewing panel comprised the principal of Lincoln College, Dr Burns, a rector from New York, and a distinguished university leader from Australia. Wilson was delighted to discover another of the candidates was Kara Puketapu, who had been part of the Wellington rugby team that had lifted the Ranfurly Shield from Canterbury back in 1956. Fittingly, Messrs Whineray and Puketapu would be the two New Zealanders awarded the Fellowships for 1967. They were required to report to Harvard University in September 1967.

Beth was thrilled for Wilson, recognizing that this was an opportunity that came the way of few New Zealanders; but she was naturally apprehensive about having to uproot the family, including three young children, from Auckland to relocate in a 'foreign' environment for two years. The second child, Kristen, had just started school. Beth knew nothing about life in America, except that they drove on the 'wrong' side of the road!

As they would need funds while in America, and because their future was now unknown, Wilson and Beth agreed to sell their home in Waikumete, a house they had had built almost a decade earlier. It was, in many respects, a traumatic time in their lives.

A month out from their September departure, Wilson was training with his club, Grammar Old Boys in Ayr Street, Parnell, when his father suddenly arrived, in a seemingly agitated state. Wilson excused himself from training to be told his youngest brother, Murray, had been piloting a Vampire jet that had crashed at Ohakea Air Force Base near Palmerston North. His brother had been rushed to hospital, where he was fighting for his life.

It was a crisis situation for the Whineray family, and after a hasty meeting it was agreed that Wilson, Grant, Bruce and their father would drive straight through to Palmerston North. Wilson was at the wheel, and they arrived some time after 10 o'clock that night, making their way directly to Palmerston North Hospital. The doctor who had been tending to Murray called the father aside and informed him that, while they had done everything possible, an hour or so before their arrival Murray had died. He was aged just 26.

Wilson, his brothers and father were devastated. Murray had chosen a career as a pilot and was making his mark with the Royal New Zealand Air Force. Married to Margaret, he had recently returned to New Zealand after a stint in Singapore, joining No. 75 Squadron, where he had become part of the Vampire aerobatic team.

On 8 August, four Vampires had performed displays in front of a group of New Zealand Second World War Spitfire veterans at Ohakea. The display went off spectacularly but, in coming into land at about 4.20pm, Murray's plane crashed.

Squadron Leader Colin Hall was on fire duty that afternoon and witnessed the accident. He would subsequently appear before the Court of Inquiry to explain the events as they unfolded. Here's how he describes, on the New Zealand Airshow Archive website, what he witnessed:

> There was . . . a loss of communication with [Murray Whineray] during the display, so they [the pilots] went into 'radio failure' routine.
>
> They then lined up to land staggered, that is one behind the other, but taking different sides of the same runway. In a normal approach, the Vampire was pretty stable if set up correctly, but the application

of power was notoriously slow with those old engines. You couldn't slam the throttle open as in *Top Gun* because the engine would stall, so the throttle had to be opened slowly, which meant power delivery could take 20 or 30 seconds to develop.

The first two aircraft landed normally, but the third was seen to stagger in the air . . . it was clear he had hit the wake turbulence of the aircraft ahead. The crash crew took off, and I can recall being on the grass before we heard the klaxon . . .

The Vampire nose went up in a typical stall manner, then dropped suddenly. At the end of [the runway] there is an earth ramp run-off and the aircraft hit that hard, bounced, and came to a halt. The impact was so severe it broke off the bottom of the aircraft . . .

The accident was probably survivable but for one unfortunate factor. There was quite a strong wind down the runway, and the aircraft came to a halt facing the way it had come, and when the fuel tank, just behind the pilot, ruptured, the resulting fire went directly over the cockpit. The pilot had no mask on, and inhaled smoke and flame in those first few seconds . . . which eventually killed him.

We initially set about releasing him by lifting him but as he was virtually sitting on the concrete . . .the boys dragged him out of the bottom of the aircraft . . . the RAAF doctor . . . stepped up and gave him . . . something pretty powerful . . .

The next morning, we heard on the radio that he had died overnight. I was at the Court of Inquiry and just told it as I saw it, and was asked what indication we had to move so quickly, before the tower sounded the alarm in fact, and I said it was obvious the aircraft was losing lift, and had virtually stalled at about fifty feet or so.

Murray Whineray's funeral service was held at St Andrew's in Epsom, and was attended by a large number of military personnel, who provided a guard of honour as the casket was carried out of the church.

10

THE HARVARD EXPERIENCE

It represented something of a journey into the unknown for Wilson and Beth and their young children — James, seven, Kristen, five, and Susan, coming up two — when in September 1967 they flew out of Auckland bound for the east coast of America. Thanks to his rugby involvement, Wilson was a seasoned world traveller, but Beth had never been outside New Zealand, and nor had any of the kids.

They broke their journey in Los Angeles to treat their children to a day out at Disneyland before flying on to Boston, from where they travelled through to Cambridge, Massachusetts, where they would be based for two years while Wilson studied at Harvard University.

Their new home was on the second floor of one of the three 21-storey accommodation towers on Peabody Terrace, from where Wilson faced only a gentle walk each morning across the river to the Harvard University Graduate School of Business Administration to attend his lectures.

The Whinerays had arranged the accommodation through the university, and a friend of Wilson's, who was living in the area, had purchased a table, chairs and some beds; otherwise, the apartment was spartan. Inevitably, the Whinerays arrived ahead of their trunk-loads of gear. They had a dishwasher, a television, and not much else. So it was down to Woolworths to purchase cutlery, towels and blankets, and enough additional furniture to make their new apartment feel like home.

Beth was soon introduced to the Harvard Dames Club, created to look after the wives of the international students. Many of the wives became homesick and found it challenging to fill in their days, which certainly wasn't a problem for Beth, who had three young children to keep her well occupied. Beth found the Americans friendly and willing to assist. And she quickly related to an Australian family living on the floor above them, who also had three young children.

The school James and Kristen would attend was close-by, but there was an initial hiccup when Beth took them along to enrol, because American children don't commence their education until the age of six. Five-year-old Kristen, who had been enjoying her school-life back in Auckland, was not unnaturally upset when told she would have to wait until the following year before she could join in. Luckily, the teacher was understanding and agreed to allow her to sit in with the six-year-olds, arranging a special desk for her in the corner.

When Kristen finally did become a *bona fide* pupil, she had difficulty understanding her teacher's American accent. She eventually tapped into the American lingo, adjusting so well that, when two years on she returned to New Zealand, her schoolmates told her she 'spoke funny'.

Among her most vivid memories were the winter snowfalls that confined the schoolchildren indoors. For an Aucklander, building a snowman was a pretty special event. Her class comprised 50 per cent Americans who lived in the area, and 50 per cent children of students who were studying at Harvard.

Cambridge, an old, established suburb of Boston, was probably 70 per cent black and, with Americans going through the transition of accepting blacks, it made it an interesting time to be living in the country. James quickly adapted to his new environment and was soon playing baseball and football (of the American variety, that is) with neighbourhood kids at the local park. Kristen developed a cluster of close friends, several of whom were black.

It was a local woman of Italian descent who introduced Beth to American supermarkets. The first time she stepped inside one her mouth dropped open. It was about eight times the size of the supermarket she'd been accustomed to shopping at back in Henderson, Auckland. She thought she'd start with washing powder, but the shelves containing packets ranging from small to absolutely giant stretched into the distance. How could she ever choose just one out of this line-up?

The Whinerays had a car provided for their private use, a flash left-hand-drive Ford Bel Air, which was much larger than any car they'd ever owned back in New Zealand. Initially, they used it — well, Wilson did, Beth opting to travel only as a passenger in the left-hand-drive car — for short sightseeing outings to check out Boston and its suburbs, an area rich in American history. One of the places they visited was Lexington, where the first battle of the Revolutionary War took place in 1775. It's where Paul Revere undertook his famous ride to warn the locals the British soldiers were coming, and it's where Captain John Parker declared, as the British approached, 'Don't fire unless fired upon, but if they mean to have a war, let it begin here.'

While the winters in the northeast of the United States were harsh, including snow, the summers were gloriously hot, and the Whinerays took advantage of Wilson's three-month summer holiday to 'discover' this great new country they were living in. With petrol — or 'gas' as the Americans called it — marvellously cheap, they drove their Bel Air right across the country, taking in the Niagara Falls and venturing as far as the Yellowstone National Park in Wyoming and Montana, towing a pop-up trailer all the way. Wilson, Beth and baby Susan slept in the trailer, while James and Kristen shared a tent. Notwithstanding a couple of punctures, their grand tour of America was completed without dramas or disasters, and ranks as one of the family's great experiences.

Boston is a city renowned for its sporting achievements, and

Wilson took advantage of this. He and James went along to watch the famous Red Sox baseball team play, and he was also able to arrange tickets to see the Boston Bruins ice hockey team and the Boston Celtics basketballers.

Television in New Zealand at the time the Whinerays embarked on their American adventure was in its infancy and screened only in black and white. So for the Whinerays, television in glorious colour was a joy to behold. Not only that, but the programmes screened 24 hours a day. A few months after their arrival, Beth woke one night to the sound of voices in the lounge. When she checked it out, she found her then two-year-old daughter Susan sitting on the side of the settee watching the late, late show!

Wilson had proven he could apply himself academically in achieving his Bachelor of Commerce, and from the moment he enrolled at Harvard he demonstrated the same commitment to his studies that had distinguished his leadership of the All Blacks. He told Beth he felt enormously privileged to have been presented with the chance to study at one of the world's most prestigious universities, and he certainly wasn't going to waste the opportunity.

Harvard, the first university founded in the United States, in the 1600s, with the Business School dating from 1908, does have a facility for undergraduates but only graduates were accepted into the School of Business — the same applied to the law and medicine schools. If Wilson, who was 32 when he arrived in the States, hadn't completed his degree, he wouldn't have been eligible for Harvard's graduate school.

The Harkness Fellowships, which were previously known as the Commonwealth Fund Fellowships and administered from New York, were established to allow British graduates to replicate the Rhodes Scholarships to Oxford and enable fellows from various countries to spend time studying in the United States. The philanthropic foundation was set up by Anna Harkness in 1918, her son Edward initiating the Commonwealth Fund Foundation in 1925. In 1927 it was widened to include Dominion Fellowships, admitting graduates from Australia, New Zealand, Canada and South Africa, with the proviso that candidates had to be under the age of 40.

The chief executive of the Harkness organization explained to Wilson and the other newcomers upon their arrival in 1967 that he wanted the recipients of the fellowships to get about and appreciate the country. He didn't want those on scholarships to feel they owed the Foundation anything. He wanted them to see as much of America as they could, and to absorb the country's history and culture so they might understand the political decisions that were made.

While in so many respects Harvard was a million miles removed from Auckland, it didn't stop Wilson's reputation preceding him. The day he signed in, one of the registrars declared, 'Mr Whineray, we know who you are and we're delighted to have you with us. We have a very good rugby team here, you know!'

Wilson didn't know, but he should have realized with the number of South Africans, Australians and Brits in attendance that rugby would feature somewhere along the way. Without ever allowing it to distract from his studies or taking it too seriously, he was soon training with an eclectic bunch of 'ruggers' from many parts of the globe. The rugby season on the northeast coast of the United States is split in two because of the severity of the winter. Players manage a couple of months of action in October and November, then effectively go into hibernation until February.

Harvard competed against other universities like Yale, Dartmouth and Holy Cross, and against clubs from Boston and New York and was competitive against most of them. The university's home field didn't bear too great a resemblance to Eden Park, for sure. Gear bags were used to mark the corners of the field, and the goalposts looked like they'd been borrowed from soccer. Some of the fields they visited had to be cleared of rubbish before play could commence. It's fair to say rugby didn't hold great status on the east coast of America! But Wilson enjoyed the exercise and the camaraderie, and the games afforded him the opportunity for relaxation away from his textbooks. After-match entertainment mostly revolved around a keg of beer out of the back of one of the players' cars. The Harvard rugby team's luxuries were few and certainly didn't extend to a clubhouse.

They were momentous times to be in the United States, with the Vietnam War in full cry. While the Whinerays were living in America, the Government changed the draft laws. Previously, anyone attending university or aged over 25 was exempt, but no longer. Suddenly, many of the Americans who were attending lectures were apprehensive that they would be called up, and some were. The university responded by allowing those who had now become eligible for the draft to study through the middle of summer, when normally all students were on holiday for three months. It was a gesture hugely appreciated, as it allowed these individuals to complete their doctorates or masters degrees before they headed for Vietnam. As a New Zealander, Wilson was fortunate that he didn't have to worry about being shipped off to the other side of the world for combat duty.

In his first year at Harvard, Wilson contended with what was essentially a compulsory package at graduates' school. It covered all the main core subjects that go towards a business degree — marketing, finance, planning, human relations, personnel, statistics, management, economics and statistics. In the second year, students selected three or four papers each semester, from the 30 or 40 that were available. Wilson settled on a broad spectrum in the core disciplines, preferring not to specialize in any one topic.

Harvard involved a lot more than merely attending lectures and studying. Anyone walking away with a Master of Business Administration had to be prepared for all manner of challenges in their business life. The students were often put into conflict situations designed to reveal their true business acumen and capacity to function under pressure. On one occasion Wilson was handed an assignment on a Friday afternoon and told he had to have it completed and on the professor's desk by Monday morning. 'Oh, and by the way, Mr

Whineray, your access to the computer will be after midnight each evening!'

Several world-shattering events occurred while the Whinerays were living in America. In April 1968, Martin Luther King was assassinated in Memphis, Tennessee, sparking a succession of riots. Just two months later, Robert Kennedy was shot at the Ambassador Hotel in Los Angeles while campaigning for the Democratic nomination for presidency of the United States. He died the next morning. In November of 1968, four men hijacked a Pan Am plane out of JFK Airport in New York and made the pilot fly to Cuba. Lyndon Baines Johnson announced he would not be seeking re-election as president, paving the way for Richard Nixon to move into the White House. And with the Vietnam War such a hot issue, there were frequent civil riots. The newspapers were seldom wanting for sensational front-page stories.

Wilson's hard work paid off. In March 1969, he had the thrill of opening a letter advising him that he had attained his MBA. Captaining the All Blacks to series victories against the Springboks and the Lions was one thing, but adding the letters MBA after his name represented probably an even greater achievement. In the 1960s the number of New Zealanders studying at universities with the status of Harvard was minuscule, and the number who graduated with MBAs would probably have not exceeded one a year.

It was a time of full employment and, with a settled economy in America, anyone with good qualifications was looking sweet. Interview booths were set up at Harvard, and for those who'd graduated it was a case of to whom you flashed your credentials. As Wilson and Beth were always planning to return to New Zealand, Wilson wasn't bothered with the job opportunities that were being flaunted. But some targeted him because word of his scholastic achievements had spread. One individual who'd played in the Harvard rugby team with

Wilson invited him to fly to Chicago where his family, who owned the company that produced Quaker Oats (one of the biggest-selling cereals not only in the States but world-wide), was based. 'Please go,' pleaded the fellow. 'It will get the family off my back.'

So Wilson flew to Chicago, inspected the company's set-up and listened with appropriate earnestness to their job offers, before gracefully declining. A lot of Harvard graduates would have given their left arm to be in his position at that point.

While he was at Harvard, Wilson enrolled for an optional course: An Introduction to Computers. Computers were in their infancy in the 1960s, but Wilson had heard someone expound that they were the way of the future. Concluding that they would probably be around for some time, he decided to familiarize himself with them. Definitely not, he would tell business colleagues years later, the worst decision he ever made in his life!

Wilson's rugby experiences at Harvard would unfortunately come to a painful conclusion. The player who had proven virtually indestructible through 240 first-class outings over more than a decade on rugby fields in New Zealand and throughout the world would tear the exterior ligaments of his knee in one of his final outings. The injury required surgery and meant he returned to New Zealand in 1969 with his leg in plaster! It was a factor in his not remaining in Cambridge for the capping ceremony.

As part of their trip home the Whinerays had scheduled a stopover in Honolulu, staying in a hotel close to Waikiki Beach. Beth and the children thought this was just fantastic, an opportunity to relax, swim and soak up some sunshine at one of the most desirable holiday resorts in the world. Wilson wasn't quite so enthusiastic, given that the large plaster cast on his leg meant progress was possible only on crutches, and he certainly couldn't immerse himself in the gorgeous Waikiki surf.

So while Beth and the kids set themselves up on the sand, Wilson shuffled along the promenade to a bar, where he made himself as comfortable as possible. An obliging barman came across, took his order and duly served him a delightfully cool Michelob beer. While all this was happening, Wilson realized to his horror that, with so many other things to concentrate on, he'd come out with only enough American cash to cover one beer.

God works in mysterious ways. About the time Wilson was downing the first mouthful, and wondering how he could make one Michelob last an afternoon, a loud Texan focused his attentions on this fellow with his leg in plaster.

'How you doing, son?' asked the Texan.

'Pretty well, apart from this,' replied Wilson, pointing to his leg.

The Texan recognized the strange accent.

'You not an American?'

'No, I'm from New Zealand.'

The Texan leant forward and shook his hand vigorously.

'My God,' he said, 'I've got the greatest admiration for you Vietnam vets. Let me buy you a beer. Michelob, is it?'

Wilson suddenly realized he was caught between a rock and a hard place. He didn't want to dampen this Texan's admiration for those who served in Vietnam, but nor was he prepared to tell a lie.

'I'm afraid I don't have enough on me to buy you one in return,' said Wilson.

'You're not buying another beer today, sonny.'

Wilson knew he'd have to confess if the Texan started asking questions about life in Vietnam. But that never happened, because the Texan retreated to his own cluster of friends, reappearing every once in a while to hand Wilson another Michelob.

A couple of hours later, Beth came up to the bar.

'Have you had a nice afternoon, dear?'

'You'll never believe how pleasant it's been,' he replied. Right at that moment his only concern was whether he could make it back to the apartment without falling off his crutches!

♣

In the early 1970s John Blackwell, a dynamic young book-publishing executive with entrepreneurial qualities, launched a company dedicated to publishing sports books. He named the company Moa — not after the extinct bird, as most New Zealanders would presume, but as an abbreviation for Mail Order Associates, which is how he marketed his first two books: the *New Zealand Rugby Annual* and the *New Zealand Cricket Annual.* Sales were modest through mail order, so he switched to more orthodox methods of retailing, publishing much sought-after annuals for rugby, cricket and racing for more than two decades.

However, the publishing concept for which Blackwell would become renowned was sports books on a grand, grand scale, of which *Men in Black* was the first. This book — written jointly by Rod Chester and Nev McMillan, and first released in 1978 — chronicles every test match played by the All Blacks from 1903. The book was published in two sizes: normal, which sat perfectly on most bookcases, and gargantuan, measuring 54 by 40 centimetres and weighing 10.6 kilograms. As one reviewer so delightfully described it, it wasn't so much a coffee table book, it *was* the coffee table! Blackwell printed 1,200 copies: 1,000 for the New Zealand market, which were fully subscribed, and 200 for export. The pre-subscribed copies sold for $295 each, the remainder for $350. The venture was a roaring success, with the standard volume having been republished several times since, with sales now in excess of 100,000 copies. And who was invited to write the introduction to this astonishingly successful publication? None other than the individual regarded as New Zealand rugby's greatest captain, Wilson Whineray.

Wilson, who had known McMillan when he had taught history at Auckland Grammar, painstakingly wrote the near 5,000-word introduction, entitled 'The highest honour', in longhand. It was a masterpiece. Here are a few extracts:

Old front row forwards have one foible — those who don't understand us would say we have several — but we will at least confess to one. I would like to say that it was something exotic like fast cars or hang gliding but, alas, this is not so. It is simply that given a chance, we will stand up in front of, or push our way into, any group willing or unwilling to listen and talk with great authority on any subject whatsoever. The quirk probably results from years of banging heads with somebody equally odd. Consequently, I am delighted to have the opportunity of writing an introduction to this outstanding book, as once again it affords me the chance of airing my opinions.

We must never forget that rugby is a very human activity, no matter how large or spectacular or publicised it becomes. The history of the game is the history of the millions of young men who, over the years, have laced up their boots and joined in the fun. Its future will ebb or flow depending on the quality and quantity of people who make up its ranks. It has a long history and tradition and has a set of standards unique among today's hard physical games.

I had the good fortune to be involved with international rugby for nine years, playing test matches both at home and abroad. It was an exciting period for me and there is little I would change, could I do it over again. I cannot go into a changing room even now and smell that unique combination of embrocation and sweat, and anticipation, without having my pulse rate quicken. It is something a sports person never loses.

The transition to All Black captain happens to some players and I think most would agree with me that it is a somewhat overrated occupation. What I found to be the least enjoyable part is that both circumstance and the position itself force you away from members of the team, many of whom are your greatest friends. In any position of authority or leadership there must be a slight 'arm's length' relationship with the group. One can never again be quite 'one of the boys' and it is foolish to try. A captain must always endeavour to conduct himself in a manner he expects the team to follow. Furthermore, the off-field demands of the UK/France tour especially can be heavy with several speeches a week at formal dinners, on top of the normal routine of meetings with the press, TV interviews, school visits etc. Most captains I know would gladly give much of it away and return to the ranks.

Training sessions . . . were aimed at co-ordinating individual skills and putting some polish on tactics and patterns. Tactics are always a difficult area, and harder to change than most people realise, once the game is under way. Most teams aim at having the game played in a way they feel gives them an advantage over the opposition by playing to your own strength and against their weakness. The idea is to control enough of the ball throughout to force the other team to play the type of game you want. All of this comes unstuck, of course, if you fail to control the ball and are forced to follow your opponents.

The other problem associated with changing tactics is that there is little time for a discussion — to get the views of other experienced players — until the half-time break. I have heard it said that the difference between the levels of differing sports is the ability of top performers to operate in a shorter and shorter time zone. This, I believe, is essentially true and certainly events move quickly in a test match. There is an urgency not apparent in lesser games.

However, hard as it is to change tactics sharply, we always practised the 'what if' situation . . . 'what if' we can't control the ball, 'what if' our defence gets mauled, 'what if' our backs are tackled out of the game, etc. I never went on to the field in a major game without two or three options that had been discussed and agreed among the team.

A habit I developed over the years was catching up on mail from 11 a.m. until lunch at 12 noon on match day. Lunch was never later than noon for a 3 p.m game and most players eat little. The steak devotees are few now as that type of meal is heavy and takes hours to digest. Many people believe it unwise to take liquid before strenuous exercise but I took the advice of Olympic gold medallist and friend Murray Halberg and would have a cup of tea laced with sugar up to 1½ hours before kick-off. I found this very helpful advice.

The team would assemble for the main team talk at 1.30 p.m. This team talk would be demanding, positive and detailed. Both Neil McPhail and Fred Allen were gifted in this area, blending 'fire' and 'detail' cleverly. Little was said then until kick-off.

It is interesting to recall changing rooms throughout the world, many seemingly designed to meet a 'most cheerless' contest. Most are tucked in the depths of concrete grandstands and are cold, dark, smelly and depressing. Before a game they exude a spotless sterility; after they are strewn with tapes, bandages, broken laces, cans, the odd bottle and various pieces of torn gear. I once found a tooth on the floor after a game in Wales and as it transpired that none of our people had lost it, I could only conclude it came from an earlier boisterous encounter.

Another fascinating piece of worthless information is that most players have a deep superstition that finds its expression at changing times. Some always go to a certain part of the room, others have lucky charms and most follow a strict pattern of changing into their playing gear. Again, many will only run on to the field at a certain place in the line and look out any newcomer who accidentally takes that position!

The history of rugby is no more than a history of the people who have been involved with the game, reflecting the hopes and attitudes of their era. We live in rapidly changing times and administrators must be aware of, and receptive to, new views emerging. Their task must surely be to move with these attitudinal changes yet at the same time preserve everything that is worthwhile in the game.

I know of one great rugby administrator/coach/manager who held every office and enjoyed every honour in New Zealand rugby who, on the occasion of his acceptance of life membership, said that he would have given it all away just to have worn the black jersey once.

Rugby in this country seems at times to be under a state of siege. From various quarters our administrators are criticised for lack of sensitivity and poor public relations; our players are accused of over-intensity; our crowds for being partisan and boorish; and our referees for being inadequate. Overlaying all of this in recent years has been the complex question of politics and sport. Fortunately, the game and its supporters have always been big enough to meet these criticisms, strengthened in the knowledge that rugby in this country has much of which to be proud. No other institution has done so much to cross social, religious, racial, cultural and economic boundaries so comprehensively and with so little pretence.

11

CHAIRMAN OF THE BOARD

During his final month at Harvard University, Wilson fielded a call from an Auckland journalist who was aware of his imminent return to New Zealand.

'Do you have a job to come home to?' the journalist inquired.

'No, I have nothing lined up at this moment,' Wilson, now with the distinctive letters MBA (Harvard) attached to his name, replied with great honesty.

The story in the *New Zealand Herald* certainly helped fix that. Wilson received three letters from well-established New Zealand firms, each offering interviews. Once settled back in Auckland, Wilson called on all three companies, which led to him joining Alex Harvey Industries (AHI). Demonstrating wonderful loyalty, he would remain with the firm, which in 1985 would become Carter Holt Harvey, for 24 years, rising to the position of chairman of the board.

When he first took up the appointment in 1969, he went into the new products division of their head office. This gave him time to comprehend all that AHI, at the time employing between 2,000 and 3,000 people, produced and marketed. At his initial interview, Wilson made it plain that, despite his MBA qualification, he didn't want to commit himself to head office administration too soon. He would prefer to garner as much practical experience as possible by working for and ultimately managing companies.

Alex Harvey wasn't prepared to leave its new shining star languishing for too long, and after three months he was appointed manager of ACE-St Regis (New Zealand) Ltd, a company that produced plastic bags, aluminium foil, and laminating products used for insulation. It was a comparatively small company, but it was in a competitive industry and provided Wilson with valuable experience. He could see the desirability of enjoying a monopoly, where you existed as a supplier and seller with little or no competition. At the time that Wilson managed ACE-St Regis, there were quite a few plastic-bag makers in the market.

Wilson rolled on to become assistant manager of Hygrade for a number of years. This company produced corrugated boxes and cartons used for holding beer, wine and ice cream. Unlike ACE-St Regis, Hygrade had several manufacturing plants around the country, operating out of Napier, Wellington and Christchurch, as well as Auckland.

Next stop for Wilson in the AHI chain was to succeed renowned mountaineer Peter Mulgrew as manager of the company's aluminium/roofing group, a position he occupied for four years. It was a sound company that produced aluminium window-frames and roofing tiles. Among those to whom the company supplied aluminium window-frames and ranch-sliders was the Karekare Surf Lifesaving Club, which operated out of a remote part of Auckland's west coast. Club captain of Karekare at the time just happened to be Bob Harvey, who later became the larger-than-life mayor of Waitakere City. Karekare's finances were stretched to the limit to pay the Alex Harvey bill, which also included new decramastic tiles on the roof, so they summoned the representatives of AHI, including Wilson, to the club for a meeting.

'It's not true we couldn't pay the bill,' recalls Bob Harvey, 'but we felt we were in a position to negotiate an arrangement satisfactory to both parties.'

Karekare's offer was a cash payment to cover most of the account, with the balance coming in the form of a handsome painting of which the club was in possession. Harvey estimated the painting's value at approximately $8,000 at the time.

The painting was by a young fellow named Peter Siddell, who had abandoned a career as an electrician to concentrate on his artistic talent. He had a bach at Karekare where he did most of his painting, often joining the boys at the club for a social drink. He occasionally offered his paintings for sale, at bargain-basement prices, and Harvey was one who, liking Siddell's work, made several purchases, a couple on behalf of the club.

Harvey was plainly a good negotiator, because the Alex Harvey representatives returned to the city in possession of the Siddell painting, which for the next several years occupied a place in the company's boardroom. When AHI was taken over, the artwork found a place in the Carter Holt Harvey boardroom, along with a handsome collection of other paintings.

While the name Siddell meant nothing to the AHI members when the painting was first handed over, Wilson, an admirer of fine art, later discovered that Siddell was being touted as one of New Zealand's most promising artists. Educated at Mount Albert Grammar, Siddell would become only the second New Zealand artist to be knighted. He would have many exhibitions in public and commercial galleries, and his works — described as 'magic realism' — are now displayed in all New Zealand's major public art galleries.

The majestic painting hung in the Carter Holt Harvey boardroom throughout Wilson's term as chairman. When he finally retired in 2003, the company said his farewell gift would be any painting he cared to select, an honour accorded in recognition of his immense contribution to the company. Not surprisingly, he selected the Siddell, which now decorates the Whineray home in Remuera.

Applying the adage that all work and no play makes Jack a dull lad, Wilson opted to balance his business commitments with some rugby coaching. Having rejoined Grammar Old Boys following his return from America, he volunteered his services as a coach in 1970, being placed in charge of the club's Colts team, which comprised players aged under 21. Under Wilson's astute guidance, they took out the championship, repeating the feat the following year.

In 1972, he took charge of the Grammar Old Boys seniors, who the previous season had finished an embarrassing 11th of 14 teams. Expectations were high that the former All Black captain would rejuvenate the club's fortunes, but few anticipated such a remarkable transformation. After qualifying second, Grammar defeated the much-fancied Ponsonby team in the first round of championship play, and went on to claim the Gallaher Shield, the trophy named after the legendary 1905 All Black captain, Dave Gallaher. Sadly, it has to be recorded here, much to the chagrin of the Grammar faithful: the club has not won the senior championship title in the 38 years since!

Wilson would have a brief stint coaching rugby in Wellington when he was seconded to help establish the New Zealand Wool Marketing Corporation. Wool had traditionally been sold via an auction system, but there was a move to introduce single-desk selling and it was Wilson's responsibility to help set this up. He spent 18 months in the capital, and for one winter linked up with his vice-captain from the 1960 tour of South Africa, Mick Bremner, at the Onslow club. The club had been struggling, but they managed to get them through to the top four.

Eden Park had always held a special place in Wilson's heart. As an 11-year-old he'd watched the celebrated 2nd New Zealand Expeditionary Force team, The Kiwis, fresh from their epic tour of Great Britain and France — and featuring such legends of the game as Bob Scott, Johnnie Smith, Fred Allen, and Charlie Saxton — play out a thrilling draw with Auckland. Later that same 1947 winter, Wilson had been on the terraces when the All Blacks staged a thrilling comeback to defeat the Wallabies, thanks to the accurate boot of Bob Scott. In 1950, Wilson had watched some of the finest athletes in the world compete at the Empire Games. And through the 1960s he'd been on centre-stage helping the Auckland rugby team create a record sequence of Ranfurly Shield defences.

So it was entirely appropriate that in 1977 he should be voted on to the Eden Park Trust Board, which at the time was under the chairmanship of Stuart Hay. Remarkably, he would serve the board for 31 years, during which Eden Park would undergo almost a complete metamorphosis.

While the stunning new stadium — with its 60,000 capacity — that will become the headquarters for the seventh Rugby World Cup in 2011 will stand comparison with any rugby venue on Earth, it's the surface at Eden Park that has brought greatest satisfaction to Wilson and his fellow board members. As Eden Park has a volcanic base, it has traditionally drained brilliantly, but the spreading of sand over the years, in the preparation of cricket pitches and rugby fields, had resulted in many of the drains becoming clogged.

Something had to be done, and the Board of Control decided to spare no expense in creating a world-class surface. They eventually spent $3 million in pursuit of this vision. Reinforced meshed nylon now holds the surface together and has created a facility second to none. Laser beams were used to create a surface so flat and true that lawn bowlers could happily operate on it (were the grass to be trimmed to bowling green proportions, that is). With state-of-art drop-in pitches now in vogue, it would be possible for Eden Park to stage a rugby match on a Saturday and a cricket contest the following day, with both sports guaranteed perfect playing conditions.

The Carter Holt Harvey company that Wilson would become deputy managing director of from 1987 to 1993, and chairman of for a further decade, was created through the merger of three prominent

New Zealand businesses, all dating back to the 1800s. Carter and Holt became leaders in New Zealand's forestry products sector, while Harvey became the country's major packaging company.

Holt dates back to the 1850s when Robert Holt built his first sawmill. When his sons John, James and Robert joined him, the company became Robert Holt & Sons. They opened a mill in Hastings and became the first New Zealand company to move logs by truck, and they were also the first to experiment with drying kilns to produce seasoned lumber. In 1961, headed by Harold Holt, the company went public. Harold encouraged the company to take a new direction by investing in renewable planted forests, shifting the emphasis away from New Zealand's dwindling native forests. With the country's timber supply running out, Holt built a mill at Jackson Bay, south of Haast on the West Coast. The company courted controversy in 1969 when it linked with two Japanese companies — Oji Paper and Sanyo Kokusaku — to exploit the concession in the southern Kaingaroa Forest, a move that led to the building of a $12.3 million sawmill at Whirinaki. Construction began in 1971, with production starting two years later.

Francis Carter built his first sawmill at Koputaroa near Levin in 1895, cutting white pine, later adding another sawmill at Rangataua near Waiouru. He demonstrated shrewd business nous by purchasing cutting rights from Maori and settlers in areas being opened up for the railway. By the 1940s, Carter had developed a network of seven associated companies, having expanded the lumber base into the production of wood products. In 1948, Alwyn Carter succeeded his father as managing director and soon set about restructuring the family's holdings, merging the various companies into Carter Consolidated.

Alexander Harvey came to New Zealand in 1866, settling in Auckland, where he established a company producing machinery and equipment. He was joined by his sons, Alexander Junior, David and William, and in 1911 the company became Alex Harvey &

Sons. After the Second World War, they expanded into packaging and tin-printing, and began producing tin containers in Wellington. They also produced cabinets for washing machines and refrigerators. Having developed into one of New Zealand's largest manufacturers of packaging and aluminium and plastic products, they became Alex Harvey Industries.

Carter and Holt merged in 1971 and were joined in 1985 by Harvey. But before Harvey became involved, there was an attempted takeover of Carter Holt in 1980 by the company's largest rival, the Fletcher Group, a bid that was staved off after a protracted legal battle. This move prompted the company to seek expansion to reduce its vulnerability, and in 1985 the New Zealand Government brokered a merger between Carter Holt and Alex Harvey Industries, which itself had been the subject of a takeover bid a year earlier, from Australian Consolidated Industries (ACI). The government was again involved as it sought to prevent foreign ownership of one of New Zealand's largest corporations. After the creation of Carter Holt Harvey, the company bought out ACI's stake for $300 million.

By the time of the merger, Wilson had risen to a position of responsibility in the Alex Harvey boardroom and he began attending Carter Holt Harvey board meetings. There, the chairman was Richard Carter; his brother Ken, the managing director. It wasn't long before Wilson was appointed deputy managing director.

It was a time of massive expansion for the company, the merger having given it increased power. When the 1987 sharemarket collapse left many companies weakened and vulnerable, Carter Holt Harvey, in rugby parlance, went on the attack. Its first major purchase was of Caxton, New Zealand's leading producer of toilet paper, and then followed a takeover of monumental proportions, of Elders Resources NZ Forest Products, at a cost of $682 million.

The purchase of NZ Forest Products boosted Carter Holt Harvey's turnover by 60 per cent to $7 billion and made it the leader in the New Zealand forestry sector. It then began turning its attention overseas, and targeted the considerable forests of Chile, in the process forming a joint venture with Chile's Angellini Group. The two companies together took a controlling stake in Copec, one of Chile's largest conglomerates, giving it access to Chile's forestry sector. The spending spree took its toll, especially when the Gulf War caused international tensions. Carter Holt Harvey's bankers sought repayment of $1.3 billion, with the company being rendered vulnerable to takeovers as its stocks fell.

Indeed, Brierley acquired a controlling stake in September 1991, but within a few months had sold part of its stake to the American company International Paper, the largest pulp paper maker in the world. International Paper later boosted its shareholding of Carter Holt Harvey to 51 per cent, thus ending the founder families' association with the company.

When International Paper was looking at buying out Brierley, two executives flew down from America, requesting a private meeting with Wilson as the deputy managing director. They insisted on secrecy and travelled incognito, choosing to leave their recognizable corporate jet back in the States. They agreed to meet Wilson at the Regent Hotel in Auckland and discuss business over dinner. When they walked in, it seemed to them that every third person in the dining room knew Wilson and stood to shake his hand. So much for the secret meeting! Being Americans, of course, they knew nothing of rugby or Wilson's iconic status as an All Black. They did, however, have immense respect for a man who had attained an MBA from Harvard. In many American businessmen's eyes, that was the ultimate.

With the Carter brothers' exit, American David Oskin became Carter Holt Harvey's new chief executive. Oskin had a reputation as a tough cookie. He'd served as an army officer in Vietnam in the mid-1960s, being part of the first American unit that went in to secure strategic positions. Oskin knew little about New Zealand, and nothing whatsoever about rugby, but was eager to learn. The very first day he set foot in Carter Holt Harvey, no one seemed to know who he was. He was standing around waiting patiently when Wilson, ever considerate, came along and introduced himself.

'Oh, David, there you are,' said Wilson. 'Now, you're going to need somewhere to sit with a phone — here, use my office.'

Oskin began to protest, but Wilson would take no notice. 'No, you stay there until we get you sorted out.' After ensuring his PA had secured their American visitor a cup of coffee, Wilson buzzed off.

The chief purpose of Oskin's visit was to interview for the position of chairman of the board, the seat Ron Carter was about to vacate. It wasn't long before he asked Wilson if he would become chairman, to which Wilson answered yes, which, of course, meant resigning his position as deputy managing director.

Oskin, who these days runs his own investment company out of the United States and sits on four boards — two in America, one in China, and one in Malaysia — lavishes praise on Wilson.

'I've been around the world to all sorts of places, and of all the people I've met he's the most approachable, helpful character. He's direct and respectful — right at the top. In Wilson's world, no one is better than anyone else and he treats them all with respect. In the whole world I've never met another Wilson Whineray.'

When Oskin assumed his role as chief executive, the company was confronted with major financial difficulties, and it was his duty, working closely with Wilson, to turn that around, which it's fair to say they achieved quite magnificently.

Oskin was enchanted by Wilson, and enjoyed nothing more than conversing with him. Having studied at Harvard, Wilson loved talking about the United States and also about the military. Wilson was to become involved with the New Zealand SAS — indeed, they would appoint him their colonel commandant in 1997 — and had enormous respect for those who fought for their country, as Oskin had done.

On one social occasion, the Whinerays and the Oskins found themselves at the same table as Sir Edmund Hillary. David's wife,

Jo-Ellen, somewhat in awe at being in the presence of the conqueror of Mount Everest, opened her purse and produced two $5 notes which, of course, featured the face of Sir Edmund. She suggested to her husband that the notes — if personally signed by the great man — would represent marvellous mementoes for their granddaughters Ashley and Alli back in the States. David agreed, but having only just met Sir Edmund was reluctant to press him.

Wilson happened to overhear their conversation. 'Ed,' he said, 'we need you to sign something.' And with that, the job was done.

'Thank you so much,' said Jo-Ellen.

'My pleasure,' said Sir Edmund, with a twinkle in his eye.

When Oskin was in the United States in 1993, looking at buying a company in Atlanta, he finished up in a sports bar and was in the process of ordering some food when he looked up at one of the many television screens — and who should be featuring but Wilson Whineray.

Incredibly — and remember, this was Atlanta where rugby doesn't register at all on the Richter scale — this wasn't a fleeting shot of the All Black captain who'd retired from international play 28 years earlier, but a documentary about the All Blacks with a reasonably lengthy segment dedicated to Wilson. Oskin sat there awestruck; and when it was finished, he rang Wilson.

'Wilson, I'm in a bar in Atlanta and guess who I'm looking at?' Wilson admitted to being as surprised as Oskin.

The board that Wilson chaired was an intriguing mix of highly qualified New Zealand independents, Americans appointed by International Paper, plus Chilean Maximo Pachenco, a delightful personality — now based in Brazil — who enhanced every meeting he attended. They would meet eight times a year, four times in Auckland, when the overseas representatives would fly in, and four times when the overseas cluster would hook up on a video conference. On one memorable occasion, the Americans and Pachenco beamed in by video from Chile, Hong Kong, Sydney, and the various parts of the United States.

The Kiwi independents were: Chris Liddell, who has gone on to win appointments as chief financial officer for Microsoft and General Motors — making him arguably the highest achieving New Zealand businessman ever; Kerry McDonald, like Wilson an accomplished rugby player who served as director of the NZ Institute of Economic Research and was chairman of both Comalco and BNZ; John Maasland, a lawyer by training who filled executive roles with ICI, Morrison PIM Holdings and Wilson and Horton, and who would succeed Wilson as chairman; and Peter Springford, who would become CEO of Carter Holt Harvey after serving as president of International Paper (Asia) Ltd, based in Hong Kong — he is still chairman of Hong Kong-listed Hung Hing Printing Group.

Wilson had a challenging role, given the sometimes differing views of the International Paper representatives whose company owned more than half of Carter Holt Harvey, and New Zealand's independent representatives. There were strong personalities on the board, but Wilson managed to get them operating constructively rather than destructively. As chairman, Wilson represented the shareholders and he knew that any decisions the board reached had to be in the shareholders' interests.

He would never allow any individual to control a meeting, but he'd do it in a way that was not controlling. John Maasland, who would succeed him, describes him as 'a most relaxed chairman but fully in control, with a lot of lovely touches'. He was impressed at how Wilson would ask probing questions that would draw people out. And he noted that he got on uncommonly well with Americans.

One of those Americans he related to brilliantly was Jonathan Mason, who in 2000, when Chris Liddell was functioning as the company's CEO, was appointed by Independent Paper as chief financial officer. Mason came from America with outstanding credentials and, indeed, went on to become chief financial officer for another of New Zealand's most powerful companies, Fonterra.

About a year after he'd settled in, Mason, in tandem with Liddell, spearheaded a major foreign exchange proposal advising the company to seek to profit long term from the exchange rate. Mason recommended a five-year hedge, which represented a gutsy move at the time, with the New Zealand dollar then equalling US$0.40.

Mason and Liddell had done their research and were confident the US dollar would increase in the following years, certainly up to US$0.50 and possibly beyond. They never in their wildest dreams imagined it would career out to US$0.70.

First, they had to 'sell' the concept to Wilson and the board, which was no certainty. If the US dollar dropped to US$0.30, say, and remained there, the company would lose hundreds of thousands of dollars. That was the worst-case scenario; conversely, if the dollar increased in value to US$0.50 there was the potential for hundreds of thousands of dollars in profits annually, and if it spiralled beyond that the profit would extend into the multi-millions. Mason explains that most companies weren't prepared to take the risk Carter Holt Harvey did. He and Liddell had done their homework and were confident that the exchange rate would favour the venture.

With Kerry McDonald and John Maasland backing them and Wilson supporting them, the board gave its blessing to the five-year hedge. Although Wilson would retire in 2003, well before the hedge matured, he was able to step aside taking plaudits as the chairman who backed one of the most audacious finance operations the country has ever witnessed.

As the US dollar bounded from 40 cents to 50 cents to 60 cents and ultimately to 70 cents, Carter Holt Harvey, with its currency hedging beautifully in place, benefited across the five years by between NZ$800 million and $1 billion. Bankers still talk about it as a classic example of how to get the foreign exchange market working for you.

While he was deputy managing director, Wilson was precluded from accepting directorships, but that changed after he was appointed chairman of the board, for the board met mostly only once a month. Given his status, Wilson, who by the time he accepted the chairmanship had become Sir Wilson, was in keen demand, and in fairly rapid succession was offered directorships of the National Bank of New Zealand Ltd, where he would become chairman, Auckland International Airport Ltd, and Nestlé NZ Ltd.

One call he wasn't expecting in this regard came from Tony O'Reilly, whom he had first befriended when the British Lions toured New Zealand in 1959. Tony had become an international celebrity, and as the managing director of HJ Heinz Co had achieved the distinction of becoming the highest-paid executive in the world — not bad for a rugby player!

The dizzying performances O'Reilly produced on the rugby field were nothing compared with his spectacular advancements as a businessman. Having secured 28 per cent of the Dublin-based Independent News & Media, publisher of Ireland's most esteemed daily newspaper, *The Independent,* he pushed the company to expand into Australia, South Africa and New Zealand, which it did in stunning fashion. At a cost of €1.3 billion, Independent purchased 38 newspapers and 70 radio stations in the three countries.

Around the time Wilson was settling in as chairman of Carter Holt Harvey, he fielded the call from O'Reilly, inviting him to become a director of the *New Zealand Herald*, New Zealand's largest-selling newspaper, a share of which O'Reilly had just purchased. The persuasive Irishman convinced his former rugby rival he would enjoy getting involved in the publishing world.

Within a couple of years, O'Reilly had purchased a controlling share in the *New Zealand Herald* through APN (Australian Provincial Newspapers), which was majority-owned by Independent News & Media. O'Reilly then invited Wilson to become a director of APN News & Media Ltd (Australia), which he accepted. What the mercurial O'Reilly also invited Wilson to become part of was an International Advisory Board he had created following his purchase of the formidable Argus Publishing Group in South Africa.

O'Reilly — being O'Reilly — had befriended Nelson Mandela who, truth be known, was flattered that a Western country was prepared to invest in the new South Africa. Naturally, Mandela was concerned that the new owners should not intrude on editorial policy, and would have expressed this sentiment to O'Reilly.

O'Reilly's reaction was to bring together a dazzling collection of overseas personalities, largely businessmen and politicians, under the banner of an International Advisory Board, who would meet once a year in Cape Town. There they would discuss issues of the day, economic trends, conflicts, and matters of immediate concern to South Africa, such as the spread of AIDS.

Wilson wasn't overly enthusiastic about flying to Cape Town, for two reasons: the arduous journey from Auckland, and the fact the titanium staples that had been inserted during the repair of his knees and hips invariably set off the metal detector when he was passing through airport security.

However, because the invitation was extended to both Wilson and his wife Beth, and because of O'Reilly's salesmanship, he accepted. He was pleased he did, because he was quite overwhelmed by the charming individuals in whose company he found himself once he arrived.

This is the list of those who featured on the panel on the four occasions Wilson was able to make it through to Cape Town:

- Ben Bradlee, chairman: former editor of the *Washington Post* (Watergate and all that)
- Ted Sorensen: US lawyer and former aide and speechwriter for John F Kennedy
- Andrew Young: former mayor of Atlanta, and President Carter's Ambassador to the United Nations (UN)
- David Dinkins: former, and first black, mayor of New York
- Charles Daly: from the Kennedy Library
- Brian Mulroney: former Prime Minister of Canada

- Kenneth Clarke: former UK Chancellor of the Exchequer
- Lord Paddy Ashdown: former leader of the UK Liberal Democrats and UN representative to Bosnia
- Baroness Jay: daughter of Jim Callaghan and Labour member of the House of Lords
- Lord Rogan: chairman of the Belfast Telegraph Board and chairman of the Ulster Unionist Party
- Maurice Hayes: Irish senator from Northern Ireland
- Dermot Gleeson: former Irish Attorney-General
- Frank Ferrari: ProVentures USA
- Eric Molobi: head of Kagiso Media and Nelson Mandela's fellow prisoner on Robben Island
- Professor Jakes Gerwel: Chancellor of Rhodes University at Port Elizabeth and former director-general of the President's office
- Anthony Sampson: author and biographer of Nelson Mandela
- Ted Harris: respected and senior Australian businessman
- Shaun Johnson: executive director of Mandela's Children's Fund and former editor and CEO of the group's South African newspapers
- Sir Thomas Sean Connery: Scottish actor and film producer most famous for his portrayals of James Bond.

John Maasland, a fellow director of Wilson's at Carter Holt Harvey — and his successor as chairman — was the only other New Zealander to be involved with the advisory panel, which finally disbanded in the late 2000s, Maasland receiving his invitation from Sir Anthony as chairman of the Wilson and Horton board.

Only Sir Anthony O'Reilly could bring such a distinguished collection of individuals together to assist in the development of the Rainbow Nation.

Four months out from the British Lions tour of New Zealand in 2005, certainly the biggest sporting event on the New Zealand calendar that year, and with tickets and hotel beds at a premium,

Wilson received a call from Tony O'Reilly.

'Wilson, I've decided the International Advisory Board should meet in Auckland during the final week of the Lions tour. Then they can see the Auckland game midweek and the final test on the Saturday. Do you think you could arrange a corporate box for them and help with some accommodation?' The total number of visitors, wives included, would extend beyond two dozen.

'I'll see what I can do, my old mate,' said Wilson.

With Wilson, Sir Wilson, in control, anything is possible and, yes, of course, Mr O'Reilly's entourage were worthily accommodated in the Queen's City — and watched both matches from a box on high. A newcomer to the advisory board was Sean Connery, who slipped quietly into Auckland and attended both matches at Eden Park. Wilson made sure he wasn't neglected.

'You'll never guess who I had the pleasure of accompanying at the rugby tonight,' he told a family member when he returned home, 'Sean Connery, Mr James Bond himself.'

'Gosh, does he know much about rugby?'

'I'm not sure. When you have the opportunity to talk with someone like Sean Connery, the last subject you want to bring up is rugby. I found talking about his career and film making much more interesting.'

The first time Peter Springford brought a proposal to the Carter Holt Harvey board, around 1994, was for the development of a $90 million medium-density fibreboard plant at Rangiora. Springford was making the presentation as the chief executive of the company's wood products division.

'OK, Pete,' said Wilson, in his most welcoming manner, 'tell us your story.' Springford remembers how Wilson contributed questions that helped him get across the strategy and rationale of the project. Approval was duly granted and the mill built; Prime Minister Jim

Bolger opening it in 1995. Now Japanese-owned, it was a successful business that exported more than 50 per cent of its production to Japan over a period of 15 years.

Around 2000, board members travelled to Adelaide in Australia, where Carter Holt Harvey had bought a tissue business, specializing in diapers and facial paper, to complement its Caxton brands. It also bought a wood product sawmill and a company that produced laminated veneer lumber.

Wilson was struggling with his knees and hips and back at the time, and there were an agonizing number of stairs at the sawmill in Adelaide, but he insisted on getting around and meeting all the people. The way he interacted with the employees, who totalled around 500, meant they all happily became part of Carter Holt Harvey.

That was Wilson's greatest strength: his ability to get on with people and relate to them. It mattered not whether the person he was beside was the most basic labourer, the managing director, a politician, or Nelson Mandela — Wilson treated them all the same, was genuinely interested in their opinions, and always left them feeling good about themselves. It is a personal characteristic that has resulted in some unexpected consequences.

When the North Auckland rugby team played Auckland at Okara Park, Whangarei, in 1965, it was a challenging occasion for the North Auckland No. 8, Laly Haddon, who played out of the Omaha club. Although good enough to have represented New Zealand Maori, he had never played against the great Wilson Whineray and on this occasion he was as nervous as he could be, because his coach, the great Ted Griffin, was explaining how the only way the team could blunt Auckland's favourite tactic from lineouts, the Willie Away, was if he, Haddon, tackled Whineray in the first few strides after he received the ball.

'If he gets away from you, Laly, we're in big trouble. You've got to put him down.'

Haddon nodded and tensed a bit more.

History will show that North Auckland won the game by 16 points to 14, not least because Haddon several times lowered Wilson as he was embarking upon potentially dangerous runs. Wilson thought enough of the North Auckland No. 8 to mention him in his after-match speech. Haddon has never forgotten it.

Three decades later Haddon was a much respected elder in the Ngatiwai tribe; indeed, he was the leader of the Omaha marae in the Rodney district north of Auckland, and chairman of the marae trust. He also had a horse-trekking business enterprise which would bring him back into contact with Wilson. Haddon's company was trying to lease approximately 1,000 acres of land in the Mangawhai Forest region and some buildings on it, but they were encountering difficulties with the owners of the land, who just happened to be Carter Holt Harvey. This was while Wilson still held the position of deputy managing director. One day, while Haddon was expressing his frustration at being unable to secure a lease on the property and the name of Carter Holt Harvey was possibly being taken in vain, someone suddenly declared, 'Hey, that's the company Wilson Whineray works for.'

Haddon had enormous respect for Wilson; on more than one occasion the two men had shared a drink at the iconic Leigh pub, just up the road from the Whinerays' holiday home at Matheson's Bay.

'I'll give Wilson a call,' said Haddon, which he proceeded to do.

Wilson listened intently to what Haddon had to say, and said that, while he was sympathetic to their situation, there was a procedure to follow.

'I can't give you any guarantees,' he said, 'but I'll look into it.'

A couple of weeks later, Haddon was asked if he would call at Carter Holt Harvey's head office to discuss his company's application. Given the length of time the issue had dragged on, he arrived with faint optimism, so was quite overcome when, within a few minutes of his arrival, he was presented with lease documents to sign. Some

15 years on, with the horse-trekking business a thriving concern, Haddon has only words of affection for Wilson.

'He never forgot his rugby buddies,' he said. 'I respect him for that.'

In 2009, when Haddon was awarded the Queens Service Medal for services to conservation, who drove up to the Omaha marae — along with fellow former All Blacks Waka Nathan and Mac Herewini — to speak and share in the celebrations, but Wilson.

Wilson was always planning to step aside as chairman in 2003, and he would naturally have preferred that the final months of his leadership unfolded harmoniously. Far from that happening, a crisis situation developed when 270 Kinleith workers went on strike over 'unsafe and unfair demands on them', effectively bringing production at the mill to a dead stop.

The paper-making mill at Kinleith was one of Carter Holt Harvey's major assets, and it brought Wilson equal measures of satisfaction and despair. It was a challenging industry to be involved in, especially operating out of a country isolated from its major markets and having to contend with currency fluctuations and high interest rates. The machinery involved to convert the logs into paper was massively expensive. It was an industry in which few survived, but Carter Holt Harvey did.

However, the company had been struggling to operate the mill profitably until International Paper brought its immense resources to bear. It is estimated that what International Paper spent in research and development annually was greater than Carter Holt Harvey's entire turnover! The Americans introduced the latest technology and sent their engineers Down Under to make the company far more efficient and competitive. Carter Holt Harvey employed well-qualified engineers, but the difference was that the Americans had done it all before.

Wilson and his board had identified that one of the problems they faced was the low rate of productivity at Kinleith. It wasn't about working harder, it was about working smarter — and that's what the Americans from International Paper were able to achieve.

Through 2002 and into 2003, when Kinleith was employing almost 700 workers, the mill was fighting for its life because it was unprofitable. To bring it into profitability, the workforce had to be trimmed by almost 300. A classic example involved the buses that operated between Tokoroa and Kinleith. None of the workers was using them. Management recommended selling the buses and redeploying the drivers into other activities, saving $120,000.

As might be expected, the Kinleith union didn't accept the management's recommendations and was determined to preserve a workforce of 700. So management came to the Carter Holt Harvey board, saying it had to stand against the union, otherwise Kinleith would probably cease to operate.

Wilson, as chairman, was literally in the hot seat. He represented the shareholders, but had to take a decision that was in the best interests of everyone. His board came out in support of the management stand. It represented probably the most challenging time in his business career. He understood the impact of people — almost 300 of them — losing their jobs, and it wasn't something he treated lightly; indeed, his family will tell you that during these troubled months Wilson was many times awake in the middle of the night pacing around his house.

The Kinleith strike was settled just a few days after Wilson presided over his final Carter Holt Harvey annual meeting in 2003, and his consummate skill in dealing with disgruntled union representatives is acknowledged by his fellow board members as one of the chief reasons the strike ended so promptly.

Business writer Brian Gaynor — of Irish heritage, and someone who'd been among the crowd cheering for Munster when Wilson's All Blacks were touring the UK in 1963–64 — captured the essence of Wilson's final board meeting delightfully in his article in the *New Zealand Herald*:

Sir Wilson Whineray retired with style on Wednesday. His skilful chairmanship of the Carter Holt Harvey annual meeting played a big part in containing a potentially inflammatory situation.

The signs were ominous when shareholders arrived at Ellerslie Racecourse. There were security guards at the gates, striking Kinleith workers and Auckland union officials outside the Convention Centre and a bevy of television cameras and other media representatives.

Union reps handed out leaflets. These claimed that the 270 Kinleith pulp and paper workers had been on strike since March 7 because the company had made unsafe and unfair demands on them.

Security was even tighter at the entrance to the Convention Centre. A large number of security guards, company employees and share registry personnel made sure that only accredited individuals could enter. Inside the meeting room, some Kinleith workers, who were also shareholders, sat together in a long line.

Sir Wilson was relaxed and in control from the beginning. He told shareholders that Kinleith had lost millions of dollars over recent years — the media notes said $26 million over the past 24 months — and this did not include any losses from the present strike.

He said more than 70 per cent of the mill's output was exported. It earned twice as much in overseas funds as the wine industry, but prices were cyclical and the mill must get to the point where it was world class and profitable.

Carter Holt Harvey uses about 3 per cent of the country's electricity and the crisis is having a big impact on its operations. The country's infrastructure problems, the rising dollar and resource act are also impacting on its investment decisions — and opportunities are more attractive in Australia.

On the positive side, the company will make about $150 million from its currency hedging operations this year and will report net earnings of about $100 million for the six months to June 30 . . . which indicates a net profit of roughly $165 million for the full year.

216 A PERFECT GENTLEMAN

Gaynor went on to say:

> The problem with boyhood sporting heroes is that they are usually a disappointment when one meets them later in life. Sir Wilson is a major exception to this rule.
>
> Carter Holt shareholders will argue that earnings and share price have been extremely disappointing in recent years. True, but it had to operate in treacherous conditions.
>
> It hasn't been pretty but Sir Wilson's team at Carter Holt has done better than any of the other domestic forestry companies, particularly Fletcher Challenge. The important point is that Carter Holt is now in a much stronger position than it was a decade ago when Sir Wilson was appointed chairman.
>
> When he retired as All Black captain in 1965, he left the team in a dominant position and they went on to win all their remaining tests in the 1960s.
>
> Carter Holt Harvey is in a similar situation — Kinleith is its one big weak spot — and all the firm needs is more favourable trading conditions for it to reach its full potential.
>
> Sir Wilson, enjoy your deck chair, glass of beer and fishing. You thoroughly deserve it.

All good things come to a conclusion, and in 2003, after a decade at the helm of the good company Carter Holt Harvey, Wilson stepped aside. Given his massive contribution over 34 years, first as an employee and manager with Alex Harvey Industries, then as a board member, deputy managing director and ultimately chairman of Carter Holt Harvey, he deserved all that was lavished upon him.

In the *New Zealand Herald*, feature writer Michelle Hewitson revealed she induced 'a little twitchiness' in Wilson when she implied his rugby and business careers were inextricably linked.

> It does bother him that, even on the occasion of his retirement as chairman from the company he joined in 1969, his captaincy is inextricably linked with his chairmanship.
>
> He can see the obit, can't he? 'Yes, I can and it does bug me

a bit. It's like Sir Edmund Hillary. No matter what Sir Edmund Hillary does, he will never not be remembered as the first guy to climb Everest.'

You can understand why the little bug bites occasionally. Although he is the first to admit that rugby has opened doors, he worked hard to get his degrees while playing rugby at amateur status, has worked hard since and 'you've really got to earn it'.

Solidly, carefully has done it. In many ways he is the same Whineray as the young man who took up the captaincy at the age of 23. He has always had what T.P. McLean called 'a streak of caution'. If he has ever done anything wildly impetuous in his life, he can't recall it.

With his knighthood and OBE, successful captaincy of the All Blacks and chairmanship of such iconic brands as Carter Holt Harvey and the National Bank of New Zealand, there didn't seem much more Wilson could aspire to as his career entered its twilight phase in the 2000s.

But the *New Zealand Herald* came up with a new one' — Governor-General.

A front-page story in November 2004 announced that Wilson was a 'hot contender' to become the next Governor-General.

The position becomes vacant in 2006 when Dame Silvia Cartwright's term finishes. The Government is looking at candidates. Sir Wilson, the longest-serving All Black captain, meets two criteria wanted by the Labour Government — he's male and he's not a judge.

Since 1980 there have been five Governors-General and three have been judges — Sir David Beattie, Sir Michael Hardie Boys and Dame Silvia.

The Government is keen to have an ordinary bloke to serve as representative of the Queen, New Zealand's Head of State.

Sir Wilson, 69, could not be contacted but it is thought he has been sounded out. Reaction yesterday indicated he would be a popular choice.

He unquestionably would have been an ideal Governor-General. John Maasland goes so far as to say he would have been 'absolutely brilliant'. To be considered for the position of Governor-General, one must allow one's name to go forward. Wilson very obviously did not permit his name to go forward.

However, Wilson did agree to stand for the position of patron of the New Zealand Rugby Union, a position he has occupied with distinction since 2003. After reappointing him annually, the NZRU decided in 2010 to install its iconic patron for a term of three years, which is hugely appropriate because it means Wilson will operate as patron at the time of the seventh Rugby World Cup in 2011. Who better to head the host nation?

12

MOVE OVER WILLIAM WEBB ELLIS

When in 2006 the IRB chose to establish an international Hall of Fame — created to preserve the heritage and cultural identity of rugby by celebrating the game's heroes and their achievements — there was much intrigue as to who the early inductees would be.

After all, the game had been played seriously in at least eight countries for well over a century, and each of those nations had produced its share of players, coaches, administrators, match officials and institutions who had made an indelible impact domestically and in most instances internationally. So where would you start?

The IRB displayed refreshing originality and uniqueness with its first intake. First cab off the rank, although he came from an era long before cabs existed, was William Webb Ellis, that enterprising young fellow who way back in 1823 daringly caught the ball and ran with it — the claim is apocryphal, but there is a modicum of evidence to support it. He and Rugby School, where it all happened, were the first pair inducted at a ceremony in Glasgow in November 2006.

Ellis, born in Salford, attended Rugby School from 1816 to 1825 and was a noted good scholar and cricketer. The incident when he is alleged to have caught the ball in his arms in a football match and run with it is thought to have happened in 1823 during a football match between Rugby and Bigside.

The sole evidence for his then shocking but now heroic behaviour came from a fellow pupil by name of Matthew Bloxam. In 1876, he wrote to *The Meteor,* the Rugby School magazine, that he had learned that a change from a kicking game to a handling game had originated with a town boy named Ellis:

> While playing Bigside in 1823, he caught the ball in his arms. Under the existing rules, he ought to have retired back as far as he pleased — because the opposition could only advance to the point where he caught the ball. The opposition were not allowed to rush until he punted the ball or placed it for someone else to kick. By these means goals were scored. Ellis disregarded this rule and on catching the ball, instead of retiring, rushed forwards with the ball in his hands towards the opposite goal, with what result I do not know.

Ellis, who is immortalized by the William Webb Ellis Cup that goes to the winner of the Rugby World Cup every four years, played cricket for Oxford University, where he graduated with a Master of Arts in 1931. He entered the church and became an Anglican clergyman. He never married, and died in the south of France in 1872, leaving an estate of £9,000.

His grave was discovered in 1958 by Ross McWhirter, who with his brother Norris famously founded the *Guinness Book of Records,* and has since been cared for by the French Rugby Union.

The second Hall of Fame induction took place in Paris in October 2007, the night following the sixth Rugby World Cup final. It featured an eclectic mix. The chosen five were Baron Pierre de Coubertin, Dr Danie Craven, John Eales, Gareth Edwards and Sir Wilson Whineray — a distinguished quintet indeed.

De Coubertin, Craven, Edwards and Eales — four remarkable achievers, all genuinely worthy of their place in rugby's Hall of Fame. So for Wilson to join that illustrious group, as effectively the founder members of the Hall of Fame, William Webb Ellis being something of an apocryphal figure, demonstrates the esteem in which he is held throughout the world. Not for nothing has Sir Anthony O'Reilly written in the foreword to this book that New Zealand is 'lucky to have him as a symbol of all that is good and upright in the land of the long, white cloud'.

In 2008, a further five personalities were inducted, and again they were an intriguing mix. Three were gifted performers — Pumas fly-half Hugo Porta, Irish and British Lions fly-half Dr Jack Kyle, and French midfielder Philippe Sella, who became the first player to notch up 100 test appearances. The other two were Ned Haig along with the Melrose club, who introduced a Sevens concept in 1883, which 126 years on has been adopted as an Olympic sport; and Joe Warbrick and his amazing 1888 New Zealand Natives team, which somehow managed to find the energy and enthusiasm to play 74 matches in the United Kingdom and a further 33 in Australia and New Zealand at either end of the tour.

New Zealand has too few iconic heroes to allow any of them to be cut down early in life. One such national figure who was tragically taken early, his death provoking shock and grief throughout the land, was Sir Peter Blake, who was murdered on board his research boat on the Amazon River in Brazil in December 2002, aged just 53.

Described as a living legend by the then Prime Minister Helen Clark, Sir Peter was New Zealand's most famous yachtsman. He had won the Whitbread Round the World race for the Jules Verne Trophy, setting the fastest time of 74 days and 22 hours, on *Enza*, and brought immense pride and joy to the nation by leading his crew to successive America's Cup victories.

The red socks he wore as New Zealand annexed the Cup in *Black Magic* at San Diego in 1995 so captured New Zealanders' imagination that it sparked a nationwide frenzy, thousands of his countrymen buying red socks to help fund the (successful) defence of the much-prized trophy four years later.

Sir Peter is buried at Warblington churchyard near Ensworth on the south coast of England. His headstone bears John Masefield's famous words: *I must go down to the sea again, the lonely sea and sky, and all I ask is a tall ship and a star to steer her by . . .'*

When Dr Mark Orams, sailor, marine scientist, friend and colleague, wrote a book entitled *Blake: Leader* as a celebration of the life and legacy of Sir Peter, he invited Wilson to write the foreword. This is what Wilson wrote:

> Leadership is an intriguing subject and one which most of us recognise more easily than we can describe. In a general sense, leadership is a complex interactive process between people who willingly work together to achieve common goals. Or put another way, leadership is a process that enables ordinary people to work together to do extraordinary things and feel good about doing them.
>
> What makes the subject so elusive is that it involves human attributes such as emotions and feelings, respect, integrity, inspiration and decision-making and this leaves little that is tangible to hang on to. But we all know that leadership is a vital ingredient in the progress of people and nations.
>
> Psychologist Dr Daniel Goleman introduced the concept of 'emotional intelligence' and argues it is critical in leadership. He defines emotional intelligence as 'the capacity for recognising our feelings and those of others — to motivate ourselves and manage emotions in a relationship. When facing a decision the sense of right or wrong is as important as any other data you might bring to the discussion. If it feels right, it probably is.'
>
> Essentially, he proposes that great leaders have an ability to understand and connect with people on an emotional level, that they have great emotional instincts. Sir Peter Blake was like this.
>
> I had the pleasure of knowing both Sir Peter and Sir Edmund Hillary, both leaders of global stature and I found much in common in their characters. Amongst these was an ability to intensely focus on whatever project captured their interest. Then a skill of pulling together the necessary resources — planning, funding and people — and in this latter regard each had a remarkable ability in

understanding people. Selecting individuals that would 'fit' and building them into a highly motivated team, making everyone feel they were valued, giving praise and caution in a quiet, firm manner and all the time having fun along the way.

As I reflected on Sir Peter's life and achievements, I suddenly became deeply saddened that his life had ended so early. He was at the height of his popularity and influence, which, had he lived longer, would have been so helpful in funding and expanding the important work he was undertaking on environmental and marine issues.

Years pass by and memories fade, and for this reason we must thank Dr Mark Orams for placing on record his memories of the years and events he shared with Peter. Mark is well placed to write this book. He has a doctorate in marine sciences and has a keen interest in leadership and leadership styles. But more importantly, he knew Peter very well, having been involved with several yachting campaigns and through this shared the good/bad times, the thrills/dangers, the wins/losses, the pressures/solitude with him. He had experiences and insights into Peter Blake the leader few others had.

Peter was always the leader; part of the team but always slightly separated from it. He led in the New Zealand way, gaining his support by deeds and actions and the respect followed. Peter never sought fame and fortune and had a dislike of pomposity and pretence. All he wanted to do at the outset was to win a yacht race. It frequently took several attempts, but the dream never faded and his focus and determination intensified.

From a supporting hero to an ambassador for environment protection, Peter attracted support because he was a proven winner, a 'safe pair of hands', a fine man and a great leader undertaking important work.

The support he had from his wife and family was enormous, and we thank Pippa, Lady Blake, for both her support and contribution to Peter's many successes.

For me, Sir Peter Blake personified the final lines from Alfred Lord Tennyson's great poem 'Ulysses' that, in many ways, seems written for him: '. . . but strong in will, to strive, to seek, to find and not to yield'.

When Auckland Grammar School opened its new sports pavilion in 2007, it sought out Sir Wilson to speak. His address is regarded as one of the finest ever delivered within the portals of the grand old school.

Here's that speech:

Many of you may reflect with me that the building that has been demolished as being out of date, inadequate and no longer useful was not even here when we were at school — which says something about our relevance and doesn't bear thinking about.

The pavilion overlooks a patch of grass that because of its history is quite unique. Without doubt, this field has helped develop more outstanding sportsmen than any other field, at any other school in New Zealand, or perhaps the world. It truly is a Field of Dreams for many boys. From the cricket block, the soccer and hockey pitches, the rugby field and the athletics track, hundreds of top-class sportsmen gained their early skills and went on to memorable national and international careers. We applaud their successes.

But they number in the hundreds. Let us also rejoice in the role sport played in the school days of thousands of boys — the lads of 3C rugby, 4B cricket, 2C soccer and 3B hockey. They wore their jerseys with pride, tried hard, gave their best, enjoyed themselves and took with them all the good things that flow from sport — mateship, rules, never quitting and learning that victory is never forever, but neither is defeat. This too was their Field of Dreams.

Children of course go to school to be educated, not just to play sport. Our last three headmasters have not only been outstanding educators but wonderful sportsmen — Henry Cooper (cricket and hockey), John Graham (All Black) and John Morris (All White). But all have, quite correctly, made it clear that the heart of the school lies in the classroom and sport like music and drama are activities that round out the education experience in its fullest sense. Our boys walk out the gate academically sound, rounded and confident.

It would be easy to think that in demolishing the old building we have lost something of the mystery and traditions built up over decades of use. Not so. Rebuilds have not changed the magic at Wembley, The Oval, Lord's, Twickenham, the MCG, Eden Park, or our pavilion. The new building instantly absorbs everything that has gone before.

Sport at Grammar has much of which to be proud. What other activity has done so much to cross social, cultural and racial divides so well with so little fuss? What other activity has engendered such a feeling of pride in our school community? Consider the contribution that sport has made to the development of character in our adolescent boys — a will to succeed, respect for the rules and ethos of the game, the mental and physical toughening that flows from bumps, bruises, a black eye, a cut lip; when you know you must get up and push on. All this lies at the heart of the game as we know it and for these reasons we continue the love affair with sport that began when we were boys.

Please join me in a toast, to suit the occasion, that will serve to open the pavilion . . . through cut lips, black eyes, bruised shins and spiked feet, to the ribbon, the silver cup, the medal, the crown of laurel leaves. More succinctly put — *Per Augusta Ad Augusta.*

13

THE ALL-PURPOSE MAN

Susan, the Whinerays' youngest child, was about five when she wandered through into the neighbours' property in Epsom one day and encountered Lorraine Marshall.

'Hello, Susan,' said the friendly neighbour.

'Hello, do you know my dad's famous?'

'Really, Susan?' replied the kindly Mrs Marshall. 'What's he famous for?'

'He painted our house!'

Lorraine Marshall chuckled at the story. She knew her illustrious neighbour was enormously famous for his exploits on the rugby field and for leading the All Blacks to epic victories over the likes of the Springboks, France and the British Lions.

And yet she appreciated there was more than an element of truth in the innocent boast of wee Susan, who knew nothing of her father's deeds as a sportsman or of his growing reputation as a businessman. Lorraine and her husband, Tom, knew better than most that Wilson, rugby and business achievements aside, was a dedicated father, husband and, perhaps most surprisingly of all, one hell of a talented home-handyman.

Rural cadetships, of the type that had seen Wilson posted to those remote farms in Southland, Wairarapa, Bay of Plenty and

Mid Canterbury, were renowned for turning boys into men. By the time Wilson graduated to an office posting, he was pretty much the ultimate DIY person. There was hardly anything, from repairing cars and tractors to building fences to replacing windows to painting houses to sawing firewood to cultivating orchids, to growing vegetables, to treating ailing animals, at which Wilson wasn't a dab hand. The exception to this impressive list of could-dos was winemaking, at which Wilson was singularly unsuccessful, his first vintage bringing a comment from one neighbour that it would make excellent paint remover. Wilson persisted, however, and achieved a breakthrough with his guava wine, which found exceptional form in Beth's kitchen as a steak marinade.

At weekends, when he wasn't involved in any rugby capacity, Wilson would get around on the home front looking like Father Brown, in shorts, paint-splattered shoes, and well-worn shirt. If there was a domestic problem, phoning for a repairman was never an option. Wilson would set out to fix it — and usually he did.

The outcome wasn't always without angst, as on the occasion a swarm of bees set up home in a tree adjacent to the Whinerays' chimney at their home in Cedar Place, Epsom. The bees started to become an infernal nuisance, especially when they began finding their way down the chimney into the lounge and dining room.

'Leave it to me,' declared Wilson, 'I'll get rid of them.' Contacting a beekeeper was never a consideration.

First, he secured a large cardboard box which he positioned directly under the hive. Then, he cut the branch off, so that the hive fell directly into the box, with masterful precision. Before the bees had a chance to react to their changing world, Wilson slammed the lid shut, sealed it with tape, placed it in the boot of his car and drove off.

The intended destination has never been revealed to the family, but as he progressed down Auckland's southern motorway, Wilson became aware that he was sharing the interior of his car with bees.

Angry bees! The relocation plan wasn't going down too well with the buzzy ones, who'd not only exited their cardboard box but had found a passageway through from the boot. Wilson hastily started opening windows, but it was obvious he was losing the battle. He pulled off the motorway, flicked open the boot, deftly removed the box, and, before the bees could take their revenge, jumped back in the car and sped away!

If the bees had behaved and confined themselves to their own territory, they would probably have survived at Whinerayville, because Wilson was extremely tolerant of animals and insects. He especially loved dogs, and when he was at Auckland Grammar he added some of his own pocket money to a cash present from a family member and bought a springer spaniel puppy, whom he named Ruff.

Ruff would be waiting at the gate with his lead in his mouth when Wilson arrived home from school. Happiness for Ruff was being let loose around the nearby Windmill Road tennis and netball courts, where he had a penchant for sniffing out tennis balls.

Wilson and Ruff developed such a strong bond that not long after Wilson, at 16, left home and took up residence on a farm at Waikaia, Ruff was transported south to join him. When a year later Wilson received his first appointment as a rural farm cadet in the Wairarapa, he realized it was impractical to retain Ruff, so his faithful friend was given to the Waikaia farm-owner's son.

There would be a Ruff 2, many, many years later after Wilson married. Springer spaniels are natural sporting dogs, and Ruff 2 enjoyed nothing more than Wilson's duck-shooting outings.

Between Ruff 1 and Ruff 2, the dogs Wilson was mostly associated with while he completed his rural cadetship were farm dogs. A large part of the time he was based at Stoney Creek in the Wairarapa, he functioned effectively as a shepherd with a pack of five dogs assisting him.

♣

Soon after their return from Boston, the Whinerays purchased a property in Cedar Road in the delightful Auckland inner-city suburb of Epsom, a large, rambling family home with generous areas of garden, to which was added a swimming pool, with scoria retaining-walls built, of course, by Wilson.

The neighbours across the back were Tom and Lorraine Marshall, Tom having followed Wilson through Auckland Grammar School; indeed, after Wilson had toured Ceylon with the New Zealand Colts in 1955, he was invited to address the Auckland Grammar First XV, a team that included Tom Marshall and Wilson's younger brother, Scott.

After a few chats across the back fence, Wilson and Tom decided to facilitate matters by cutting a hole in said fence, and, when Denis and Adrienne Harding moved in immediately beside the Marshalls a couple of years later, it wasn't long before another opening was created.

Tom Marshall was a GP, and Denis Harding, whose property featured a tennis court, was an ear, nose and throat specialist. To say the three families complemented each other would be a severe understatement. They functioned in a marvellous communal atmosphere. The Marshalls and their three kids — Nicky, Hamish and Juliet — and the Hardings and their four sons — Geoff, James, Peter and Cameron — had *carte blanche* access to the Whineray pool; in return, the Harding tennis court was always available to the neighbours when not booked. All three properties were possessed of mature fruit trees, which made for delightful pickings for all the kids when the produce started to ripen.

Having a GP and an ear, nose and throat specialist next door meant first-class medical treatment was instantly available if misfortune befell any of the Whineray clan. When Kristen fell out of an oak tree and broke her arm, Tom Marshall was there in a flash to minister to her needs. And when Susan developed asthma — a mild version of it, fortunately — Tom made certain she received the appropriate medication.

While the three families survived in perfect harmony, there existed an intense rivalry that manifested itself each summer when it came to tomato-growing. No titles were more keenly sought than those annually awarded for the first ripe tomato, the most abundant crop and the biggest single specimen. 'Best at Show' was about to be declared one year when a closer inspection of the whopper in question revealed that the skin of a tomato bought from the fruiterers had been stitched on. Name suppression has been granted to the offending party!

Tom, Denis and Wilson shared a number of projects, including helping to paint each other's houses. On the occasion of the painting of the Whineray house, after morning tea had been served at 10.30, Wilson suddenly declared he was off to golf; not that he was a serious golfer, but there was a celebrity tournament to which he had committed himself.

'Thanks, guys — see you later,' he said, and with a wave disappeared down the driveway, leaving Tom and Denis to complete the chore.

When the three of them were painting Tom's house, Tom fielded a call from the maternity ward. 'Oops,' he said, 'one of my patients is in labour — gotta go.' On this occasion, Wilson and Tom completed the project.

Denis was the only one to put in a full day's toil on his own house!

Back in the 1970s, the three of them were keen squash players and many epic contests took place, until Wilson began complaining of a sore thumb. Unsympathetic, Tom told him to stop complaining.

'It's really sore and uncomfortable,' said Wilson.

Knowing that Wilson had an extremely high pain threshold, Tom arranged for the hand to be X-rayed, which revealed there had been a fracture at the base of the thumb.

'Do you ever recall having a broken thumb?' Tom asked him.

'Well, yes, actually, in South Africa in 1960. That pesky Piet du Toit was giving our team a lot of problems in the Boland game because of his illegal tactics, and to stop him, I clouted him.'

Wilson explained to Tom that he thought at the time that he might have broken the thumb, but he'd never reported it because his team couldn't afford another front-row injury, having lost hooker Ron Hemi in that same Boland game with broken ribs. The record books reveal that Wilson stood down from the 'fifth test' against Northern Transvaal seven days later because of a 'sprained thumb' but played a further eight times on tour, including all four internationals, with his thumb fractured.

The wives of Wilson, Tom and Denis were not only close friends, they all, as it happened, drove Morris Minors. This was in the days when you could run a petrol account at the local service station, which the Whinerays, the Marshalls and the Hardings all did. This led to mild chaos, with workers at the service station regularly confusing the wives. The bills all got paid, but sometimes the Whinerays knew they were writing out a cheque for the Marshalls' or the Hardings' purchases, and vice versa!

Wilson was certainly multi-talented. He watched a programme on television in which various items, from yachts to plants, were inserted through the narrow neck of a bottle and then assembled or permitted to grow, causing wonderment to viewers. Wilson was intrigued and accepted the challenge. After a few unsuccessful experiments he eventually got a fig tree to flourish in the bottle, which drew admiration from visitors.

The title of this book, *A Perfect Gentleman*, might imply that Wilson is indeed a faultless human being, pretty much perfect in every way, and in many respects that is true. However, there was one challenge that Wilson never quite mastered: skiing.

The Turoa Ski Field at Mount Ruapehu came under the Carter Holt Harvey banner, so Wilson, as the then deputy managing director, reasoned it would be entirely appropriate if he and his family checked out its facilities. The kids were naturals, and were soon whizzing this way and that and loving every second of their time on the slippery slopes. Beth also showed herself to be surprisingly adept at the art. But poor Wilson regularly had to admit defeat. The batterings his body had taken working in the outback and being bucked from horses as a youth, and the medial ligament he'd ruptured in Boston in 1968, reduced him to ordinariness on the ski slopes. He could ski, it's true, but his lack of agility and flexibility meant he often came to grief.

He was still prepared to give it a go. For unaccomplished skiers, exiting the chair-lift can represent a traumatic challenge — as Wilson demonstrated in spectacular fashion on one occasion. He got his two skis hopelessly tangled, and, although managing to clear the exit zone before the next skier arrived, found himself slithering uncontrollably down the slope. Some 70 metres later he came to a halt close to a café, where a group of players from his Grammar Old Boys rugby club back in Auckland were milling around.

'Well, hello, boys,' said Wilson, as nonchalantly as possible.

'Hello, Wilson . . . Enjoying your day?'

'Couldn't be better!'

On another occasion at Turoa, when youngest daughter Susan, then a teenager at Epsom Girls Grammar and a pretty cool skier, was trying to impress some boys, who just happened to be from King's College, her father, 50 or so metres up the slope, suddenly lost his footing. Skis, ski pole and Wilson all departed in different directions. Gravity and the slippery slope once again delivered Wilson to an unintended destination, this time just a few metres from Susan, who was putting on her no-I've-never-seen-him-before-in-my-life face.

As Wilson strove manfully to bring himself into a stable, vertical state, he focused on the intrigued audience.

'I'm her father,' he said. 'She doesn't want to admit she knows me.'

♣

The Whinerays often holidayed at Brown's Bay in Auckland's North Shore when the children were young, in the days when a trip across the Auckland Harbour Bridge was still regarded as a novel experience. Because of traffic congestion, most people try to avoid the Harbour Bridge these days. Wilson's sporting and business commitments meant that Beth was the one who heroically got the family organized and safely to their destination and ensured there was sufficient food to feed everyone.

Wilson ultimately became the champion organizer of family holidays at Christmas-time, a role he fulfilled with great energy and efficiency. Around September he would begin scanning newspapers, looking for holiday homes available over the vacation period. Thanks to his diligent research and organization, the family holidayed at such special beach resorts as Taipa, Cooks Beach, Waihau Bay, and even — one summer in partnership with the Hardings — at Arid Island behind Great Barrier. Denis Harding was related to All Black coach Bryce Rope, whose family owned the island. The farmer who managed Arid Island told the Whinerays to pitch their camp at sea level, not atop any of the island's hillocks. They ignored him — and their tent was promptly blown down in the middle of the night. Eventually, Wilson would purchase a holiday home — a bach as North Islanders call them, or a crib in southern lingo — at Matheson's Bay, about 90 minutes' drive north of Auckland. But before then, Wilson and his family enjoyed their summer breaks at a rich variety of destinations, hardly ever returning to the same place twice.

Wilson was the ultimate mentor for his children. He taught them to snorkel and dive, to body-surf, to dig up pipis, and, after acquiring a small boat named *Kapiti*, he also showed them how to water-ski and fish. No matter how many children were on board *Kapiti*, they all experienced the joy of landing a fish, *Kapiti* earning a reputation as a particularly lucky boat. Regardless of how many fish were landed, there never seemed to be more than half a dozen when the Whinerays returned to their base. It was many years before the truth was revealed: Wilson used to recycle the caught specimens when the children weren't looking, reattaching them to the hook. He didn't want any kid to go home without experiencing the thrill of catching a fish!

Ian Smeaton became a dear, personal friend of Wilson's and, ultimately, the whole family. Ian and Wilson had first encountered each other at Auckland Grammar, where they played in the First XV — Ian at prop, Wilson at halfback — extending the friendship when they found themselves as rural field cadets based together at Lincoln College.

Ian ultimately bought a farm at South Kaipara Head, where the Whinerays were always welcome. Truth be known, Wilson would have loved to have farmed, but his career took him away from the land and into high-pressure corporate boardrooms. He relished the opportunity to visit the Smeaton farm, where he would help Ian with his drenching and tailing and fence repairs. The Whinerays would almost always head for South Kaipara as the duck-shooting season approached each year and help Ian build maimais, and, of course, they'd be back on the opening day when Ian and Wilson, with assistance from his trusty dog Ruff 2, would become hopeful hunters.

Often they were joined by Jim Bracewell, Wilson's First XV coach from Auckland Grammar, who became a lifelong friend of both Wilson and Ian. The three of them would often sit on the balcony of Ian's farmhouse in the evening, reviewing and solving many of the world's most challenging problems.

One year, the Whinerays agreed to look after the farm while the Smeatons holidayed in the South Island. Everything went swimmingly until a bull died, which shocked Wilson, who had to dig an exceedingly large hole and, not without a major effort, bury it. He decided not to break the news to Ian until he returned home, not wanting to spoil his holiday.

'I've got some terrible news, Ian, I'm afraid: one of your bulls died.'

'Oh don't worry — that bull had been crook for some time. I didn't expect him to survive long. I should have told you!'

Notwithstanding his rugby and work commitments, Wilson was possessed of great patience and was always available to help his children with their homework. A lesser father would have grumpily redirected his kids towards their mother because he had 'things to do', but Wilson would quietly put his pen down and say, 'Yes, how can I help you?'

He was most animated when the homework challenge involved mathematics, because he was gifted at mental arithmetic and could solve most problems in his head. Percentages and fractions were his particular strength. If the problem involved art or more basic subjects, he would hastily redirect his children to Beth. Art was her strength.

Wilson raised his children to believe they could do anything. He encouraged them all to participate in sport and be part of a team, but wasn't concerned whether they were hugely successful or not. The participating was the important thing.

Wilson appreciated that a son bearing the name of Whineray was always going to be under pressure if he played rugby, as James did, and so he engaged his son in a heart-to-heart discussion when James was beginning to make his way at Auckland Grammar.

'You're not the same build as I was,' said Wilson, 'so therefore you will probably not be so successful. Enjoy your rugby, but don't feel you have to reach the same heights I did.'

Without ever threatening to emulate his father's amazing achievements, James was a talented rugby player in his own right. He represented Auckland West Roller Mills while at primary school, and made it into the Auckland Grammar School First XV in 1978 as a hooker (weighing 11½ stone — 73 kilograms) where his coach was a certain Graham Henry and his teammates included Grant Fox and John Buchan, who would go on to become All Blacks. Under Graham

Henry's astute guidance, and with Foxy already demonstrating the skills that would later have him installed as a rugby legend, they shared the title that season.

When James enrolled at Otago University, initially in search of a degree in medicine but later to complete a commerce degree, he naturally made himself available to the University club rugby selectors. He played one game for University A, against Pirates in the main encounter at Carisbrook — which he regards as the highlight of his playing career — and five games for University B.

James could have persisted and perhaps graduated to rep status, but he took a realistic appraisal of his talents, or more accurately, his attitude. Physically, he considered he wasn't equipped to survive countless poundings in the front row, and, while extended sessions at the gym might have remedied this, he admitted to himself that, frankly, he wasn't hard-nosed enough. Long days of lectures and a cold Dunedin flat somehow weren't compatible with evening training and beer-swilling sessions in the clubhouse afterwards. James concluded that his future lay in business, not in playing rugby. It was a decision he would never regret.

After graduating, he would operate as a money market dealer with NZI before serving as a treasurer for six years with the Owens Group. In 1993, the year his father became chairman of the board, he became assistant treasurer of Carter Holt Harvey, later — over a period of nine years — progressing to investor relations manager and new ventures manager. Since 2004, he has operated as a private advisor for JB Were.

James never severed his links with rugby, and for a number of years turned out for the Grammar Old Boys Restricted (under-85 kilogram) team. Occasionally, just occasionally, he would get his father along for an inspirational team talk.

Wilson probably struggled a little more in dealing with his daughters, having grown up as one of five sons. He certainly found discussions with his son easier than with his daughters, who, as one of them admits, could burst into tears at the drop of a hat.

Yet he gave them just as much love and attention as James. Susan recalls how when she received her first two-wheel bicycle, it sported exactly the same colour purple paint that had speckled her father's fair hair just a few days previously. And whenever Kristen drove her trusty Morris Oxford the near 500 kilometres home from Massey University in Palmerston North, where she was studying to become a vet, Wilson would always insist she check the car in for a service. Out of Kristen's earshot, he would phone the serviceman and instruct him to go over the car with a fine-tooth comb, repair everything, including replacing the rust with fibreglass, and make sure the bill was sent to him.

Kristen studied at Massey University for five years, remarkably boarding in the same hostel her father had stayed in a quarter of a century earlier, and graduated with a degree in veterinary science. She gained experience working on farms, then spent 13 years practising her profession in Auckland. She now works as a consultant in the pharmaceutical world.

Susan studied medical laboratory science at Auckland University of Technology and worked for a number of years in London.

Wilson was knighted at a ceremony at Government House, Wellington, in 1998, the investiture being conducted by the Governor-General Sir Michael Hardie Boys. The citation acknowledged that the award was for his services to business and sport.

It not only represented the climax of a remarkable career as a sportsman and businessman for Wilson, but was also a wonderful occasion for rugby, for never before had an All Black been knighted for his services to the game.

The occasion was celebrated worthily, not publicly, not with women's magazine photographers fighting for the exclusive pic, but in a manner entirely appropriate to a Whineray event, with the achiever surrounded by his family. The children were there, the grandchildren were there, the brothers were there to salute Sir Wilson and Lady Whineray.

Youngest daughter, Susan, was so moved by the occasion that she wrote a poem. It went like this:

THE BALLAD OF SIR COLONEL

A long time ago namely three score and some
We cast back to Epsom where this ballad began
Where number three son out of five lively lads
Were born unto Ida with Bruce as their dad

Legend says Wilson got up to some tricks
So kept busy with sports his energy fixed
But soccer and swimming and boxing and gym
While conquered came second to rugby with him

At fifteen he set off to seek his fortune
He mustered his flock under a high country noon
A love of the farming life beat in his chest
So at Lincoln and Massey he put to the test

By now he impressed by both action and pen
His character mighty, a leader of men
In the national game he was king of the pack
Triumphing far and wide, dressed in All Black

The lovely Beth stole his heart by and by
He wanted to keep her fore'er by his side
So in Palmerston North one March day took her hand
And hurried her back to his native Auckland

Late the next year she bore him a son
And two daughters followed they came one by one
He took to this duty like everything else
Giving only the best of himself

Harvard lay beckoning for fellowship men
Took two years in Boston for Beth and children
Then with AHI his career started to fly
Through CHH Wilson could reach for the sky

Chivalrous deeds long the way he did do
For children and sportsmen and other groups too
For charities and funding he golfed and he spoke
The legend it grew — he was a jolly fine bloke

More precious gems came to Wilson and wife
Grandchildren blessed them a new time of life
Nana and Grandad or 'Joker' to some
Loved them and taught them and treasured their fun

Semi-retired now the game that he chose
Chairman and boards of directors 'mongst those
The SAS chose him as titular head
They called him the Colonel and marched where he led

Queen's Birthday honours duly swung past
They made him a knight many said well at last
For goodness and trueness and work beyond call
The adventurer Knight-Errant shines on us all

We marvel at all of the caps you have worn
Just son, brother, nephew to a few when born
Then captain and Mr and my favourite dad
Joker, Sir Colonel, you're one heck of a lad!

Collectively, Jim, Kristen and Susan had presented their parents with
five grandchildren as of early 2010. Jim has a daughter, Sally (who is
a Year 11 student at Diocesan College); Kristen has two boys, Peter
(who is pursuing a physical education degree at Teachers Training
College) and Alan (a Year 12 student at Auckland Grammar); and
Susan has a daughter, Kendall (a Year 9 student at Diocesan College)
and son, Elliot (who is in Year 6).

Wilson was in the habit of hosting end-of-season parties for his Grammar Old Boys rugby colleagues. They were fun-filled occasions with many of the season's contests being vividly replayed as the partygoers relaxed.

It's fair to say that few rugby players, coaches and officials know when to go home, and Wilson would often have to provide a little encouragement. He didn't favour sergeant-major-type announcements. He was much more subtle. He took to playing records — of Welsh hymns. Loudly. Initially, it worked like magic; but after a time he found his visitors were starting to familiarize themselves with the Welsh music and began singing along. So he switched to records of Martin Luther King speeches — 'I have a dream . . .' — and that got rid of his visitors double-quick!

Had Wilson been so inclined, he could have become a politician. He confessed to radio's National Programme, in a series entitled 'Distinguished New Zealanders', that he was invited by both National and Labour to stand as an MP.

'I don't know if I would have been a good politician,' he told the interviewer. 'I had no aspirations to enter politics. And to be honest, I could never have contemplated being away from my family to work in Wellington.'

However, Wilson was always astutely aware of developments in the business and sporting world and, as it happened back in the early 1970s, in the world of education. When Auckland Grammar School was seeking to appoint a new headmaster in 1973, to replace long-serving Henry Cooper, Wilson thought of his ex-All Black teammate John Graham, who was head of social studies at Linwood High School in Christchurch, and gave him a call.

'Auckland Grammar is re-advertising the principal's position,' said Wilson. 'Why don't you apply?'

John Graham gave him an exceedingly good reason why he wasn't intending to apply — not that he even knew the position was up for grabs — and that was because he'd been turned down by New Plymouth Boys' High School.

'As you know, I'm not a good loser,' he told Wilson, 'and after the New Plymouth experience I vowed I would never apply for another headmaster's position.'

He explained to Wilson what had happened in New Plymouth. 'I missed the job because I refused to answer the way they wanted me to answer. I told them I would not have school councils, that I would rely on the senior boys instead. Then they asked me if I believed in cadets, and I assured them boys loved discipline and cadets were a great way to get them disciplined, as long as it was all part of the education policy. At the conclusion of the interview, they asked me to describe myself and I said, "I'm a dictator." That probably wasn't the smartest answer, although everyone laughed at the time. But they appointed someone else.'

Wilson said he couldn't give any guarantees, but he felt his old rugby mate should apply. 'All I'm doing is trying to help the old school,' said Wilson.

Notwithstanding Wilson's encouragement, Graham didn't rush an application to Auckland. He mulled over the opportunity for several days, finally discussing it with Jim Orman, the principal of Linwood High.

'If I couldn't get New Plymouth, I'm not going to get Auckland Grammar,' he told Orman, who disagreed. 'I think you've got an excellent chance — go for it.'

He did, and as history shows, he won the appointment. It would be 21 years before he would finally step aside as principal of Auckland Grammar, after making a contribution of massive proportions.

In 1994, he would be made a Commander of the Order of the British Empire for services to education and the community, he would serve as the chancellor of the University of Auckland from

1999 to 2004, and in 1999 he would be named New Zealander of the Year by *North and South* magazine. The magazine lauded him as 'All Black captain, headmaster of Auckland Grammar for 21 years, rugby coach, company director, businessman, commissioner of the troubled Nga Tapuwae College, manager of the New Zealand cricket team, Renaissance man and chancellor of the University of Auckland.'

Wilson and John Graham are both men of integrity and conviction. In 1981, they individually decided they would not attend any of the matches played by the Springboks on their tumultuous, extremely controversial, tour of New Zealand. Yet neither went public with their views; indeed, to this day only a minuscule percentage of the population would be aware of their stand. Graham would later say of his trip with the All Blacks to South Africa in 1960 that: 'If we had any conscience or feeling for humanity, we should not have been touring South Africa.'

Wilson has never spoken about his decision to stay away from the 1981 matches. It's not his way. He told his family that he believed the Springbok tour was not good for New Zealand, and for that reason he declined to get himself involved in any way. He made a silent protest.

Three decades on, in his chapter in Gordon McLauchlan's book *Loving All Of It*, Wilson would write: 'I've learnt to be wary of extremists — political, financial, religious, environmental. They create problems, never solve them. But it is important their voices are heard.'

In 1988, 25 years on from the famous 'Willie Away' tour of the United Kingdom and France, a reunion was organized for the All Blacks, an occasion much appreciated by the players. It prompted Auckland journalist Peter Devlin to go into raptures in recalling the team's achievements for the *8 O'Clock*. Wilson's epic try against the

Barbarians was made possible, Devlin asserted, by a gigantic sidestep that completely flummoxed the last defender, Mick Flynn.

Wilson seized the opportunity. His letter to the *8 O'Clock* was published:

> My Dear Devlin
>
> My purpose in entering into correspondence with you is to congratulate you on being the only person as far as I am aware of noticing the sidestep I unleashed on poor Flynn.
>
> Throughout my career, I felt I was under-recognised for my sidestep, which I flashed from time to time, the only possible explanation being that the speed of the manoeuvre was too rapid for human eyes in the days prior to slow-motion replays.
>
> The sidestep was my main attacking weapon and I used it liberally, which accounts for my six tries in 496 senior level or above fixtures.
>
> The secret, which I pass on to you, is left foot over right — then right over left — in such a manner to avoid a reef-knot in the region of the knees, which is not only embarrassing but extremely painful in the region of the groin. I usually wore a cricket box to prevent permanent injury.
>
> Yours,
> Wilson

In addition to his directorships of the National Bank of New Zealand, APN News & Media, Auckland International Airport, and Nestlé NZ, Wilson served on numerous trusts and committees, including the Halberg Trust for Children, the Northern Cochlear Implant Trust, the Wishbone Trust for Orthopaedic Research, Mercy Hospice, the Peter Blake Trust, Business in the Community, Special Olympics, and the Dilworth Trust.

Of these, the one that brought him greatest satisfaction was the Dilworth Trust, where he became involved with children whose families had fallen on troubled times. Wilson would interview the children, some who had lost both parents, and give them guidance and personal encouragement. Often he would take individuals under his wing and be on the sideline for them when they were playing sport. He would comment to his family that he regarded it as the single most important thing he had done in his life.

He stepped aside from the Dilworth Trust only in 2009, after serving it for a full decade. He also a patron of the Palmerston North-based Rugby Museum, a position he has held for more than a decade.

Although rugby is the sport with which Wilson is synonymous, for six years from 1995 he chaired the Hillary Commission, the government-appointed body responsible for providing funding for sporting organizations. He succeeded Sir Ron Scott, and would in turn be replaced by Sir Brian Lochore, who had also followed him into the All Black leadership three decades earlier.

When Wilson first became involved — having to travel to Wellington for meetings — he admitted surprise at finding there were no guidelines as to how the funding should be allocated, and that it wasn't just sporting organizations that were applying for handouts, but rose-growing societies and ham-radio outfits as well. Under his leadership, the Commission became a far more streamlined organization, eventually settling on a formula that allocated one-third of available funding to high-performance sportspeople, and two-thirds to grass-roots sport. At the time Wilson became involved, the Commission received $28 million annually from the government; that figure is now closer to $100 million.

Operating simultaneously with the Hillary Commission, at the time Wilson first became involved, was the New Zealand Sports Foundation, which had been set up by prominent sports administrator Graham Davy with the objective of funding élite sportsmen and sports teams.

Without government funding, the Foundation, chaired in the 1990s by Sir David Beattie — and created with the best of intentions to help New Zealand sportspeople compete on a more level playing field against the likes of Australia, which had an Institute of Sport — relied on grants from charitable institutions to operate. But it suffered a setback of cataclysmic proportions when its CEO, Keith Hancox, the swimmer who had conquered Cook Strait, was found guilty of embezzlement and sentenced to four years' imprisonment, and it eventually folded.

As chairman, Wilson operated under three different Ministers of Sport — John Banks, Murray McCully, and Trevor Mallard — the committee members who served with him being elected at the behest of the government.

♣

Wilson had always held a passionate interest in matters military, and devoured many books and movies on wartime events. So it was not entirely unexpected when in 1997 he was installed as the new titular head of the New Zealand Army's élite Special Air Service (SAS). They made him their colonel commandant.

Appointing a civilian marked a significant break with tradition for the unit, which is housed in high security at the Hobsonville military base northwest of Auckland. His predecessor was Brigadier Ian 'Buzz' Burrows.

Wilson's only previous involvement with the armed forces was as a compulsory military trainee during his youth, although of course his brother Murray was a Vampire jet pilot until his tragically early death in 1967.

Being born in 1935, Wilson had of course grown up during the war years. While New Zealand itself was mercifully distanced from the conflict, there were frequent reminders that endless immunity was never guaranteed. Wilson's family had to endure blackouts, and air-raid drills were practised at school. At the sound of a bell,

Wilson and his classmates headed to a designated area, placed corks between their teeth, put plugs in their ears, and lay face-down until the 'emergency' was over.

From a young age Wilson developed a massive respect for those who fought for his country. He honoured the legacy they left: that freedom had to be valued, defended, and if necessary fought for.

The appointment gave Wilson no command authority, and nor was he entitled to wear the SAS uniform; rather, his new role was as a mentor or patron. He told a reporter he would be supporting from the sidelines. 'These are very fit people, and there is no way I could contemplate taking part,' he said. 'Goodness me, with my knee surgery I doubt I could lead them anywhere.'

The Army chief, Major-General Piers Reid, said he was pleased the SAS could be associated with a civilian who had attained such success in his own field. It had been important to find a successor to Brigadier Burrows who would personify the aims and aspirations of all those who served the unit.

Wilson adapted to his new role passionately and spent many contented times in the SAS soldiers' presence. On one memorable occasion they decided to treat him to some real-life SAS drama, a small group kidnapping him and secreting him away in a military base. He was eventually rescued after a smoke-bomb attack!

Wilson had many personal conversations with Willie Apiata, the SAS corporal who became the first recipient of the Victoria Cross for New Zealand (replacing the British Victoria Cross), his medal being awarded for bravery under fire during the Afghanistan conflict in 2004.

Apiata, who was 32 at the time, carried a gravely wounded comrade across a battlefield under fire to safety. He was part of a small group who were being attacked by some 20 enemy fighters. They were holed up for the night in a remote, rocky area. Rocket-propelled grenades had destroyed one of their vehicles and immobilised another. This was followed by sustained machine-gun and automatic rifle fire.

A grenade blew Apiata off the vehicle where he had been sleeping. Two other soldiers were wounded by shrapnel, one — a corporal — seriously. He had life-threatening arterial bleeding. Apiata assumed command, deciding all three needed to rejoin their troops 70 metres to the rear. Apiata decided his only option was to carry the corporal to safety. None of the three was hit during the retreat. Apiata rejoined the firefight after getting the corporal to safety.

The marvellous camaraderie that exists among All Blacks past and present was never better exemplified than in 2001, when a luncheon was organized at Eden Park in honour of Don 'The Boot' Clarke, who had been diagnosed with cancer.

Clarke had lived in South Africa for 25 years, and, although he had kept in touch with some of his former teammates, he had largely become isolated from New Zealand rugby. But when the news broke that he had melanoma, the irrepressible Pat Walsh — his teammate against the 1956 Springboks and 1959 Lions, and on the tour of the United Kingdom and France in 1963–64 — sprung into action.

What a luncheon it was, with 480 attending, more than 80 of them former All Blacks. Some said it was the greatest collection of All Blacks ever assembled. There were even a couple of Wallabies, Des Connor and Terry Curley, in attendance.

Clarke's omnipotence as a fullback and goal-kicker was recalled by several speakers. Sir Brian Lochore talked of getting off the All Black bus, scanning lines of autograph-hunters, and saying, 'Don Clarke is coming.' He was a bigger attraction even than Whineray, Meads, Tremain and the rest.

Joseph Romanos, reviewing the event in the *New Zealand Listener*, described Wilson's performance as 'magnificent'.

> He rated Clarke and Meads as the two special players of his time. After singing along to the strains of 'Scottish Soldier' Whineray spoke of the opening scene of *Chariots of Fire* and the line: It doesn't seem

so long ago that we had wings on our heels and hope in our hearts. That brought a lump to the throat. Whineray described Clarke as the team anchor at fullback, a top gun as a kicker and real treasure. He mentioned a few of Clarke's most memorable performances — the six penalty goals in the 18–17 win over the Lions at Dunedin in 1959, his pinpoint kicking in the inferno of test rugby in South Africa in 1960, the incredible match-winning conversion against France during an Athletic Park gale in 1961. In an afternoon of fine speeches, Whineray's stood out. As Clarke said, 'When you see your captain shedding a few tears, it makes you feel very, very humble.'

Clarke died in Johannesburg 16 months later.

Wilson was chuffed when his old Grammar Old Boys club invited him along to present jerseys to a team of kids aged 12 and 13 who had adopted the name Grammar Whineray. Although Grammar and Carlton had amalgamated and operated as Grammar Carlton, with some of the younger grades the two clubs retained their original identity.

Around the time Wilson turned up to make the presentation, the Blues, under Pat Lam's guidance, were enduring a fearful run in the Super 14, losing more matches than they were winning. They weren't playing well, and that was being reflected in the results. Before the boys commenced training in their new jerseys, Wilson addressed the assembly.

'Have you boys been watching the Blues?'

The answer was almost a unanimous yes.

'They haven't been going too well, have they?' said Wilson. 'What do you think the problem is?'

The hands went up.

'They keep dropping the ball.'

'They can't tackle.'

'They can't catch the ball.'

'They lose too many turnovers.'

'They're not scoring tries.'

'So,' said Wilson. 'If you drop the ball, don't tackle, can't catch the ball, concede turnovers and don't score tries, you're not going to win games, are you?'

'No.'

'Well, let me tell you, you win games by scoring more points than the opposition. But that's the tricky part — how do you score more points? You do it by eliminating mistakes, playing the game at the other team's end of the field and supporting the player next to you.

'Righto, guys, good luck for the season ahead.'

In February 2010, Wilson took great delight in attending his old All Black coach Fred Allen's 90th birthday celebration. The function was held in the Auckland Town Hall, and more than 150 went along to honour the great man. Like the Don Clarke luncheon nine years earlier, it was a hugely nostalgic occasion.

Allen in his prime was renowned for goading individuals into action. Wilson recalled an occasion at Hataitai Park in Wellington in 1965, in the lead-up to the inter-island game, when Fred, one year out from becoming All Black coach and dealing with the nation's élite players for the first time, had a captive audience prior to training. He gave both barrels to Kevin Briscoe for a recent shoddy performance, he lambasted Colin Meads for not jumping in the lineouts, assuring him not even a thin book would slide under his feet when he was supposedly airborne, he heaped scorn on Kel Tremain, insisting he was more of a spectator at the breakdowns than a competitor, and he told Bruce McLeod he'd been running around in games like a chook with his head cut off. It was one of Fred's most rip-roaring sessions.

Barry Thomas, a powerful prop, had been preparing for the All Black trial that was featuring as curtain-raiser to the North–South game, but had been summoned to join Fred's North Island team following an injury to Ken Gray. When he was still 50 metres away from the clubrooms at Hataitai Park, Thomas could hear Allen berating his players. Of course, he was well familiar with Allen's often boisterous sessions, having been part of his Auckland team since 1958.

Just as Thomas was entering the room, Allen boomed, 'And where's that bloody Barry Thomas?'

In the interests of self-preservation, Thomas swivelled around and tiptoed back out of the room. Unfortunately, the sniggers of a couple of the players alerted Allen to his whereabouts. Allen advanced through the door into the changing room, where Thomas was trying to make himself invisible behind a tackle bag.

'Oh, there you are, Fred. I wasn't sure whether you wanted me at the meeting or not.'

'Get in there!'

Thomas trudged in reluctantly to take his medicine.

Actually, it can now be revealed that the very same Barry 'Bear' Thomas is the individual who gave Fred Allen the nickname of 'The Needle'. In fact, it has grated with Thomas down the years that other people have been given the credit.

'It all started,' says Thomas, 'when I was in the Auckland third grade representative side and we had a manager named Fred Audley who was tall and thin — needle-like. So I called him Fred the Needle, which was kind of a play on words, as in Thread the Needle. When I progressed to the Auckland team and finished up with a coach called Fred, being one of the troublemakers down the back of the bus, I started calling him Fred the Needle. Others picked it up and it stuck — and became terribly appropriate the more he needled players.'

Late in the evening at Fred Allen's party, a photographer managed to organize a special pic of Fred with rugby's three distinguished knights — Sir Brian Lochore, Sir Colin Meads, and Wilson. As he was coaxing the four into position, the photographer said to Fred

Allen, 'These three have been knighted — how come you haven't?'

Pinetree Meads replied on Fred's behalf: 'He should have been the first one knighted.'

And no one disagreed with that.

In a fitting footnote to this story, Fred Allen received his knighthood in the 2010 Queen's Birthday Honours List, appropriately becoming the fourth New Zealand rugby person so honoured.

In 2010, when it seemed there were precious few honours left to bestow on Wilson, he was presented with an honorary doctorate from the University of Waikato. The citation said he was recognized for the outstanding contributions made to New Zealand rugby and New Zealand business. 'He has demonstrated leadership, commitment and outstanding service in both the sporting and business fields.'

Wilson and Beth live a comfortable existence in a stylish apartment in one of Auckland's more charming suburbs, Remuera. Although it is just a gentle walk from the main shopping complex, it's fair to say that with his creaky knees, hips and back, Wilson doesn't indulge in excess walking these days.

As he's matured, Wilson has come to appreciate art, music, ballet and opera. He's been to many of the world's great art galleries and watched most of the classic operas and ballets.

In the enlightening chapter he wrote for Gordon McLauchlan's book *Loving All Of It* in 2010, Wilson describes himself as happy and optimistic. 'I'm happy because I've had a rich, interesting life with nothing of moment unfulfilled — other than flying a glider, making a parachute jump, playing an instrument and painting a decent picture. I've grown with time to appreciate the treasures of art, music, ballet and opera. My own attempts at painting were dismal, but I had the reward of being able to further appreciate art once I realised how hard it was.'

The perfect day for Wilson in his 75th year is receiving and answering his emails, watching (courtesy of MySky — he's no technophile, but he can operate MySky) any significant rugby fixture that has been played in the middle of the night, reading the *New Zealand Herald* and a selection of newspapers worldwide online (including *The Times*, the *Guardian* and the *New York Times*), sharing lunch and conversation with his darling Beth, sharing time with his children and grandchildren (and their pets) when they call in, and drinking wine with his dinner. His radio station of choice is the National Programme.

Although neither Wilson nor Beth consume much red meat these days, if asked to declare his favourite meal for a special occasion, Wilson will almost always nominate steak — cooked medium/rare.

While he loves reliving memorable moments and solving the present-day problems confronting All Black selectors and the government, when left alone he will more often than not gravitate to television's History channel if there's no compelling sporting event demanding his attention. *Midsomer Murders* and *M*A*S*H* are two of his favourite TV programmes.

He's been a prolific reader of books, with a preference for non-fiction works, but these days he is mostly content to immerse himself in a good detective story, his current favourite — along with countless millions around the globe — being Lee Child's Jack Reacher thrillers.

When socializing, he never forgets names, he has a wonderful way of putting others at ease and leaving them feeling special. And always, he keeps a protective eye on Beth, his Beth.

He really is . . . a perfect gentleman.

FOR THE RECORD

FIRST-CLASS APPEARANCES BY SIR WILSON WHINERAY

Team	Matches
New Zealand	77
Wairarapa	3
Mid Canterbury	9
Manawatu	7
Canterbury	16
Waikato	7
Auckland	61
South Island	1
North Island	6
New Zealand Colts	8
North Island Colts	1
New Zealand Under-23	9
New Zealand Under-23 trial	1
New Zealand XV	2
New Zealand trials	15
New Zealand Universities	4
North Island Universities	1
South Island Universities	2
Wilson Whineray XV	2
South Africa Jubilee games	3
New Zealand Barbarians	3
Centurions	2
Total	**240**

SIR WILSON WHINERAY'S ALL BLACK RECORD

Date	Opponent	Result
1957		
May 18	v New South Wales, Sydney	won 19–3
May 25	v Australia, Sydney	won 25–11
May 28	v Queensland, Brisbane	won 30–0
June 1	v Australia, Brisbane	won 22–9
June 5	v New England, Gunnedah	won 38–14
June 15	v ACT, Canberra	won 40–8
June 17	v Australian Barbarians, Sydney	won 23–6
June 26	v South Australia, Adelaide	won 51–3
June 29	v Canterbury, Christchurch	lost 9–11
1958		
August 23	v Australia, Wellington	won 25–3
September 6	v Australia, Christchurch	lost 3–6
September 20	v Australia, Auckland	won 17–8
1959		
July 18	v British Lions, Dunedin	won 18–17
August 15	v British Lions, Wellington	won 11–8
August 29	v British Lions, Christchurch	won 22–8
September 19	v British Lions, Auckland	lost 6–9
1960		
May 14	v New South Wales, Sydney	won 27–0
May 17	v NSW Country, Orange	won 38–6
May 28	v Northern Universities, Potchefstroom	won 45–6
May 31	v Natal, Durban	drew 6–6
June 8	v South West Africa, Windhoek	won 27–3

June 11	v Boland, Wellington	won 16–0
June 25	v South Africa, Johannesburg	lost 0–13
June 29	v Rhodesian XV, Kitwe	won 13–9
July 6	v Orange Free State, Bloemfontein	lost 8–9
July 9	v Junior Springboks, Durban	won 20–6
July 16	v Western Province, Cape Town	won 20–8
July 23	v South Africa, Cape Town	won 11–3
July 30	v Eastern Transvaal, Springs	won 11–6
August 3	v SA Combined Services, Pretoria	lost 3–8
August 9	v Western Transvaal, Potchefstroom	won 28–3
August 13	v South Africa, Bloemfontein	drew 11–11
August 20	v Border, East London	won 30–3
August 27	v South Africa, Port Elizabeth	lost 3–8
October 1	v Rest of New Zealand, Wellington	won 20–8

1961

July 22	v France, Auckland	won 13–6
August 5	v France, Wellington	won 5–3
August 19	v France, Christchurch	won 32–3

1962

May 16	v Central West, Bathurst	won 41–6
May 19	v New South Wales, Sydney	lost 11–12
May 26	v Australia, Brisbane	won 20–6
June 4	v Australia, Sydney	won 14–5
June 9	v Southern NSW, Canberra	won 58–6
August 25	v Australia, Wellington	drew 9–9
September 8	v Australia, Dunedin	won 3–0
September 22	v Australia, Auckland	won 16–8

1963–1964

May 25	v England, Auckland	won 21–11
June 1	v England, Christchurch	won 9–6
October 23	v Oxford University, Oxford	won 19–3
October 30	v Newport, Newport	lost 0–3
November 2	v Neath & Aberavon, Port Talbot	won 11–6
November 9	v London Counties, Twickenham	won 27–0
November 13	v Cambridge University, Cambridge	won 20–6
November 16	v South of Scotland, Hawick	won 8–0
November 23	v Cardiff, Cardiff	won 6–5
November 30	v South West Counties, Exeter	won 38–6
December 3	v Midland Counties, Coventry	won 37–9
December 7	v Ireland, Dublin	won 6–5
December 14	v Swansea, Swansea	won 16–9
December 21	v Wales, Cardiff	won 6–0
December 28	v Midland Counties, Leicester	won 14–6
December 31	v Llanelli, Llanelli	won 22–8
January 4	v England, Twickenham	won 14–0
January 11	v North East Counties, Harrogate	won 17–11
January 14	v North of Scotland, Aberdeen	won 15–3
January 18	v Scotland, Edinburgh	drew 0–0
January 22	v Leinster, Dublin	won 11–8
January 25	v Ulster, Belfast	won 24–5
February 1	v France B, Toulon	won 17–8
February 5	v South West France, Bordeaux	won 23–0
February 8	v France, Paris	won 12–3
February 15	v Barbarians, Cardiff	won 36–3
February 24	v British Columbia, Vancouver	won 39–3

1965

July 31	v South Africa, Wellington	won 6–3
August 21	v South Africa, Dunedin	won 13–0
September 4	v South Africa, Christchurch	lost 16–19
September 18	v South Africa, Auckland	won 20–3

IRB HALL OF FAME

2006 INDUCTEES

Ellis, William Webb
See Chapter 12.

Rugby School
See Chapter 12.

2007 INDUCTEES

Craven, Danie

Dr Danie Craven was for several decades the face of South African rugby. That was long after he had won recognition as the best player in the world, a scrum-half who perfected the dive pass but who played tests in three other positions, including No. 8!

The South African selectors boldly chose him for the 1931–32 tour of Great Britain as a 20-year-old before he had played provincial rugby. He made his test debut against Wales, after which Syd Nicholls, brother of former All Black captain Mark Nicholls, described it as the best game he had ever seen played by a halfback in an international match. 'He carried South Africa on his shoulders,' he said. Craven played two more tests on that tour, and remained South Africa's first-choice scrum-half until the outbreak of war in 1939 curtailed his career.

He starred in the Springboks' series win against the All Blacks in 1937 — many regarding that Bok team as one of the finest ever to tour New Zealand — and again in the series triumph over the 1938 British Lions.

When the Springboks resumed international play following the war, after a break of more than a decade, Craven was the coach. Under his guidance, the Springboks played 23 tests, winning 17. They whitewashed Fred Allen's All Blacks in 1949, then swept through Great Britain in 1951–52, losing just one match. Not until the momentous tour of New Zealand in 1956 did his team experience a series loss.

He was president of the South African Rugby Board from 1956 until his death in 1993; he was a coaching guru, an innovator, a lawmaker of renown, and, as Paul Dobson wrote in his book, *The Chosen,* 'When Danie Craven spoke, world rugby sat down, shut up and listened.'

De Coubertin, Pierre

New Zealanders are well familiar with the achievements of Craven, Eales, Edwards, and their own hero Wilson, but most would be surprised to find de Coubertin (the legendary founder of the modern Olympic Games) featuring in a rugby context. Yet his contribution to the game, most significantly in France, was massive. Having learnt the game at Rugby School in the 1880s, he became fascinated with it and promoted it vigorously back in France, chairing the commission that led the campaign to have rugby accepted by schools, clubs and government. He instigated the expansion of rugby among leading schools in Paris, refereed the first French championship final in 1892, helped organize the earliest French tours to England and Scotland, wrote valuable articles about the game, and promoted it vigorously.

An historian and essayist, he wrote intriguingly that what was admirable about rugby was 'the perpetual mix of individualism and discipline, the necessity for each man to think, anticipate, take a decision and at the same time subordinate one's reasoning, thoughts and decisions to those of the captain. Foot-ball is truly the reflection of life, a lesson experimenting in the real world, a first-rate educational tool'.

Largely through his efforts, rugby was included in the Olympic Games in 1900 at Paris, 1908 at London, 1920 at Antwerp and 1924 at Paris. Significantly, following his retirement from the Olympic movement in 1925, rugby was dropped from the Olympic programme.

Eales, John

John Eales was a freak, you would have to concede. Most players who stand 2.01 metres tall (6 feet 7 inches) know their place in rugby, which is invariably in the middle of the lineout and the second row of the scrum. They're rarely the captain, they're certainly never the goal-kicker, and they're seldom the hero.

But Eales was every one of those things. There wasn't anything he couldn't do. One of the most successful captains the game has known, he's one of only six players, as of 2010, to celebrate two World Cup triumphs, the others being fellow Wallabies Tim Horan, Jason Little, Phil Kearns and Dan Crowley, and Springbok Os du Randt.

Starting in 1991 against Wales, he made 86 test appearances for the Wallabies, the record until George Smith overtook him, and was given the nickname of Nobody — as in 'Nobody's Perfect'.

With Eales at the helm, the Wallabies dominated the Bledisloe Cup contests from 1998 to 2001, the All Blacks not winning the prized trophy back until after Eales had retired, and he achieved Australia's first series win over the British Lions.

Not only did Eales captain Australia on 55 occasions, he scored 173 points in his international career from two tries, 34 penalty goals and 61 conversions, making him the highest-scoring forward in the history of the game. New Zealanders will never forget the wide-angle penalty goal he kicked in injury time (when Australia's first-choice kicker Stirling Mortlock was off the field with cramp) to deny the All Blacks victory and, as it turned out, the Bledisloe

Cup, at Wellington in 2001.

The John Eales Medal is awarded annually to the best Australian rugby player, and in 1999 he was made a Member of the Order of Australia for his services to rugby and the community. He is a founder of Mettle Group, a cultural and leadership consultancy, while his own company is John Eales 5, part of International Quarterback, a sports marketing and events company.

Edwards, Gareth

In 2003, a poll of international rugby players, conducted by *Rugby World* magazine, selected Welsh halfback Gareth Edwards as the greatest player of all time. And in 2007, Will Carling listed his 50 greatest rugby players in the *Daily Telegraph* and placed Edwards at number one. 'He was a supreme athlete with supreme skills, the complete package,' said Carling. 'He sits astride the whole of rugby as the ultimate athlete on the pitch.'

First capped against France in Paris at the tender age of 19, in 1967, Edwards won 53 caps in succession for Wales before his career ended in 1978. He captained Wales on 13 occasions; the first time, against Scotland in 1968, at the age of 20.

A brilliant finisher blessed with great pace and strength, he scored 20 test tries, and created countless others. He combined brilliantly with Barry John and Phil Bennett, and had a major influence on Wales dominating the Five Nations, winning five titles, including three Grand Slams, in seven years.

He played 10 times for the British Lions, sharing in the groundbreaking series victory over the All Blacks in 1971, and starring in the amazing unbeaten tour of South Africa three years later, when the Lions won the first three tests 12–3, 28–9 and 26–9, before drawing the final test 13-all.

Leading South African rugby scribe Gerhard Burger wrote of Edwards's second test performance at Pretoria that 'in demoralising the home team with tactical kicking and passes which put Phil Bennett miles out of reach, he was once again the Lions' hero'.

The try he scored for the Barbarians against the All Blacks at Cardiff in 1973 is arguably the greatest try ever scored; it came from a move started near the Barbarians' goalposts. In 2001, he was voted the Greatest Welsh Player of All Time, and there is a sculpture of him in St David's Centre, Cardiff. These days, he commentates on international matches, serves as a director of Cardiff Blues, is a director of the Mercedes dealership, Euro Commercials Ltd, and is president of the Cardiff Institute for the Blind.

Whineray, Wilson
See Chapter 12.

2008 INDUCTEES

Kyle, Jack
Dr Jack Kyle is so revered as a player in Ireland that in 2002 the Irish Rugby Union named him the Greatest Ever Irish Rugby Player, and given that this is a nation that has produced such imposing performers as Willie John McBride, Syd Millar and Mike Gibson, that's quite something.

Kyle studied medicine at Queen's University, Belfast, graduating in 1951, the year following his successful tour of New Zealand and Australia with the British Lions. The *New Zealand Rugby Almanack*, edited at the time by Arthur Carman, Read Masters and Arthur Swan, named him one of the players of the year. Of the gifted fly-half, who appeared in 20 of the 29 matches on tour, they wrote: 'Quickly establishing his reputation as the outstanding genius of the British Isles side, Kyle enjoyed a most successful New Zealand tour. He was primarily an excellent team man. The fact he so often measured up as in the class of AE 'Bert' Cooke and other stars of the past, indicates the impression he left behind — the complete footballer.'

Kyle, who first represented Ireland during the war years, made 46 test appearances from 1947 to 1958. He is credited with masterminding Ireland's Grand Slam success in 1948, Ireland also achieving the Triple Crown in 1949 and 1951.

After he scored a spectacular solo try against France in 1953, one journalist was inspired to pen this poem:

> They seek him here, they seek him there
> Those Frenchies seek him everywhere
> That paragon of pace and guile
> That damned elusive Jackie Kyle

After retiring from rugby, Dr Kyle did humanitarian work in Sumatra and Indonesia and later worked as a consultant surgeon in Zambia. In 1991, he was awarded an honorary doctorate by Queen's University and in 2007 received a Lifetime Achievement Award from the *Irish Journal of Medical Science* and the Royal Academy of Medicine in Ireland.

The Melrose Club and Ned Haig

Ned Haig wasn't thinking about greatness when he came up with his Sevens rugby concept in the 1880s. The Melrose club, which he had joined after moving from Jedburgh to work as a butcher, was in danger of going broke and his novel idea was purely to help the club allay its financial difficulties.

'Want of money made us rack our brains as to what was to be done to keep the club from going to the wall,' he would write two decades on. 'The idea struck me that a football tournament might prove attractive, but it was hopeless to think of having several games in one afternoon with fifteen players on each side. So teams were reduced to seven with matches lasting just fifteen minutes.'

Originally, the seven comprised a fullback, two quarter-backs and four forwards, but with the development of the running game, forwards were cut to three.

In the inaugural Melrose tournament, which took place in 1883, Melrose, as the fresher team, defeated Gala in the final, but not without controversy. After 15 minutes, no points had been scored, so it was agreed an extra 15 minutes would be played. After 10 minutes, D Sanderson scored a try for Melrose, whereupon the Melrose players left the field. Their right to do so was challenged by Gala on the grounds the game was not finished. However, the referee ruled in Melrose's favour.

The seven teams that participated in that original Sevens competition — which was part of a wider sports day — were Melrose, Gala, Selkirk, St Cuthbert's, Earlston, St Ronans and Gala Forest. The immediate success of the tournament meant other clubs in the Borders region set up their own Sevens tournaments.

Ned Haig, who lived to the ripe old age of 81, was part of the Melrose team that won. Though not originally enthusiastic about rugby when he first came to the town, he cemented a place in Melrose's senior team and went on to represent South.

Porta, Hugo

Hugo Porta was a player in a million, an individual who almost single-handedly guided Argentina from obscurity to world standing as a rugby nation. If it seemed his international career went on forever, it effectively did. He played his first test for the Pumas against Chile as a 20-year-old and incredibly made his farewell test appearance against a World XV in Buenos Aires in 1999, at the gentlemanly age of 48! By then, he had served a term as Argentina's ambassador to South Africa and been appointed Argentina's sport minister.

Porta was talented enough to play soccer at the highest level, but chose rugby instead, to the everlasting benefit of Argentinian and world rugby. In 1985 he won his country's Sportsman of the Year award, an amazing achievement in a soccer-mad nation.

Porta's massive contribution to Pumas rugby is vividly illustrated statistically. In the 60 tests he played for his country, he personally accounted for 49 per cent of the points scored, his tally including 11 tries and 26 dropped goals. Of those 60 tests, 27 were won, 28 lost and five drawn. One of the draws was against the All Blacks in Buenos Aires in 1985 when three second-half dropped goals by Porta, all of them magnificent efforts, allowed his team to come from nine points down to finish level at 21-all.

Sella, Phillipe

The most test appearances by a centre for the All Blacks is 54 by Frank Bunce, so for Philippe Sella, the dasher from Agen, to appear in 111 internationals (the first half-dozen, admittedly, as a winger) is truly remarkable and demonstrates amazing resilience. When he finally quit the international scene and moved across the Channel to play for Saracens, he had made more test match appearances than any player in the history of the game.

French coach Jacques Fouroux described Sella as a player with 'the strength of a bull and the touch of a piano player'. He scored 30 test tries, his favourite the 70-metre intercept effort to beat England at Twickenham in 1957. He is one of only five players to score a try in every game during a Five Nations season. He played in the inaugural World Cup final at Eden Park in 1987, contributed to France's historic series victory over the All Blacks in 1994, and shared in six Five Nation championship wins.

Warbrick, Joe; and the New Zealand Native team

When it comes to trail-blazers there is nothing to compare with the 1888 New Zealand Native team, which was boldly pieced together by an English businessman, Tom Eyton, and a talented rugby player of nomadic tendencies, Joe Warbrick. Warbrick, who hailed from Rotorua but who also played rugby in Auckland, Wellington and Hawke's Bay, featured as organizer, selector and captain of the Natives.

The original concept was for a New Zealand Maori team to tour, but when several contenders dropped out, Eyton and Warbrick — who'd toured with the first All Black team to Australia in 1884 — chose five Pakeha who looked Maori to complete the touring party of 26. The tour cost each player £62.

If this seemed exorbitant, what an experience lay ahead for those who toured. After 16 matches in Melbourne, 15 of which were won, the team sailed for the United Kingdom, helping out in the boiler room! The team played 74 matches in England, Ireland, Scotland and Wales. It wasn't the same structured, high-tempo rugby game we know today. When hail teemed down during the second half of the match at Carlisle, the backs donned raincoats, and such was the hospitality prior to the Middlesex game at Lord Sheffield's estate, that several players were inebriated when the game kicked off. Their condition would hardly have improved when champagne was served at half-time!

So rigorous was the itinerary that the team rarely had more than 20 fit players, yet lost only 20 of the 74 matches it played in the United Kingdom. Tries at the time were worth one point; conversions two; and penalty goals, dropped goals and goals from a mark three points. Davey Gage, an iron man if ever there was one, took the field in 68 of the 74 matches in the United Kingdom.

Warbrick, whose involvement was restricted because of injuries, died at the age of 41 while working as a guide in Rotorua. He was one of four people killed when the Waimungu Geyser erupted unexpectedly.

2009 INDUCTEES

du Preez, Frik

Frik du Preez stood just 6 foot 2 inches (1.9 metres) tall, so it's hard to understand how he became an international lock. Even in the 1960s, when he played most of his 38 tests, he was typically 10 centimetres shorter than most of his lineout opponents. But he possessed extraordinary athleticism that allowed him to out-jump them. And such was his pace, he could stay with, or even outrun, most backs.

Danie Craven described him as a back and forward rolled into one. 'To my mind, he could have played anywhere on the field with equal brilliance,' said South Africa's Mr Rugby. Which is why Andy Colquhoun and Paul Dobson, in ranking their 50 greatest Springboks of all time in their wonderful book, *The Chosen*, placed Du Preez at number two (behind only Danie Gerber). In a poll of newspaper readers in the Republic in 2000 he was named South African Player of the Century.

He competed against and ranked alongside the two other commanding locks of his era, Colin Meads and Willie John McBride. But he could do something they never managed — kick goals. Remarkably, on his test debut, against England at Twickenham in 1962, he was entrusted with the goal-kicking, landing a conversion from the sideline. And in his second test he kicked two penalty goals against Scotland.

Heatlie, 'Fairy'

'Fairy' Heatlie is regarded as the greatest forward produced by South Africa, and that's saying something given some of the mighty individuals who have taunted the All Blacks down the years. A massive man for his era, significantly taller and heavier than his adversaries — he stood 1.91 metres and weighed 95 kilograms — he gave South Africa its myrtle green jersey. Not that it was easy to find a jersey to fit him back in the 1890s when he first played for South Africa. All the photos of the time suggest the jerseys he wore were at least one size too small.

He was still a student at Bishops College in Cape Town, aged

19, when first selected to play against the 1891 British touring team. He remains, well over a century later, the youngest forward to play for his country. In 1896, when Britain toured again, he was made captain for the final test in Cape Town. With the captaincy went the right to select the team as well as the jersey to be worn. As Paul Dobson wrote in *The Chosen*, he got it monumentally right! The colours he chose, predominantly green, were those of his club, Old Diocesans. A decade later, those colours were adopted by the South African Rugby Board.

And that unflattering nickname? It apparently related to a comment by one of his teachers one day: 'Whose fairy footsteps do I hear?'

McBride, Willie John

Willie John McBride, the other great Ballymena international, who infamously decked Pinetree Meads in the Irish test in 1963 — after which Wilson hauled Meads to his feet, saying, 'Come on, don't let him know you're injured' — wasn't a player to be trifled with. He belonged to the get-your-retaliation-in-first school; in fact, he may have been their patron saint!

McBride was the captain of the British Lions team to South Africa in 1974, a team renowned for two sensational happenings: an unbeaten sweep of the series against the once invincible Springboks, and the infamous 999 call that provoked scenes of mayhem on the field. Aware that the Springboks, the forwards in particular, had intimidated more than a few previous touring teams, McBride's Lions decided to get their retaliation in first. In those delightfully 'innocent' amateur days before touch judges and video umpires began monitoring foul play, the referee was the sole judge of on-field incidents. Reasoning that no referee — and this was in the days when home-town arbiters controlled internationals in their own countries — would order an entire pack of forwards from the field, the Lions decided the best way to defuse aggression from the opposition was to attack each and every Springbok forward simultaneously!

You can just imagine the chaos. The moment the Lions felt a Springbok had stepped over the line, in terms of aggression, 999 was called, a signal to each and every Lions forward to lay into his opponent. In some respects, it was the rugby equivalent of the infamous 'bodyline' series in cricket. It certainly flummoxed the Springboks, not to mention the referee, and unquestionably played a part in enabling McBride's team to complete the 22-match tour undefeated.

McBride, who didn't play rugby until he was 17 because his father died when he was five, possessed skill, strength and resilience in copious quantities, appearing in 80 test matches (25 more than Meads), a record for a lock. He made five tours with the British Lions, a record later equalled by another Irish player, Mike Gibson. McBride went on to coach Ireland and manage the 1983 Lions to New Zealand, and in 2004 was named Heineken Rugby Personality of the Century.

McGeechan, Ian

Ian McGeechan, a high-achieving Scotsman, is synonymous with the British Lions; indeed, no other individual has contributed more to the Lions' cause. He played for them in 1974 and 1977, coached them in 1989, 1993, 1997 and 2009, and was one of Sir Clive Woodward's assistant coaches in New Zealand in 2005. But he is first and foremost a Scot, having represented his country in 32 tests at fly-half and centre from 1972. In nine of those tests he was the captain. He was at centre in all four tests in the Lions' amazing unbeaten trek through South Africa in 1974.

McGeechan, a schoolteacher when rugby wasn't intruding, also coached Scotland to Grand Slam glory in 1990 — and that's something that doesn't happen often! — as well as guiding the Wasps to the Anglo-Welsh title in 2005 and Heineken Cup glory a year later.

Maclagan, Bill

Bill Maclagan is one of the grand old men of Scottish rugby. Born way back in 1858, when New Zealand was barely settled by Europeans, he had the distinction of playing in the first Calcutta Cup match against England in 1879. That game might have been played a couple of years earlier, but England had refused to join the IRB when it was formed in 1887 because it was still fuming over a disputed try in the 1884 contest against Scotland, which had resulted in a major fallout between the two unions.

Maclagan, who played most of his rugby on the wing, captained the first British Isles team on tour, to South Africa in 1891. He returned in triumph, his team winning all 20 of its matches, Maclagan appearing in 19 of them. Prior to departure for South Africa, aboard the *Cunard Castle*, Maclagan was presented with a handsome gold cup by the head of the Castle Shipping Line, Donald Currie, with the request that his team present it to the opponent that produced the best performance. Well, none of the South African sides managed a victory but, in the opinion of Maclagan's side, Griqualand West turned in the best effort, so they were duly awarded the Currie Cup. Griqualand West most honourably bequeathed the beautiful trophy to the South African Board for inter-provincial competition. The Currie Cup has been South Africa's premier rugby trophy ever since.

Maclagan, a stockbroker, settled in London in 1880 and helped establish the London Scottish club, as a player and official.

Millar, Syd

Millar represented Ireland in 37 tests as a specialist prop and made nine appearances for the British Lions. He played at club level until his mid-40s. As a coach, his finest achievement was in guiding the Lions (captained by another Ballymena man, Willie John McBride) through their undefeated tour of South Africa in 1974, when a controversial refereeing decision in the final test, which ended in a 13-all draw, denied them a clean sweep of the series. He returned to South Africa in 1980 as manager of the Lions, and also managed Ireland at the inaugural World Cup in New Zealand in 1987.

He has recently retired after serving as chairman of the IRB.

Precious few 'foreigners' receive France's highest decoration, the Légion d'honneur, but Millar managed it, joining a select group that includes Winston Churchill, Sean Connery, Arsene Wenger, Bono, and Elizabeth Arden. He received the award at a ceremony at the Ballymena Rugby Club in Northern Ireland, the presentation being made by Bernard Lapasset, his successor as IRB chairman.

He's been involved with the game for more than 50 years, two new hips and a triple bypass not diminishing his commitment and passion for the game he loves. He's been granted the freedom of the town of Ballymena, prompting Gerald Davies to say that wherever he goes he takes Ballymena with him.

Morgan, Cliff

Although Wilson's CV shows that he landed a dropped goal in a match in France in 1964, neither Pinetree nor Willie John ever contemplated such a thing. Their role in rugby was far less onerous. Their job was to neutralize opponents and secure possession so that backs, not daydreaming forwards, could score points.

Cliff Morgan wasn't at Bordeaux in 1964 when the All Black captain audaciously drop-kicked his goal, but if he had been, no one would have described it more deliciously than he. However, Morgan was elected to the Hall of Fame for his exploits on the rugby field, not for the mellifluous voice that wowed listeners worldwide when he later became one of the BBC's most admired and respected commentators.

Morgan's achievements as a player were legendary. After debuting for Wales as a fly-half in 1951, he shared in the Grand Slam achievement of 1952, and became captain in 1956. Adored by the Welsh, the rugby world became aware of his exceptional talent when he toured South Africa with the British Lions in 1955. His first test try helped the Lions win the first test 23–22 in one of the most exciting internationals ever played. He captained the Lions to a 9–6 victory in the third test, which allowed his team to share the series. One South African journalist dubbed him Magnificent Morgan.

In 1958, he joined BBC Wales as a sports organizer, making an instant impact. He went on to produce *Grandstand* and *Sportsnight* and feature in *A Question of Sport*. He became a leading BBC executive, being appointed Head of Outside Broadcasts in 1974 and later Head of Sport and Outside Broadcasts, which is about as high as you can aspire to as a sportsperson in the wonderful world of broadcasting in the United Kingdom.

In 1987, after retiring, he returned to radio. In 1988, he was the subject of *This is Your Life*. He was awarded the Order of the British Empire and made a Commander of the Royal Victorian Order for his contributions to broadcasting.

O'Reilly, Tony

Tony O'Reilly, now Sir Anthony, who so willingly wrote the foreword for this book, probably ranks as the highest-achieving rugby individual of all time. He was a showstopper as a player, a winger renowned for his short, tight-fitting shorts back in the 1950s as much as for his exceptional try-scoring talent — his 16 tries in South Africa and 17 in New Zealand on successive Lions tours both being records; indeed, his total of 33 tries remains a Lions record. One UK journalist wrote of him, exquisitely, that he 'turned the toes of defenders and the heads of women with equal facility'. He won 29 caps for Ireland after debuting as an 18-year-old and went on to make a record 30 appearances for the Barbarians, in which he scored 38 tries.

O'Reilly has been an even greater achiever as a businessman, becoming Ireland's first billionaire. He qualified as a solicitor at University College, Dublin, but never practised, instead becoming chairman of a major solicitors' firm. He also achieved a PhD in agricultural marketing.

In 1969, he joined Heinz, soon moving to Pittsburgh in the United States where he became first president, then CEO and ultimately chairman — the first non-Heinz family member to hold that post. Under his guidance, the company's value increased from US$908 million to US$11 billion. He left the company in 1998.

In 1973, he bought into Independent News and Media (currently owning 28 per cent of the shares) and pushed for expansion overseas. The company eventually bought into South Africa, Australia and New Zealand, acquiring 38 newspaper titles and 70 radio stations at a cost of €1.3 billion. It also bought the *Independent* newspaper in the United Kingdom. It's said he's earned €110 million since 2000 just from Independent News and Media.

His first wife, Susan Cameron, the daughter of a wealthy Australian mining figure, bore him six children, including triplets. They separated in the late 1980s, and in 1991 he married Greek shipping heiress Chryss Goulandris, who breeds and races thoroughbred horses. At the time of their wedding she was reportedly worth more than O'Reilly.

O'Reilly was knighted in 2001 for his services to Northern Ireland. In 2008, he was listed as the 677th richest person in the world, worth US$1.8 billion, excluding his wife's wealth, although his losses during the recession in 2009 drastically eroded his fortune.

Osler, Bennie

A master tactician who represented the Springboks in 17 consecutive tests from 1924 to 1933, Bennie Osler was so revered that whenever Danie Craven played alongside him, even at international level, he called him Mr Osler on the field! Craven was emphatic that Osler was the greatest Springbok captain. 'He was a man of few words,' said Craven. 'He rather led by example, but then again, he was a genius.'

In his time Osler changed the way rugby was played. He developed the art of tactical kicking and became famous for his up-

and-unders, cross-punts to the wings, box kicks and dropped goals. Also, he is credited with the invention of the grubber kick. The 1928 All Blacks came to respect his boot. He kicked 14 points in South Africa's first test 17-nil victory, a points-scoring record that was to stand for 21 years.

Leading South African author 'Ace' Parker would write of him that 'Osler was and remains the greatest individual match winner and tactical master that South African rugby football has produced. Osler imposed his personality and technique on South African rugby in the manner of a ruthlessly efficient dictator.'

Sir Wilson continues to follow rugby passionately — as you would expect of the NZRU patron — and proffer sage comment on trends and results. With a twinkle in his eye, he will tell you that 'forwards still win matches — the backs just determine how much you win by!'